STUDIES

IN THE

SOCIAL ASPECTS

OF THE

DEPRESSION

Studies in the Social Aspects of the Depression

Advisory Editor: *ALEX BASKIN*

State University of New York at Stony Brook

RESEARCH MEMORANDUM ON MINORITY PEOPLES IN THE DEPRESSION

By DONALD YOUNG

ARNO PRESS

A NEW YORK TIMES COMPANY

75-09310

Reprint Edition 1972 by Arno Press Inc.

Reprinted from a copy in The Newark Public Library

LC# 74-162841
ISBN 0-405-00844-9

Studies in the Social Aspects of the Depression
ISBN for complete set: 0-405-00840-6
See last pages of this volume for tifles.

Manufactured in the United States of America

Preface to the New Edition

THE WAVES OF IMMIGRANTS who crossed oceans to reach America dared to dream of a better and, in many cases, freer life. Dissatisfied with their circumstances in the land of their birth, and fired by stories of success told them by *landsleit* and countrymen who returned for brief visits, the courageous, the young, and the oppressed abandoned their families, familiar faces, and known cultural patterns in search of better lives. In the main, the driving motive was economic. But the Depression scuttled many dreams and tossed some weary travelers into the chasm of despair. In the 1930's the flow of migration was out of this country and back to Europe and other homelands. The one exception was those escaping from the genocidal madness of Nazism.

As competition for jobs heightened, minority peoples, both foreign and domestic, came under sharp and unfriendly attack. Native-born whites resented immigrants whose presence might deprive them of employment which they felt was rightly theirs. Instances of mob violence grew and nativist utterings were heard more widely in the land. Negroes, Indians and other minority groups felt keenly the pressure of the fiscal crisis. The impact and response of these people to the Depression is the subject of Mr. Young's investigation. His examination of the influence of radicalism, crime, education and religion as they affected minority group behavior contributes substantially to our knowledge of the period. His analysis of racial unrest and minority group ethnocentricity is as readable and understandable in the 1970's as it was four decades earlier. Indeed, they help to explain the basis for many views and attitudes held today.

Alex Baskin
Stony Brook, New York, 1971

BULLETIN 31

1937

RESEARCH MEMORANDUM ON MINORITY PEOPLES IN THE DEPRESSION

By DONALD YOUNG
Professor of Sociology
University of Pennsylvania

PREPARED UNDER THE DIRECTION OF THE
COMMITTEE ON STUDIES IN SOCIAL
ASPECTS OF THE DEPRESSION

SOCIAL SCIENCE RESEARCH COUNCIL
230 PARK AVENUE   NEW YORK NY

The Social Science Research Council was organized in 1923 and formally incorporated in 1924, composed of representatives chosen from the seven constituent societies and from time to time from related disciplines such as law, geography, psychiatry, medicine, and others. It is the purpose of the Council to plan, foster, promote, and develop research in the social field.

CONSTITUENT ORGANIZATIONS

American Anthropological Association

American Economic Association

American Historical Association

American Political Science Association

American Psychological Association

American Sociological Society

American Statistical Association

FOREWORD

By the Committee on Studies in
Social Aspects of the Depression

THIS monograph on research pertaining to minority peoples in the depression is one of a series of thirteen sponsored by the Social Science Research Council to stimulate the study of depression effects on various social institutions. The full list of titles is on page ii.

The depression of the early 1930's was like the explosion of a bomb dropped in the midst of society. All the major social institutions, such as the government, family, church, and school, obviously were profoundly affected and the repercussions were so far reaching that scarcely any type of human activity was untouched. The facts about the impact of the depression on social life, however, have been only partially recorded. It would be valuable to have assembled the vast record of influence of this economic depression on society. Such a record would constitute an especially important preparation for meeting the shock of the next depression, if and when it comes. Theories must be discussed and explored now, if much of the information to test them is not to be lost amid ephemeral sources.

The field is so broad that selection has been necessary. In keeping with its mandate from the Social Science Research Council, the Committee sponsored no studies of an exclusively economic or political nature. The subjects chosen for inclusion were limited in number by resources. The final selection was made by the Committee from a larger number of proposed subjects, on the basis of social importance and available personnel.

Although the monographs clearly reveal a uniformity of goal, they differ in the manner in which the various authors sought to attain that goal. This is a consequence of the Committee's belief that the promotion of research could best be served by not imposing rigid restrictions on the organization of materials by the contributors. It is felt that the encouraged freedom in approach and organization has resulted in the enrichment of the individual reports and of the series as a whole.

A common goal without rigidity in procedure was secured by requesting each author to examine critically the literature on the depression for the purpose of locating existing data and interpretations already reasonably well established, of discovering the more serious inadequacies in information, and of formulating research problems feasible for study. He was not expected to do this research himself. Nor was he expected to compile a full and systematically treated record of the depression as experienced in his field. Nevertheless, in indicating the new research which is needed, the writers found it necessary to report to some extent on what is known. These volumes actually contain much information on the social influences of the depression, in addition to their analyses of pressing research questions.

The undertaking was under the staff direction of Dr. Samuel A. Stouffer, who worked under the restrictions of a short time limit in order that prompt publication might be assured. He was assisted by Mr. Philip M. Hauser and Mr. A. J. Jaffe. The Committee wishes to express appreciation to the authors, who contributed their time and effort without remuneration, and to the many other individuals who generously lent aid and materials.

William F. Ogburn   Chairman
Shelby M. Harrison
Malcolm M. Willey

ACKNOWLEDGMENTS

FOREMOST among those who gave assistance in the preparation of this monograph is Dr. J. P. Shalloo of the Department of Sociology of the University of Pennsylvania. In addition to his preliminary search of public and private sources for materials bearing on the experiences of minority peoples in the depression, he contributed the first draft of the section on the family in Chapter VII and also many ideas incorporated in other sections. It is with sincere thanks that the author gives appreciative acknowledgment of Dr. Shalloo's aid.

Dr. Melville J. Herskovits, Dr. Louis Wirth, Dr. Frank A. Ross, Dr. Malcolm M. Willey and Dr. Samuel A. Stouffer each read the manuscript in its entirety in inexcusably rough form. Each made innumerable corrections and suggestions which were gratefully incorporated. It is an understatement to say that changes of great importance were made in the manuscript as a consequence of attention being called to errors and omissions by these five colleagues and friends.

To the individual members of the Committee on Social Aspects of the Depression appreciation is also expressed for their encouragement, their helpful criticism and their patient forbearance with a refractory contributor to their series.

Donald Young

CONTENTS

Chapter I

Minorities as a Field for Research

A NATIONAL economic crisis does not strike equally at all of the people of any country. If minutiae be considered, it strikes no two individuals with identical impact. Yet if a reasonable understanding of past depressions is to be attained in the hope of achieving a less blind mode of coping with those to come, individuals must be grouped for study as a matter of mental convenience. All such groupings must be relatively arbitrary and tangled with cross classifications. Their possible number is without limit other than the purpose of the investigator. The group here selected for consideration with relation to the recent depression may be simply defined as those persons in the United States of minority status because of their racial or national origin.[1]

The Census of 1930, fortunately taken early in the depression, gives us a numerical statement of the size of the major groups of such minority peoples in that year (Table I). This summary census table offers much too simple a classification of American minority peoples.[2] Thus, while it is possible to attempt generali-

---

[1] Such terms as "minority," "minority peoples," "American minorities," and "minority status," as used in this monograph, never refer either to a political or a purely numerical relationship. The minorities here considered are those population groups distinguished from the dominant element by differentiating biological features of racial origin or by alien cultural traits, or a combination of both. It is unfortunate that there is no English word which with entire philological propriety may be applied to all such groups. For discussion of the concept of minorities in the present sense see Young, Donald. *American Minority Peoples.* New York: Harper & Brothers. 1932. *Passim*

[2] The appendix contains a series of selected quotations indicating the diffi-

1

zations of some scientific and social utility concerning the foreign-born white population in the United States, the differential characteristics of subgroups within this classification require at the very least an analysis as to the country of birth which, given

TABLE I

POPULATION BY RACIAL OR NATIVITY GROUPS: UNITED STATES, 1930[a]

RACE OR NATIVITY	NUMBER	PER CENT
Total population.	122,775,046	100
White.	108,864,207	88.7
Native	95,497,800	
Native Parentage	70,136,614	
Foreign Parentage.	16,999,221	
Mixed Parentage	8,361,965	
Foreign-born	13,366,407	
Negro.	11,891,143	9.7
Mexican	1,422,533	1.2
Indian.	332,397	0.3
Chinese	74,954	0.1
Japanese	138,834	0.1
Filipino	45,208	
Hindu.	3,130	
Korean	1,860	
All other	780	

[a] U. S. Bureau of the Census. *Fifteenth Census of the United States*, 1930

in Table II, is also derived from the Census of 1930.

The country of origin of the foreign-born in the United States is important because it offers some index of the cultural problems which face specific groups of immigrants.[3] It has further impor-

culty encountered by statisticians in attempting to define with both clarity and social significance who should be enumerated as members of various American minority groups of racial and national origin.

No effort will be made to refer to all the important government publications containing data on minority peoples. For information on the nature and extent of printed material issued by the federal government see Schmeckebier, L. F. *Government Publications and Their Use*. Washington, D.C.: The Brookings Institution. 1936. Pp. xiii+446

[3] For brief statements of the differentiated cultural backgrounds of the major immigrant groups see Fairchild, H. P. (Editor) *Immigrant Backgrounds*. New York: John Wiley & Sons. 1927. Pp. x+269

tance because the circumstances of immigration from various countries have caused these groups to differ with regard to such characteristics as age, sex, geographical distribution, occupation, length of residence in the United States, and degree of

TABLE II

FOREIGN-BORN WHITE POPULATION OF THE UNITED STATES
BY COUNTRY OF BIRTH: 1930[a]

COUNTRY OF BIRTH	1930
All countries	13,366,407
England	808,672
Scotland.	354,323
Wales	60,205
Northern Ireland	178,832
Irish Free State.	744,810
Norway	347,852
Sweden	595,250
Denmark	179,474
Germany	1,608,814
Poland	1,268,583
Czechoslovakia	491,638
Austria	370,914
Hungary.	274,450
Yugoslavia	211,416
Russia.	1,153,624
Latvia and Estonia.	24,223
Lithuania	193,606
Greece.	174,526
Italy	1,790,424
Canada—French	370,852
Canada—Other.	907,569
Mexico	23,743
All other countries	1,232,607

[a] U. S. Bureau of the Census. *Fifteenth Census of the United States*, 1930

assimilation. Finally, it may in some cases be used as a crude index of race in the biological sense, though for this study only the degree to which racial features set a group apart because of social visibility is of concern.

In using the country of origin as a classification basis for the differentiation of minority peoples the temptation with regard to white stocks is to emphasize the foreign-born and the first American-born generation, to the neglect of groups characterized by distinct alien cultures and related problems of intergroup relations in spite of the birth of several generations in the United States. This is a consequence of the unavailability of statistical data, for no official records are kept of individual national origin beyond the first generation born on American soil. In a sense, there is an exception to this rule in the special listing in many types of public records of colored peoples whose national origin may be inferred, within limitations, from their racial characteristics. There is no logical reason for limiting the concept of minority groups, as used in this memorandum, on the basis of the time of arrival in the country of a family line.

If the country of origin of American minorities has importance because of the possibility of use as an index of group characteristics, it is also obviously true that immigrant origin classifications on both crossnational and subnational bases need to be made. The outstanding case of crossnational minority classification is the Jew, who has come to the United States since Colonial days from many nations in varying proportions. Very rough estimates suggest that in 1930 there were some 4,500,000 Jews in the United States, more or less, depending on the degree of cultural similarity and blood identity required by the definition of a Jew. The total Jewish population must also be subdivided for purposes of social research, into Portuguese, German, Russian or other regional origin, or on a basis of religious behavior, or in accord with some other category most useful for an immediate purpose. Still other crossnational classifications can be utilized, such as the "old immigration" from northwestern Europe and the "new immigration" from southern and eastern Europe, the Occidental and the Oriental, or such groupings of peoples as the Scandinavians, the Latins. or the English-speaking immigrants.

Subnational classifications may be equally valuable for specific research purposes, although usually the necessary data are more difficult to obtain. The fact that populations are rarely distributed evenly throughout a nation, that cultural divergencies between intranational regions are practically without limit, taken in conjunction with the fact that emigrants are never a random sample of a country's population, makes it essential on occasion that North Italians be distinguished from South Italians, the Northern Ireland from the Irish Free State immigrants, the English-speaking Canadians from the French-Canadians, the Bavarians from the Prussians. That materials of this order are meager is regrettable, but seems unavoidable.

Further consideration of Tables I and II shows the necessity for reclassification of not only the foreign-born white population but also of all other minorities listed, with the possible exception of those groups so small as not to warrant too fine an analysis. As has often been remarked, no sentence beginning with "All Germans" or "All Frenchmen" is true, and the same may be said of any statement which attempts to include all of any nationality or race.[4] The possibility of true generalization, however, increases in direct proportion with the use of valid subgroup definitions. The native white peoples of foreign parentage, of mixed parentage, and even of native parentage, must for most

---

[4] The following quotation is in point: "The Indians today are not a distinct ethnic group which has maintained its original racial characteristics and social customs. Contact with the general population has resulted in a blending of races, modification of customs, and increasing economic dependence on the white man. The impact of white civilization, however, has been quite uneven in its effect. In sections of the Southwest and in Florida the Indian lives very much as he did when found by the early Spanish settlers, while in many parts of Oklahoma the Indians and whites may live on adjoining property and participate equally in political and social affairs. The occasional Indian interspersed among the general population of the United States does not differ very much from the average citizen of the community." Mountin, Joseph W. and Townsend, J. G. *Observations on Indian Health Problems and Facilities.* U. S. Treasury Department, Public Health Service, Public Health Bulletin No. 223. Washington, D.C.: U. S. Government Printing Office. February 1936. P. 1

research purposes be divided in accordance with their blood and cultural heritage. Nothing of universal application may with accuracy be said about all men known as Negroes; little of general application can be said about the American Negro. Only when the Negroes of the United States are classified according to their specific histories, as on the basis of birthplace in this country or in the Caribbean region, economic or educational status, or record of residence and migration, may accurate research results be expected.

In the same manner it may be desirable to know whether a group of Mexicans is of recent immigrant or of old southwestern United States stock, the relative proportion of Indian, white, and Negro ancestry in its members, whether they came from Jalisco or Zacatecas, or whether their culture is predominantly Indian or Spanish. Many native Indians have been so thoroughly assimilated that not to differentiate them in a study of the people so designated by the Census would be an elementary research error; others retain elements of diverse tribal cultures in varying states of dissolution. China is a country more heterogeneous in population and culture than the United States. Japanese caste distinctions have not been destroyed by migration to this country. The Philippines have not sent to the United States a fair sample of their varied peoples. Only one thoroughly familiar with specific minorities, their history and present situation, may hope to use, let alone devise, classifications not to be found in general statistical tables.

To state that all classifications of people, including those based on racial and national origins, are to some extent arbitrary, is to express a truism, but it does not follow that a specific classification may not be useful in terms of a designated purpose. The purpose of the monograph series in which this bulletin is included is to aid through social research in an understanding of the impact of the most recent economic crisis in the United States. It is common knowledge that the effects of the depression have been felt unevenly throughout the population because of differences in regional and personal resources, and that there is a direct relationship between resources capable of cushioning or intensifying the consequences of economic maladjustment and minority status.

Inherited physical features which distinguish the members of one race from another, for example, although not known to be indicative of inherent limitations in potential capacity, operate as a classification basis for the limitation of development of personal resources. Regardless of the disputed problem of the comparative native ability of peoples of different color, the sheer superficial racial features of the American Negro, Oriental, Mexican, Russian Jew, South Italian, and Indian lead through consequent social visibility to differential opportunities in employment and other economic activity, in education, in location of residence, in political participation, and to resulting differences in personality and modes of behavior and thought. In time of general unemployment people so differentiated must naturally be influenced in a different manner from those of the general population.

Recent alien origin, including at least the first and in some instances later American-born generations, also tends to produce a high social visibility and is the cause of variations with regard to depression resources similar to those growing out of race distinctions, even though these are not always so severe and lasting. Furthermore, this factor sometimes implies cultural divergencies likely to be a severe handicap in economic and social life. At the same time, certain aspects of some alien cultures, such as strong family ties and group solidarity, may be powerful weapons in fighting common adversity. Where alien cultural standards and distinctive physical characteristics are combined, in a minority group as is commonly the case, the differentiation in group resources is most sharp. There is, therefore, a clear justification for the separate study of minority peoples in mapping the field of research in the social aspects of the depression.

It may indeed be inquired with propriety why such diverse minorities as Negroes, Germans, Indians, Jews, and others should even be grouped together for study. In answer, it must first be said that though they cannot be indiscriminately so grouped in any single well-defined research project—a point of view which has been emphasized previously in the discussion of the need for careful classification and subclassification of minority peoples with reference to specific research objectives—there is none the less a common ground of underlying problems, processes and research methods which on occasion makes it essential that all be subsumed under the single heading "minority peoples."

For example, this common ground has in the past been far too little recognized by students as well as laymen interested in what are ordinarily referred to as "race relations." The problems have been too complex, the available materials and techniques too frail; the city, it might be said, could not be seen because of the buildings, the lack of a telescope, and the existence of a strong motive not to look at the panorama as a whole because of a reform interest pointed in some one direction. Relatively recent developments in the fundamental disciplines such as anthropology, psychology, and sociology, the increasing availability of data, and perhaps a popular change in point of view toward a recognition of the common elements in the circumstances of minorities in general, now demand an integrated attack on minorities as minorities—that is, on Negroes, immigrants, and Jews as minorities, as well as the more conventional studies of Negroes as Negroes, immigrants as immigrants, or Jews as Jews.

That there is common ground in all minority situations which demands integrated, parallel research is suggested by the increasing use of the term minority peoples. One factor never absent is social visibility; history teaches that a minority without such visibility because of racial characteristics, cultural differentiation, or some externally enforced means of identification, such as caste distinction in dress, does not long maintain its minority status.

An element of competition with the majority, either real or fancied, and usually of an economic nature, is also the rule where minority status is a matter of importance. The idea of a superior-inferior group status may, of course, be borrowed by one region from another, by one social class or caste from another, or be carried over from one period of time to another as a matter of tradition, without appreciable concurrent social visibility or competition. Such a transfer, however, is ordinarily of short duration unless kept alive or revived from time to time by special circumstances such as, for example, a deliberate campaign of propaganda. Thus without either social visibility or competition, minority status tends to lose significance and disappear.

Minorities, apart from the fact that their cultures frequently vary significantly from the culture of the dominant majority because of foreign origin, may also be expected to develop special cultural norms of their own as a result of minority status as such. These may result partly from the fact that they live and work under special circumstances, partly because they are forced to invent patterns of defensive behavior because of their status, and partly for the reason that the inevitable adoption of majority standards involves both a lag and a warping. In the process of cultural growth it is not unnatural that widely divergent minorities should experience some common directional bias resulting in similar modes of behavior, particularly if they live in the same region and are dominated by the same majority.

It is also to be expected that dominating majorities in various regions, when faced with the problem of what to think and do about minorities, will fail to be sufficiently inventive to create unique schemes of relationships and action. Variations in intensity of restriction and oppression, special techniques in maintaining superior status, and other adaptations to the local scene will always be found, but the choice of fundamental patterns of dominance in majority-minority relations is limited by the nature of man and his circumstances.[5]

Although the approach from the point of view both of research and of social action implicit in the designation "minority peoples" has obtained wide acceptance in recent years, and is the approach underlying the present exposition, it is still supported only by rough observation and scanty scientific evidence. With but few interested, and fewer still reasonably well trained in much more than the elementary manipulation of superficial quantitative data on gross group differentials—such as comparative employment, education, crime, distribution, and vital statistics—postulates concerning minority peoples have yet to achieve that degree of substantiation required for acceptance as more than likely hypotheses. There are, however, an increasing number of students in the field who recognize the need for special research training, to some extent interdisciplinary, preparatory to work with any minority.

With the new trend of development in the field—an intelligent supplementation of the drive for social action by a parallel drive for scientific understanding which takes into account a neglected wealth of approaches, materials and techniques— there has been opened a vast and enticing prospect of urgent research questions concerning the fundamental nature of minorities. The temptation is strong to urge their immediate attack, but the present task must be restricted by mandate to the acceptance as a starting point of the established and likely facts

[5] For further elaboration of this point of view and supporting evidence see, for example: Miller, Herbert A. *Races, Nations and Classes*. Philadelphia: J. B. Lippincott Company. 1924. Pp. xvii+196; Muntz, Earl Edward. *Race Contact*. New York: The Century Company. 1927. Pp. xiv+407; Schrieke, B. *Alien Americans*. New York: The Viking Press. 1936. Pp. xi+208; Young, Donald. *American Minority Peoples*. New York: Harper & Brothers. 1932. Pp. xv+621

and hypotheses concerning minorities as such, so that the less inclusive problems of American minorities in the last depression can be sketched in bold outline.

Logically this mandate requires a statement of what is definitely known concerning minorities and the depression as a result of research, suggestions concerning the outstanding feasible research questions in the field, and some indication of research techniques and sources of data. As is so often the case, however, circumstances do not permit a balanced adherence to this formula. Practically nothing of scientific value is known about American minorities in depression, a circumstance which is not surprising in view of the fact that so little is known with certainty about minorities in previous periods.[6] Crude statistics exist in abundance, especially for census years, and there have been numerous sample surveys during the depression itself, involving separate races and nationalities, productive of scattered data concerning gross differentials in such matters as housing, land tenure, education, employment and income, and so forth. A few of these surveys, practically all completed with government support, offer data susceptible of scientific reworking, more are suggestive of problems of importance, but in none of them is there

[6] For present purposes the depression may be defined with reasonable chronological accuracy as the period of unusual economic maladjustment following 1929, but not without some question concerning the propriety of including a vague prior period when it was in the making, and even more uncertainty concerning its end. It may also be observed that rural depression conditions were evident long before their urban counterpart. Of greater difficulty, moreover, is the problem of determining whether a given observed minority phenomenon during the depression period may be considered a depression phenomenon or whether it might not have occurred in any event, perhaps being merely slightly or not at all influenced by the crisis. Such cases of doubt are more than peripheral, and must be handled instance by instance in the absence of any satisfactory fixed principle of discrimination. It is important not to think of the depression as a flat bottomed economic valley with abrupt sides like the Grand Canyon, but rather as an irregular valley of varying depth, width, and slope of sides, depending on the cross section viewed.

any serious attempt to go beyond simple description and test hypotheses of possible general application. As a consequence of the scarcity of reliable depression studies of minorities other than those which involve mere counting—and even in these cases often questionable in their use of sampling and other techniques—illustrative citations of such material as is available will be reported not in a separate section but distributed throughout the entire discussion. In further explanation of this mode of treatment, it is necessary to state emphatically that regardless of any scepticism shown as to the possible scientific value of such materials, there is no intention to belittle any considerable proportion of them from an emergency administrative point of view. It is rather a reflection on social scientists that better information could not be furnished with the unusual facilities available.

Almost the entire discussion will point toward research questions. Since these questions take on full meaning only in terms of the background from which they arose and if viewed with relation to each other and the field as a whole, they will be presented with a minimum of supporting data and interpretation. Thus where it will be necessary to quote or refer to pertinent statistics, illustrative cases will be cited, and various proffered explanations of situations and relationships under discussion will be mentioned. The principal end in view, however, is not to define a social trend or even to report a particular situation; the spade work preliminary to such effort remains to be done. The hope of this memorandum is rather to facilitate in some small measure some of that research without which our knowledge must remain at the most elementary level.

It is, incidentally, not a difficult matter to propose projects of the census or survey types which involve only the counting of selected items in a selected area. Without disparaging such procedures, it can be indicated that in spite of their values to administration and reform, as well as their utility in the preliminary stages of social research, it is only under unusual circumstances that they have been so framed in the past as to produce results of more than local and ephemeral application. Further, their possible number is so great that their mere listing is out of the question. Omission is consequently indicated, except for occasional outstanding illustrations.

There thus remain to be treated in this study two distinct types of problems which are intimately related. More obvious of the two is a great cluster of problems in which the central interest is material differences shown between two or more minorities in the depression and between minorities and the majority group. Of no less importance, but far more subtle and difficult of understanding, is a second cluster having to do with the less tangible differences found in cultural patterns and standards of thought and behavior. Inseparably bound together as are these two sets of problems, their distinction in research is perhaps more justified by historically divergent methods of description and analysis than by any logic of fact.

Material differentials, because they are more readily observable, and because of their value as evidence of discrimination, have received the greater attention. It is a commonplace that minority workers tend to be employed for relatively low wages and under inferior laboring conditions, that their housing and other tangible living circumstances tend to be below par, that the physical facilities for their education and recreation lag behind those of the majority, that their possession of goods either in terms of ownership or of use indicates a comparatively low plane of living. Continued effort, however, is necessary to refine and supplement such casual observations and to establish relationships with a smaller margin of error than is now possible. Once material differentials have been so analyzed, it is then possible to utilize such knowledge either as a basis for ameliorative social action or as data from which generalizations concerning their cultural foundations and repercussions may be deduced.

The less tangible cluster of cultural differentials may be attacked directly as well as by such a roundabout deductive process. The available research techniques for the direct approach, borrowed mainly with adaptations from cultural anthropology and social psychology, are inadequate for good workmanship and of questionable reliability in use. Few students of race relations have sufficient familiarity with their proper handling. For example, although practically any advanced graduate student in sociology with a research interest in the Negro may be expected with confidence to carry through competently a study of colored housing facilities, it is a rare person who can even undertake an intelligent analysis of the attitudes, beliefs, and standards of a particular Negro community as these may be related to the problems of family functioning in a segregated, congested area. Similarly, it is a relatively easy matter to determine the proportion of Italian immigrant families on relief to whom wine is so important that more nourishing food staples are sacrificed in its favor, but study of the cultural complex involved is far from equally simple. As a third illustration, reference may be made to the relative facility with which a project could be planned to determine the extent and nature of material sacrifice by a given group of Russian Jewish parents for their children, in comparison with a group, say, of second generation German Jewish parents, but a direct comparison of the cultural patterns having to do with the parent-child relationship would tax the ingenuity and technical skill of the most advanced specialist in the field. There is no reason to believe, however, that the difficulties referred to are insuperable. The promise of superior results justifies the extra effort required for the development of tools and personnel.

It would be folly if in the effort to develop neglected lines of research, other approaches which have long yielded some profit, however slight, should in turn be neglected. Increasing knowledge of minority material differentials will have increasing research as well as practical social value, and will ultimately serve as a check and supplement to any understanding which may be obtained of minority problems by approaches as yet undeveloped. The fact that the cultural approach to the study of the American Negro is still in a stage of naïvete is all the more reason why there must be no reduction in the more old-fashioned type of research project. If, for further example, the study of the process of acculturation of the European or Oriental immigrant has been halting and fumbling, perhaps largely characterized by shrewd guesswork backed up by selected illustrations, it is the more essential that all possible data be worked up by whatever methods may be available, old-fashioned or pioneer.

To minimize the danger of appearing to separate too sharply two foci of minority research which could perhaps be better described as two points on a continuous line, there may be cited the intermediate group of research studies starting with overt behavior rather than with either material differentials or cultural patterns. Studies of immigrant, Indian, and Negro crime, of variants in sex behavior, of achievement in the arts, of leisure time activities, and even of economic behavior, as a rule fall between these two poles and thus have some relationship to both, the emphasis depending on the research bias of the student. Thus analyses of minority crime may on the one hand stress the material amount of social damage or the material causative influences or, on the other hand, the emphasis may be on the factor of cultural conditioning or of cultural conflict; while not infrequently in more careful studies, both types of approach are used. The most serious criticism of the group who do this kind of middle-of-the-road research is their tendency to do no more than classify and count forms of overt behavior, apparently on the theory that such procedure meets the test of objectivity. This may be a means for obtaining objéctivity, but it also guarantees minimum scientific and practical utility through avoidance of any attempt to forge the links between minority behavior and their cultural and environmental circumstances. In other words, the result is superficial description without the possibility of causal inference. The eclectic approach is unpopular with some students, to whom it appears as a form of compromise, but this seems an ill-considered criticism until more is known concerning the relative merits of the possible extreme positions. In any event, no feasible research approach will be slighted in this study, but attention will be directed to the advantages and limitations of each.

Every research problem suggested in the following pages should be first tested by two criteria: Is it a depression phenomenon and is it also a phenomenon of significance in the life of minority peoples as such? It must be obvious that the application of these criteria is rarely easy and frequently impossible. They are, however, the adopted standards for inclusion and exclusion in this monograph, and are used with the full recognition that in certain instances their application must remain of doubtful validity in the present stage of knowledge concerning the social phenomena involved.

It must also be recognized that the depression created no new minority problems or programs for social action. Every depression modification in the circumstances of minority living, whether unplanned or the consequence of purposeful action, could be described either as a change in degree rather than one of kind, or as a predepression latent possibility which has been afforded an opportunity for development by the economic crisis. This denial to the depression of an originally creative rôle, however, is not to be construed as a refusal to recognize fundamental shifts in emphasis and even reversals of·trends in minority life when these are really consequences of the depression.

Chapter II

Social Stratification

FOR more than a century and a half the law of the United States has described the social structure of this country as democratic, with free opportunity for all. Class legislation restricting the liberty of accepted residents has been forbidden with such major exceptions as restrictions on convicts, on redemptioners in our early history, on slaves until the time of the Civil War, and the regulation of tribal Indians. Democratic safeguards have been increased since the founding of the nation. School children have been taught to believe that all citizens by birth have a chance of election to the Presidency. Thus political, economic, and social democracy have gained acceptance as national symbols which it is dangerous to question.

Popular behavior, however, in contrast with verbal professions, establishes the existence of numerous lines of class distinction and even some rigid caste groups. In parts of Europe, the revolutionary post-World War changes in governmental forms, which were political expressions of fundamental modifications in social structure, show a strong tendency toward formal recognition of caste and class distinctions. The depression has apparently encouraged similar tendencies in the United States toward the destruction of historic symbols of democracy and the open avowal of class conflict.

MINORITIES AS SOCIAL CLASSES AND CASTES

The phenomena of race prejudice and of minority discrimination are a variety of class and caste phenomena. These in turn are a variety of interest group phenomena. Thus, a social class may be said to be an interest group to which public opinion attaches a higher or lower status with reference to some other social class or classes. To illustrate, medical doctors, manufacturing exporters, stock brokers, wild life conservationists, or golfers may constitute interest groups, but such classifications do not necessarily imply any important comparison of social status. On the other hand, social status is significantly involved in such designations as middle class, labor, capitalist, or "the four hundred." Membership in an interest group denotes little more than a common objective on the part of its component units which may be furthered by some degree of cooperation; class membership also implies some common interest, if only defensive, but with an added status classification. When a group membership with status implications is rigid to the extent that social rank may be lost but not gained, the term "caste" may be applied.[1] The circumstances of birth determine the highest rank achievable by an individual in a caste system; there is theoretically no limit to the height in a class system to which any man may climb during his lifetime.

In accordance with these definitions, some nationalities in the United States may be referred to as interest groups, such as the Germans, the English-speaking Canadians, or the English. Others constitute social classes, such as the Portuguese, the French Canadians, and various South and Central European nationalities commonly referred to as "new" immigrants. The Negro, the Oriental, and the Jew, since they can rise out of their original group status only if they are able to hide their origin or only under other exceptional circumstances, constitute castes.

---

[1] For a statement of Negro-white class and caste relationships which differs in some respects from the position taken in this chapter see Warner, Lloyd W. "American Caste and Class." *American Journal of Sociology.* 42:234-237. No. 2. September 1936

For a detailed study of a southern town in terms of Negro-white status relationships see Dollard, John. *Caste and Class in a Southern Community.* New Haven: Yale University Press. 1937. Pp. 502

The American Indian, once constituting an inferior caste in the social hierarchy, now constitutes little more than a social class, since today his inferior status may be sloughed off by the process of cultural assimilation. It is perhaps unnecessary to remark that class and caste distinctions do not apply with uniformity throughout the communities and regions of the country, or that there are extensive variations in individual privilege, right, and status within each grouping.

With the example of European crisis experience before us, it may with reason be inquired whether there is support for the hypothesis that depression influences tend to give emphasis to interest group, class, and caste distinctions. By a priori logic alone, it would appear likely that groups characterized by common physical features or culture, by common discrimination, oppression, or exploitation, should in time of want band together more closely in order to secure as large a share as possible of available goods and services. This theory does not minimize the probability that many individuals of inferior status will endeavor to escape by passing into a higher social classification. Such a mode of escape, however, is not feasible for more than very few persons of minority status. Sharper group alignments and closer group cohesion for attack and protection are to be expected. This hypothesis may be tested by study of what the depression did to the bases of social stratification, by examining the objective behavior of the various social strata, and investigating group attitudes as they are given verbal expression.

The measurable bases of social stratification, i.e., the essential observable marks of group distinction, include hereditary physical features (the color of the Negro), ancestral achievement (scions of Colonial families or recent immigrants), material possessions (landed estates), the possession of authority (military, political, or judicial authority), personal qualities (cultural traits, education, or the social graces), and individual achievement (the poet or the financier). Obviously the depression has done nothing to alter the racial features of any stock, nor has it changed the ancestry of any one. It has, however, modified the distribution of capital, income, and prestige, and in so doing may have modified the social structure of the nation.[2] Such changes in social rank, however, have probably been greatest within the dominant white majority, many of whom were undoubtedly brought closer to minority economic levels. Minority norms themselves were probably at the same time reduced. In the absence of definitive analyses of economic data with reference to minority-majority relationships, it may be assumed that this factor has not weakened, but may actually have bolstered class feeling through increased economic uncertainty and competition and restriction of opportunity and mobility.

Authority is a function of public and private positions held irrespective of the fact that there may be unseen powers behind the throne. Suggestions bearing on this point will be made later in the appropriate sections, but it may be mentioned here that there has been no pronounced trend toward the placing of minority leaders in important positions in civil, military, or private life. If anything, general observation suggests that such positions were during the depression more zealously guarded for the use of the majority than in the preceding years, excepting perhaps in communities containing important blocs of minority voters.

So with the other bases of social stratification as they apply to majority-minority relations. Individual personal qualities are rarely made more attractive by inadequate wages or prolonged unemployment. The level of group achievement is not raised by poverty. In general, the reasonable assumption is that on the whole the depression increased the gaps between minority handicaps and majority advantages.

Consideration of the behavior which characterizes the various

---

[2] See, for example, Lynd, Robert S. and Helen M. *Middletown in Transition.* New York: Harcourt, Brace and Co. 1937. Pp. xviii+604

social strata seems to support this contention. Failure for any reason, even though personal responsibility therefor is minimized, encourages substitute symbols of success. The family in poverty or on relief has extra need for a badge of worth, for the maintenance of self-confidence, for ego gratification, for symbols of quality proving superiority with which to face the world. What simpler device is there for such a purpose than identification with a superior social class or caste? Minorities themselves, as well as ruling peoples, commonly find or invent unique virtues characteristic of their group, and thus vicariously obtain that success which is denied them as individuals and in real life. Practically every large minority except the American Negro has claimed in some sense to be a chosen people. The principle is the same whether it be used to rationalize minority or majority failures. Its effect on class and caste may be expected to be one of reënforcement of existing stratification.

Studies of the various forms of competition for recognition in terms of group identification, in contrast with that for purely individual achievement, could throw much light on race and nationality distinctions as class and caste phenomena. Did the depression make it more necessary than in earlier times for individuals not sure of themselves to be seen in the "right" places, to display knowledge of the "right" books, to wear the "right" clothes, to drive the "right" car, to live in the "right" neighborhood or apartment, to belong to the "right" political party and social clubs, to call social items to the attention of society editors, and otherwise flaunt marks of group identification? How did behavior in such matters differ between majority and minority, and between minorities and subdivisions of minorities? What was the history during the depression of class restrictions in admissions to schools, clubs, residential areas, resorts, and the like? Were there more or fewer intermarriages?[3] Or, on the other

---

[3] Because of the research already done on the subject of intergroup marriage and of the existence as a matter of public record of concrete data concerning the

hand, did the depression afford an easy excuse for behavior which would have been considered below class standards in more prosperous times? Was there abnormal defensive bragging about money lost, about triumphant economies, about hard luck in general? To what extent was there effort to avoid declassing by evading friends, by moving and by otherwise concealing identity? What were the last things, material or social, sacrificed by those overwhelmed by disaster, and were they in any way indicative of group status? Data on such questions is perhaps the most direct source of information on the problem of the influence of the depression on any form of social stratification; for our purposes it must be correlated with the behavior of interracial and international groups.

Such correlation requires the careful classification as to race or nationality of each individual concerning whom information is secured, and the interpretation of this information with due regard for cultural standards and the specific social situation in

marriage status of identifiable individuals, the further study of minority-majority and of inter-minority marriages during the depression offers perhaps as good an index of changes in class and caste relationships as any available approach. Inter-group extramarital sex relations should be simultaneously investigated, but their naturally clandestine nature makes this exceptionally difficult.

The following references are offered as sources both of factual data on inter-marriage and of methodological suggestions: Adams, Romanzo. *Interracial Marriage in Hawaii.* New York: The Macmillan Co. 1937. Pp. xvii+353; Drachsler, Julius. *Intermarriage in New York City.* New York: The Macmillan Co. 1920. Pp. xii+275; Wessel, Bessie Bloom. *An Ethnic Survey of Woonsocket, R.I.* Chicago: University of Chicago Press. 1931. Pp. xxi+290; Herskovits, Melville J. *The American Negro: A Study in Racial Crossing.* New York: Alfred A. Knopf. 1928. Pp. xiv+92; Herskovits, Melville J. *The Anthropometry of the American Negro.* New York: Columbia University Press. 1930. Pp. xiv+283; Kolehmainen, John I. "A Study of Marriage in a Finnish Community." *The American Journal of Sociology.* 42: 371-382. No. 3. November 1936; Mead, Margaret. "Notes on the Possibility of Studying the Mixed-Blood Situation," Chapter XV, *The Changing Culture of an Indian Tribe.* New York: Columbia University Press. 1932. For further suggestions for research bearing on the depression see Stouffer, Samuel A. and Lazarsfeld, Paul F. *Research Memorandum on the Family in the Depression.* (monograph in this series)

point. The methodology called for is primarily that of the social historian accustomed to studying recent history through the use of newspapers, private and institutional records, along with the memories of the living. The historical approach is demanded by the necessity for comparative materials from predepression days. The social theory involved and the high proportion of the data to be obtained from living persons requires supplementary familiarity with the germane working concepts and techniques of social psychology, sociology, and social anthropology. Although few social historians now possess such training, such studies should not be difficult of attainment through the collaboration of colleagues in the disciplines mentioned.

As a substitute for direct investigation of overt behavior indicative of group status, or as a supplement to such an attack, verbal expressions of social attitudes toward class distinctions may be utilized. The individual with keen insight and interpretative genius may reconstruct with significant accuracy interclass attitudes from such written sources as the plays, novels, stories, motion pictures, editorials, news items, cartoons, humor, and personal writings in both minority and majority publications of a period.[4] For example, in the course of American history there

---

[4] Any list of periodical publications intended for minority readers or for a wider audience interested in minority affairs sufficiently comprehensive to be useful in research would be far too difficult of compilation and too long for inclusion here. Minority newspapers and magazines, annual and occasional reports issued by minority welfare and social action agencies, and ephemera concerned with various aspects of minority life are being published constantly in large volume. Such material must be regarded as a major source of research data.

By way of illustration, reference may be made to the material on the Negro issued by the National Association for the Advancement of Colored People, the Association for the Study of Negro Life and History, and the National Urban League; the periodicals *The Crisis, The Journal of Negro History,* and *Opportunity* published by these organizations in the order listed, *The Journal of Negro Education,* and the Negro newspapers published in such cities as New York, Philadelphia, Baltimore, and Chicago. The book reviews and notes on publications bearing on the Negro regularly contained in the *Journal of Negro History* cover an unusually wide range of material and may be used as a bibliographical guide.

have been striking shifts in the prevailing stereotypes of minority appearance and qualities in all forms of popular literature and art. Has there been any such shift during the depression which could illuminate minority-majority class relationships? Material for this type of investigation is almost too plentiful. No means, however, has as yet been devised to reduce it to numerical or chart form for the facilitation of manipulation and understanding. Nevertheless, there is no reason to believe that it may not be reduced to comprehension and generalization by the mind of the keen scholar—as reliable a procedure as is needed in the absence of standardized techniques.

The method of measuring social attitudes by the question and answer technique developed by the social psychologists is more standardized and more readily checked and extended in use by the average scientific workman despite the fact that this method is still in a state of flux. Using procedures varying from simple rank order correlations of answers concerning group preferences to complicated adaptations of technique borrowed from psychophysics, studies have been made on the borderland between psychology and sociology of the interracial and international attitudes of fragmentary populations in both depression and predepression times. It is possible that the best of these might be pieced together for the purpose of suggesting if not of establishing depression fluctuations.

For the years that are gone, attitude tests can of course be useful for our purposes only where scattering tests dealing with minority-majority relationships were made before and during the depression. It is, however, still possible to construct and apply a test designed to indicate present status discrimination between groups of differing racial and national origin, and at the same time relate current attitudes to depression experiences. The task not only presents no unique methodological problems, but offers in addition a rare opportunity for the analysis of depression influences on subsequent attitudes toward minorities.

The scars of a crisis may reveal the cause and course of the illness.

STATUS DIFFERENCES WITHIN MINORITY GROUPS

The human tendency to classify strangers by traits which distinguish them most strikingly has made for the neglect of the complicated class stratification which exists within each minority, no matter how lowly its position on the national social scale. Whatever the white man's view, Negroes are not just Negroes to each other; a multitude of status lines crisscrosses colored social relationships, marking distinctions which are no less important humanly and scientifically than those to be found in white Boston or Baltimore. Similarly, Mexicans are not just Mexicans to each other, nor Jews just Jews, Japanese just Japanese, French Canadians just French Canadians, Italians just Italians. The existence of minority stratification has long been known to students of race relations familiar with their subjects of study as people rather than as distant sources of statistics. Only scanty research data, however, are available concerning this phenomenon of minority status classifications and it is consequently difficult to establish a base line for the study of the influence of the depression on minority social classes. There are, nevertheless, a few cases of minority subcastes which were reasonably well familiar to the specialist before the beginning of the depression, and to these we can turn with some prospect of reward in our search for tendencies.

Jews in America, for example, have long maintained a remarkably effective caste system within their number by distinguishing emphatically between the Spanish-Portuguese, the German, and the Eastern and South-Eastern European Jews. There has, of course, been appreciable blurring of the lines between these groups, but it is not essential to the definition of a caste that there should be no friendly relations or even intermarriages between castes under any circumstances. Behavior is rarely so rigidly confined. It is enough to know that there is among the Jews powerful disapproval within each group mentioned against mingling with the subgroups who are held inferior in the order listed. Such matters are relative, and the fact that group membership is determined by birth and that rising on the scale is an impossibility except in the sense of acceptance of individuals for most social relations—though always with a mental reservation because of different caste origin—requires the designation of subcaste.

There is also a subcaste system in operation among American Negroes based on skin color and other physical features. As is true of all minorities of long residence in the United States, the Negro has unconsciously drifted toward the acceptance of the characteristics of the dominant white majority as the most desirable, and colored individuals acquire status by the biological accident of their degree of resemblance to the white race. To some extent this resemblance may be increased by hair straighteners and skin bleaches, but since this mark of status is biological it is of course impossible to rise on this particular scale. The situation is confused, it must be observed, by the fact that equally high or even superior status may be achieved by dark-complexioned Negroes on the basis of achievement, but this is a class phenomenon which does not contradict the coexistence of a caste on a different foundation, even though intermarriage of individuals of relatively parallel position in subcaste and subclass is permitted. Although still in a formative stage, this seems to be a rare instance of a color caste in development where the individual rather than the family is the unit of membership, and intermarriage of members of different castes does not mean absolute demotion for the spouse of superior status.

A third minority subcaste system may be found among the Japanese in the United States. This is a survival of the caste system in Japan, and seems to be in the process of rapid disintegration because of the cultural assimilation of the American-born generations. A fourth system is to be found among the Mexican immigrants in this country, among whom color barriers to status improvement may be observed. The number of white Mexican immigrants, however, is so small in proportion to those of Indian or mixed origin that their relative practical significance is slight.

In addition to these minority subcastes, selected for emphasis here because of their relative ease of contemporary observation and historical comparison, there are any number of minority social classes. They correspond roughly in foundation and function to those which stratify comparable white populations. There are the minority laboring classes, the capitalists, the middle classes, the professional people, those relying on their birth and the achievements of their ancestors, those relying on their own achievements, and many others.

It may be tentatively suggested that the depression has strengthened rather than weakened caste and class lines within American minorities, for reasons similar to those mentioned in connection with the previous discussion of class and caste barriers between minorities and the dominant majority. There may be strength in union, but relatively small proportions of the colored and immigrant peoples in the United States seem to have been able to make any practical use of this principle in fighting the depression. In so far as cleavages within minorities bear any relation to economic opportunity and success in competition for any objective, it is probable that the exceptional economic stress has operated to increase the struggle between subgroups. In the case of distinctions based on social visibility, such as color or cultural peculiarities, it is likely that the more common tendency would be for those with the least degree of visibility to be reluctant to identify themselves with less favored members of their group. Status alignments are not the products of reason, nor do they lend themselves readily to rational manipulation for intergroup advantage. Sensible as it might be to pay less attention to group prestige in combatting hard times, the tendency appears to be to lay even greater than normal stress on lines of social cleavage during periods of economic distress. This hypothesis, of course, is a generalization that is not intended to apply to all individuals or to all types of social stratification.[5] The problem is to discover and explore the degree of truth which it may contain. This perhaps may be accomplished, but not without difficulty at this late date, by the use of sources and procedures similar to those suggested above in connection with the discussion of minority-majority status relationships, though special precautions will have to be taken against misunderstanding arising out of the cultural peculiarities of any given minority. Any phase of human relations of sufficient social importance to be regulated by sanctions of custom may offer research opportunities of this type.

A few exceptional possibilities for the study of minority status groups may be pointed out. The comparative social rank of business partners, associates, executives, and various grades of employees before and during the depression for firms controlled by minorities is capable of investigation. The names on payroll records, for illustration, may be a source of information both by virtue of the obvious class significance of certain ones and because of the possibility of investigating the social status of their bearers. It is not assumed in this connection that parity in business associations implies equality in social status, but it is suggested that any significant change in the status grouping of individuals brought into close association during the depression period—let us say in Jewish companies—would illuminate the stratification of that minority. Similar analyses might also

---

[5] As an extreme example of contrary behavior, reference may be made to the well-known fact that occasionally persons of unmixed white ancestry have deliberately passed themselves off as Negroes, presumably in the main because of a preference for Negro associations and for employment opportunities, as in a colored orchestra. Whether the depression increased such instances is an interesting question, but there is little hope that it will ever be answered.

be made of the membership of minority religious congregations, since all minorities have individual units of worship to which status implications are attached. Minority enrollment in private and parochial schools with class connotations also offers opportunity to investigate social distinctions. Jewish and Negro college fraternities, and clubs of all kinds that are found among minorities, should be particularly fruitful sources of information concerning the influence of the depression on status classifications.

Most diagnostic of all should be the facts concerning intermarriage of members of minority subgroups, since marriage is a legally recorded change in a human relationship in which social status is a prime factor. Has there been any change since the beginning of the depression in the comparative pigmentation of Negro couples which might throw light on our problem? Have there been more or fewer intermarriages between Negroes born in the United States and colored immigrants, groups which have a history of deep-seated conflict? Have the old, established Negro families in such cities as Philadelphia, Boston, Baltimore, and Washington shown more or less of a tendency to marry into migrant and other socially inferior Negro families since 1929? Are American-born children of immigrants more commonly marrying immigrants of their particular national origin than before the depression? What of intermarriage between members of the various Jewish castes and classes? Some information on questions of this type could be obtained from no more than the names of persons securing marriage licenses. In most cases, however, it is necessary to make use of additional personal data, some of which may be found recorded in connection with the license, such as color, place of birth, citizenship, place of residence, names of parents, occupation, and the like.

In studying minority status groups it is perhaps wisest, and most convenient, not to concentrate on any one or two of the sources just suggested. For no one of them does it seem feasible to secure a representative nationwide sample of data, and no one type of data has been shown to be such as to permit the student to draw definitive conclusions. Furthermore, it is not likely that the status cleavages of any fair-sized, well-dispersed minority will be found to be even relatively uniform throughout the country. The most workable procedure would appear to be to confine individual studies to clearly defined local communities, or perhaps, if facilities permit, to a series of communities selected for comparative purposes. If the resources at hand for a particular study do not allow even a complete community analysis, it should be profitable to study one type of institution within a community, such as the schools or the minority churches, or even a single institution, perhaps—one school or one church. The hope of ultimate understanding of minority group status in the depression lies not in large scale projects but in the eventual summation of a multitude of reasonably comparable and additive investigations each in itself feasible for the competent scholar of modest means.

Chapter III

Distribution

IN THE hands of specialists, the field of population has shown a tendency to stress statistical techniques in the study of the numbers, race, nationality, sex, and age of people in a given area, their changes in residence, their death rates and their birth rates, to the end that in describing these situations quantitatively they may eventually establish relationships of various sorts between these categories. Raw data of this order are available in abundance.[1] It is not improbable, however, that the mere availability of census data has been of more importance in determining the

---

[1] The Census of 1930 naturally contains the best data available concerning the geographical distribution of American minority peoples for use as a base in studying depression influences. Attention is called not only to the general 1930 Census report on population but also to the *Special Report on Foreign-Born White Families by Country of Birth of Head* for the same year prepared under the supervision of Dr. Leon E. Truesdell and published by the Bureau of the Census in 1933. This report contains an appendix "giving statistics for Mexican, Indian, Chinese, and Japanese families." Jews, however, are not enumerated by the census as such, although limited inferences may be drawn from the data on the Yiddish-speaking population, and for the geographical distribution in their case the data collected by H. S. Linfield for 1927 may be utilized. These data may be found in Schneiderman, Harry. (Editor) *American Jewish Yearbook.* Vol. 36. Philadelphia: American Jewish Committee, The Jewish Publication Society of America. 1936. Pp. 370ff. The bulletin *Age of the Foreign-Born White Population by Country of Birth* for the year 1930 published by the Bureau of the Census in 1933 contains data on the mother tongue of immigrants.

For summaries and analyses of current population problems and data see Dublin, Louis I. (Editor). "The American People." *The Annals* of the American Academy of Political and Social Science. Vol. 188. Philadelphia, November, 1936. This symposium deals with "the composition, distribution and growth of the population, and its relation to resources in the United States."

content of population studies than is warranted by the logic of the problems investigated. The Carl Smith who has been enumerated as born in Germany in 1888, arriving in New York in 1908, marrying in 1918, moving to San Francisco in 1928, and finally dying there in 1931, may not be understood as a person from these facts, nor do these facts offer a basis for the interpretation of a nation, community, or historical period even if multiplied by a million, except in so far as they are projected against a background of material and cultural description. It is well to bear this limitation of population statistics in mind as the problems of minority distribution are considered.

POPULATION DISTRIBUTION AND RESOURCES

In considering the distribution of minorities two questions present themselves: (1) Since no minority population has distributed itself with anything that approximates evenness throughout the total population, did the predepression regional concentrations of minority peoples deflect or intensify the impact of the depression because of residential relations to material and cultural resources, and in what ways? and (2) How did minority population movements during the depression influence the effects of the depression?

The first of these two questions has already received an answer in its larger aspects as a byproduct of a study of the possibilities of population redistribution as a defense against depression.[2] That this study paid only incidental attention to minority peoples in carrying out its mandate to examine the possibility of improving the economic situation through population shifts must in itself be taken as evidence of considered judgment that their distribution was not an important factor in the crisis.

American minority peoples have been noted for a mobility which has enabled them to follow where economic opportunity

[2] Goodrich, Carter, and Others. *Migration and Economic Opportunity.* Philadelphia: University of Pennsylvania Press. 1932. Pp. xvii+763

led, and thus provide a flexible labor supply where it is most needed.[3] The Indian, of course, has not been mobile since the settlement of the West, but his numbers are far too small to be of national economic significance. The Negro, ordinarily thought of as a relatively stabilized population element, has actually since his first arrival on this continent moved with the work available to him; southwestward with specialized agricultural development until the World War, and then northward to cities as industry found itself unable to fill its needs from the supply of immigrant and native white labor. Immigrants, coming to the United States for work and without personal resources, naturally located where work was most abundant. It may be argued that the minority labor supply—workers characterized as cheap, tractable, and mobile—aided industrial overexpansion and thus intensified the subsequent depression, but such reasoning suggests the search for a scapegoat. It is, however, the only line of reasoning in which the depression is connected with minorities as a causal factor.

The first part of the population distribution study referred to above examines intensively the economic need for migration with particular reference to regional economic levels, the distribution of resources, industrial location, and trends in the need for labor. The data—compiled by counties—concerning agricultural income, planes of living as indicated by income tax returns (1928), residence telephones (1930), families reporting radio sets (1930), and persons on relief (1933-1934), do not suggest any possibility of generalizing concerning the relation of the depression to minority population distribution. They do, however, suggest the desirability of further intensive study, minority group by minority group and county by county. Such a study, involving the comparison of each minority population by coun-

---

[3] *Population Index,* published quarterly by the School of Public Affairs, Princeton University, a continuation of *Population Literature,* regularly contains a section devoted to bibliographical notices on migration.

ties with the data prepared by Professor Goodrich and his associates, when taken in conjunction with such pertinent data for
the Census year 1930 as each county's economic characteristics,
minority population occupations, age and sex distribution, family structure, education, and the like, would do much to provide
bases for clarifying any discussion of minorities in later years.

Referring to his "plane-of-living" map, Professor Goodrich
observes that:

It may be asked whether any race or nationality groups are regularly
associated with the poorer colors on this map. The European and Asiatic
immigrants are too well distributed among the population for any influence they may have to be visible by counties. The areas of high Negro
population[4] coincide fairly well with our "red"[5] counties in certain sections, as in northern Louisiana and in much of South Carolina, but on the
whole the agreement is not striking. These Negro areas do not invariably
fall in a worse color than others, probably for the reason that the items
used in making this map do not distinguish between the poor and the
very poor.

The influence of the Mexicans and Indians of the Southwest is almost
as hard to isolate. Our poorest counties in Utah, Arizona and New Mexico have usually a high percentage of Indians to the population (Apache,
Arizona, 66 per cent), or a high percentage of Mexicans (Dona Ana,
N.M., 54 per cent). Some have many of each. But other factors combine
to make some counties seem fairly good, despite large Indian or Mexican
groups. Conconino, Arizona, with 52 per cent of both, is such a county;
Grand Canyon is there. Yavapai, Gila and Cochise, Arizona, have not
only mining, but cities of some importance, and thus stand well, though
each has over 30 per cent of Indians and Mexicans.

Rio Arriba and Taos, "red" counties in New Mexico, report few
Indians and almost no Mexicans among the population, whereas those
who know the country believe these counties to contain nearly as many
as McKinley, which has 60 per cent of both. There is reason to believe
that the census enumeration in these and certain other counties has
failed to count as such large numbers of Mexicans and Indians. It is said

---

[4] Paullin, C. O. and Wright, J. K. *Atlas of the Historical Geography of the
United States*. Plate 70B. Carnegie Institute of Washington publication No. 401,
1932

[5] This refers to the colors in which the map was done, red indicating very
poor counties, and other shades toward the opposite end of the spectrum showing
those of progressively greater resources.

that Mexican enumerators sometimes list Mexicans as native white. Imperial, the California county with 35.5 per cent of its population Mexican, falls below neighboring counties, though its land is rich. But this may be partly for lack of large cities, rather than from the presence of Mexicans. In western and southern Texas, it is hard to see any correlation between the percentage of Mexicans and the colors shown. On the other hand, there is always the possibility that many Mexicans, as in the New Mexico counties, were not counted as such.

Indian populations elsewhere in the country stand out much more clearly, except in Oklahoma. In Utah, San Juan, the one county having over 25 per cent Indians, is one of two in the lowest plane-of-living class. In Montana, the two counties of largest Indian population—Glacier and Big Horn—stand as low as any, and lower than all but one. Sioux County, North Dakota, with 30 per cent of Indians, stands in the lowest North Dakota class. The two lowest South Dakota counties have 82 per cent and 88 per cent of Indian population—the highest in the State. The six remaining counties having over 25 per cent of Indians fall either in the next higher class, or barely within the class above that. And only Ziebach County in the second class has a negligible percentage of Indians. In Minnesota, the worst county is the only one having a large proportion of Indians: 26 per cent of the population.

Thus we see the Indian counties usually poorer than others; though whether the Indians made them poor, or found them that way, may be questioned. Such measures as we have used are less applicable to Indians, however, than to others who perhaps take more interest in radios and have more use for telephones.[6]

This quotation, minimizing the possible use of plane-of-living data in connection with the study of minority population concentrations as a cause of the economic situations found in various counties, is given here at length because, in spite of its understatements, it excites curiosity concerning correlations which might be made. For example, Professor Goodrich brushed aside European and Asiatic immigrants, as quoted above, as "too well distributed among the population for any influence they may have to be visible by counties." It may be true that these immigrants do not have a sufficiently uneven distribution to justify county by county analysis, and that an analysis of them to establish a beginning-of-the-depression base and make possible later

---

[6] Goodrich, Carter. *Op. cit.* Pp. 25-26

comparisons is not feasible. Yet such an attempt is obviously called for in the case of each minority, if only because Professor Goodrich has given us such an excellent start in the matter of economics and total population.

It is, of course, both possible and desirable to compare minority population concentrations not only by county but also by major national regions, states, metropolitan areas, or whatever other units are available in a given case, with a much wider range of economic indexes than those used by Professor Goodrich. This is a matter of choice with reference to particular problems. The county, however, remains the one relatively small, clearly-defined politico-geographical unit for which it is possible to obtain data on a national scale concerning both the composition of the population and economic indexes. For this reason it is the one practical working unit for mapping minority population distributions throughout the entire United States in relation to local economic conditions before and during the depression.

Granted the validity of the hypothesis that minority workers during their predepression history demonstrated exceptional sensitivity to differential regional labor demands and thus distributed themselves throughout the country with primary reference to local economic opportunities, there still remains the problem of economic adjustment by migration as a consequence of regional and occupational irregularity of depression impact. Was minority mobility such during the depression that it aided rather than hindered the resolution of economic problems? This question calls for consideration of national immigration and emigration and of internal population shifts during the depression.

INTERNATIONAL MIGRATION

Men move because they believe they will be better satisfied in some other place. Before moving they must be dissatisfied with their location and hopeful of finding a better one for their purposes at a transportation cost and cost of readjustment not anticipated to exceed expected gains of migration. Dissatisfaction may be with material or cultural circumstances, or both, and so may the attractions of a new home. The move may be voluntary or compulsory, or a combination of these to varying degrees. Historically, the main motive behind migration has been economic, complicated with secondary drives and rationalizations of failure at home. Those who make good financially at home rarely decide to start over again in some other community, as is witnessed by the poverty of migrants, which shows how reliable a clue this is to the most widely found motive for migration in or out of depression.

It may consequently be assumed that a severe economic depression in a given region discourages outsiders from attempting to locate in that region, except those who may be worse off where they are or who may expect in their new place of residence greater cultural congeniality or special assistance by friends or relatives. As a corollary, it may also be assumed that the entrance of outsiders into a depression area will be regarded with strong disfavor by its residents. From this it might be expected to follow as a matter of a priori logic that with reference to the United States during the depression:

(1) The pressure of immigration from foreign countries should have been severely reduced, with the exception of individuals having personal connections in the United States which promised sentimental satisfactions or support. Further, this reduction in immigration as between different countries of origin should bear a direct relation to their respective economic conditions and to that of the United States.

(2) Increased emigration, including legal deportation, voluntary repatriation, and assisted repatriation, should have been expected.

(3) The attitude of residents in the United States should have been markedly less friendly toward immigrants during the

depression than previously. Earlier rationalizations favoring immigration, such as the concept of the United States as a "haven of refuge" for the oppressed of the world, should have lost much of their popular appeal and have been in large measure replaced by such nativist slogans as "America for the Americans."

(4) There should have been a practical cessation of internal migration of minorities toward predepression employment centers, particularly toward urban centers, and increased hostility on the part of the people of regions of heavy minority concentration against further minority additions to the population.

(5) There should have been a noticeable, but far from complete, reversal of previous internal migration trends back toward original home regions for reasons of previous experience, sentiment, and for family and group support. There should also have been new internal migration movements toward refuge areas, including marginal lands, centers of relief generosity, and to regions reported to be in better condition.

(6) There should have been an increase in transient and aimless internal migration.

(7) There should have been increased problems of minority congestion.

(8) Excepting transients, migrants motivated by differences in local relief policy, and individuals misled by reports of better conditions in some other community, there should have been increased family and group solidarity among minority internal migrants—and even improved personal integration—as a result of a depression trend back to familiar scenes and people after the disappearance of employment opportunities causing predepression migration.

It is, of course, hardly necessary to observe that these hypotheses, together with the basic assumptions on which they rest. may not be accepted without much more support than the reasoning process and fragmentary observation which now support them, and that it is not anticipated that they will ever be established as at present baldly stated without obviously necessary qualifications. They are all, however, susceptible of proof or disproof, in whole or in part.

That immigration from foreign countries has practically ceased during the depression in comparison with its volume in previous years is a commonplace observation which can be established by no more than a casual survey of the records of the Bureau of Immigration and Naturalization.[7]

Such a crude comparison, however, tells practically nothing about the relation between immigration and the depression. What nations and subregions in them have sent the United States the comparatively few immigrants who have arrived since 1929? To what extent did the streams of emigration from the various human export nations of the word dry to a trickle because of homeland conditions, particularly economic and political, and to what extent was it decreased because of diversion to other immigrant-receiving countries? What can be inferred concerning depression migration by comparisons of economic levels

[7] The most comprehensive source of international migration data covering the period immediately prior to the depression is: Willcox, Walter F. (Editor). "Statistics," *International Migrations*. Vol. I, compiled on behalf of the International Labour Office, Geneva, with introduction and notes by Imre Ferenczi. Pp. 1112; Vol. II, "Interpretations," by a group of scholars in different countries. New York: National Bureau of Economic Research. 1931. Pp. 715. These two volumes constitute the finest possible guide to available materials. See also *World Statistics of Aliens*. Geneva: International Labour Office. Studies and Reports, Series O (Migration). No. 6. 1936. Pp. vii+251

It is also suggested that various publications concerned with the larger aspects of population movements be consulted in planning research on problems of international migration. Among these, the following may be suggested as especially valuable: Carr-Saunders, A. M. *World Population*. Oxford: The Clarendon Press. 1936. Pp. xv+336; Davie, Maurice R. *World Immigration*. New York: The Macmillan Co. 1936. Pp. x+588; Taft, Donald R. *Human Migration*. New York: The Ronald Press Co. 1936. Pp. xxiii+590; Thompson, Warren S. *Population Problems*. New York: McGraw-Hill Book Company. 1930. Pp. xi+462; Dublin, Louis I. (Editor) *Population Problems*. Boston: Houghton, Mifflin Co. 1926. Pp. xi+318

and social conditions in countries of origin and of destination? To what extent was international migration artificially limited during the depression more than before it by legal measures aimed at damming the flow? In short, may not a breaking down of the gross figures of international movements of peoples which involve a relatively permanent change in official residence provide a reliable test of the validity of the hypothesis that the depression tended to limit immigration by reducing differences in the economic levels of the sending and receiving countries?

Previous studies of immigration into the United States in pre-depression times give support to this hypothesis.[8] Since 1921, however, the situation has been complicated by numerically restrictive legislation and administrative procedures. Before that time any number of immigrants could enter the country as long as they met a few simple individual, qualitative tests of personal desirability, and any change in volume could be correlated with conditions suspected of bearing on migration motives. Since then the immigration acts of 1921 and of 1924, together with the extended administrative interpretation of the old law barring aliens likely to become public charges—which came to be read so as to include economic conditions in the United States as well as immigrant personal handicaps as a basis for denying visas— have put an end to the use of gross immigration figures in the analysis of migration volume as a natural flow. There is, however, no apparent reason to believe that the recent depression has exerted any different influence on immigration than previous ones, unless conditions abroad may this time have been somewhat different than in previous American depressions.

Adequate data have not yet been presented to serve as a guide to immigration legislation designed to protect both this country and potential immigrants when later depressions arrive. Would

---

[8] Jerome, Harry. *Migration and Business Cycles.* New York: National Bureau of Economic Research. 1926. Pp. 256; Thomas, Dorothy S. *Social Aspects of the Business Cycle.* New York: Alfred A. Knopf. 1927. Pp. xiv+217

a flexible quota system subject to both upward and downward revision in accordance with periodic economic indexes be an improvement over the present system? If so, when should quotas be changed, on what basis, and through what administrative procedures? What account may be taken of the fact that because of cultural similarities certain immigrants may be more readily absorbed than others? What humane exceptions to general regulations need be considered to allow for personal, family, and political exigencies? What necessity is there for national protection against the arrival of many immigrants motivated by previous prosperity during the early stages of a depression? All such questions may be settled by flat decree that no immigrants are wanted so long as there is an unemployed man in the country, or by such patchwork legislative and administrative barriers as are at present in force. A rationalized system of immigration regulation must be postponed until just such questions as those listed have received trustworthy answers.

As immigration decreased, emigration increased during the depression. American conditions which failed to attract new immigrants naturally also failed to hold tens of thousands of earlier arrivals. It is noteworthy, however, that the depression was not sufficiently severe to drive out any appreciable number of native-born citizens. The greater number of depression emigrants were people who returned to an earlier homeland as a refuge, and not persons who left this country to take their chances in a new and strange home. Furthermore, although the emigration totals during the depression years are impressive when compared with immigration of the same groups during the same years, they lose importance when a comparison is made between them and similar national origin groups resident in this country.

More rigid enforcement of deportation laws accounts for some of this emigration during difficult days. In the absence of any evidence of marked increase in anti-social or disloyal conduct on the part of immigrants during the depression, it must be assumed that increased national unfriendliness toward aliens was responsible for the increased deportation activity, and that the legally-assigned causes of deportation in innumerable instances, although literally accurate, were in a sense utilized in deportation prosecutions because of anti-alien sentiment reinforced by the depression. It has never been a secret from government officials that for decades there have been hundreds of thousands of aliens illegally resident in the United States, but not until the troublesome times following the World War, and particularly during the depression, did deportation sentiment become really effective in stimulating action.[9] The relation between the depression and increased deportations seems so clear that what is required is not further statistical and legal studies but rather historical and sociological examination of the rise of public sentiment supporting the more severe recent policies.

Voluntary departures of immigrants, usually repatriations, are far more important numerically and for analytical purposes than deportations. What tendencies, great or small, did the various nationalities show to return to their land of birth during the depression, and how do the depression repatriation tendencies compare with those of predepression days? Are there differences in native cultures which may explain differences in repatriation rates, as between the rates, for example, of the Italians and the Swedes? To what extent is repatriation a function of comparative economic conditions in the homeland or of social pressures

---

[9] For analyses of the administration of deportation legislation see: Van Vleck, William C. *The Administrative Control of Aliens*. New York: The Commonwealth Fund. 1932. Pp. ix+260; Clark, Jane Perry. *Deportation of Aliens from the United States to Europe*. New York: Columbia University Press. 1931. Pp. 524; National Commission on Law Observance and Enforcement. *The Administration of the Deportation Laws of the United States*. Washington, D.C.: Government Printing Office. 1931. Pp. 179; Panunzio, Constantine M. *The Deportation Cases of 1919-1920*. Federal Council of Churches of Christ in America. 1921. Pp. 104

in the United States? What were the individual characteristics of the immigrants who left the country both before and during the depression? How many of them had made and saved enough money to live comfortably in their country of birth? How did their savings, their general adjustment to life in the United States compare with that of their compatriots who did not leave the country? Were the repatriates drawn from the least assimilated of the immigrants in the United States? What of their age distribution, their family structure and ties, their ability to use English, their level of education, their length of residence in this country, their age at immigration, and their occupations abroad and here? In other words, is it possible to characterize repatriates or groups of repatriates in terms of the economic, political, or cultural characteristics of their country of origin, of individual qualities, of achievement in the United States, or of economic and social pressures exerted against them?

A special study of "assisted repatriation" is also called for. In spite of extreme official reluctance for any publicity concerning this matter there is no question but that appreciable numbers of aliens left the United States "voluntarily" during the depression, with both public and private financial assistance and even under coercion. This statement does not refer to those individuals probably subject to legal deportation who were allowed to leave at their own expense to save the government trouble and money or to permit later legal reëntry if desired. Specific reference is made to the large number of Mexicans who without legally recognized cause or procedure were, in effect, forced back to Mexico with the tacit approval of state and local officials, public and private relief workers, by employers who had recruited them and even by self-appointed guardians of the nation, with or without financial assistance. Furthermore, how many children of these coerced voluntary repatriates, born in and citizens of the United States, were also forced out of the country with no legal justification and with considerable consequent confusion concerning their subsequent citizenship status? In this connection it is not without significance that in one district in the Southwest a new category of relief clients was created, that of "citizens by birth only," referring to children of aliens born in this country. From the point of view of relief administration, there is no reason for inquiring or recording either the race or citizenship of relief applicants, since in theory at least all legal residents of the United States are legally entitled to relief if in need. Yet there is good reason to believe that the citizenship status of alien relief applicants, particularly in the Southwest, was taken into account to the extent of encouraging and even forcing repatriation. There was appreciable public sentiment in favor of such action as a means of saving money and ridding the country of alleged undesirable aliens. The subject deserves study, if only for the light it may throw on the power of nativistic forces to accomplish an extra-legal objective in time of national crisis.

Primary attention to the problem of any depression change in popular attitude toward minorities of alien origin will be given in a later section devoted to nationalism and nativism during the depression. It is, however, to the point to raise here the question of the influence of the depression on public opinion concerning immigration as such. During most of its history the United States has welcomed the immigrant, at least as far as those who made the country's immigration laws were concerned. Competing native workers, of course, have long been sceptical of the immigrant's desirability. Nevertheless, so long as abundant cheap land was thought to need development to ensure the nation's prosperity or, later, so long as expanding industry needed vast quantities of cheap labor, this country prided itself for its record as a haven of refuge for the politically, religiously, economically, and otherwise oppressed of the world, especially if they were white people. Except in the case of Orientals— because their earlier restriction, beginning timidly in 1882 and culminating in 1924, is a special case complicated by distinctive color and culture differences—quantitative immigation restriction sentiment was ineffective until the passage of the first quota act in 1921. Not until the depression did this sentiment reach the point where the nation could be said to have reversed its earlier attitude and to have taken the position that immigration as such was a threat to national welfare.

Most verbalized arguments for and against immigration and immigrants are apparent to the student to have been popular rationalizations of national and class interests. A majority of the population saw progress, prosperity and personal profit, first in driving back the frontier and later in the presence of a large labor supply. They were convinced that a rapidly increasing population was desirable, that immigrants were fine people, and that American tradition demanded that they be welcomed with open arms. National symbolic phrases, such as "land of opportunity," "refuge of the oppressed," and "right of asylum" were the all-powerful shibboleths. It now appears that the depression has destroyed the power of such phrases, and put in their place slogans such as "America for the Americans" condemning immigration and immigrants per se. The beginnings of this change were evident long before the depression, but it was during the depression that the movement reached its culmination.

What rôle was played by rationalized arguments and national symbols in the regulation of international migration? To what extent was the discarding of old and the acceptance of new immigration attitudes in the depression a natural, unplanned product of conditions, and to what extent was it fostered by organized propaganda? What facts, figures, analogies, rallying cries, and appeals to tradition, true or false, were used to translate national woes into immigration restriction? What were the personal and organizational sources of propaganda, and what channels of communication were most effectively utilized? The need is for full information concerning the entire process whereby material depression phenomena produce immigration barriers and alien deportations. Future control of immigration is dependent on detailed understanding of this process.

INTERNAL MIGRATION[10]

Turning from international to internal migration, it may first be observed that at the beginning of the depression minorities of recent alien origin were most heavily concentrated in those sections of the United States with the greatest economic opportunities during prosperity and which were probably better able than the rest to take care of their populations during the depression.[11] This is merely the natural consequence of the combination of the mobility and economic motivation of the immigrant. Owing to the tendency of people to settle down and take root in a region to which they have once been attracted, it is understandable that it is among the groups with the longest residence in this country that economically stranded populations are most likely to be found. Centers of economic prosperity have shifted from time to time during the natural course of economic history and left behind disinherited populations attached to decadent areas. Recently arrived aliens have not yet had time to be stranded or to lose their mobility. With remarkable uniformity, after landing on our shores, they have gone promptly to prosperous regions and have later moved about somewhat more freely than the native population as opportunity beckoned.

This does not mean that immigrant distribution in relation to economic opportunity has been perfect. French Canadian immigrants have perhaps stayed too near the eastern Canadian border. Mexican immigrants, spreading in the states bordering their country and drifting up the Pacific Coast and the Missis-

---

[10] The subject of internal migration, in general, is treated at greater length by Thompson, Warren S. *Research Memorandum on Internal Migration in the Depression.* See also Sanderson, Dwight. *Research Memorandum on Rural Life in the Depression.* (monographs in this series)

[11] Goodrich, Carter. *Op. cit.* Particularly Ch. IX, "The Record of Unguided Migration," and Appendix A, "The Analysis of Past Migration."

sippi Valley, with but sparse penetration of the industrial East and Lake States, have undoubtedly missed many of the better labor opportunities by accepting those more accessible to them. All nationalities show tendencies to restrict mobility by forming concentrated colonies. The restricting influences of distance, easiest routes of travel, and this tendency for nationals to congregate in special areas do not, however, contradict the general observation that alien minorities as a whole were relatively fortunate in their pattern of distribution in relation to resources when the depression began.

The Negro and Indian, on the other hand, as minorities of long residence in the United States, did not find themselves so well situated when the depression arrived. It is true, of course, that beginning with the World War the Negro migrated in extraordinarily large numbers to industrial centers in response to demands for labor.[12] Most Negroes, however, remained in the less favorably situated southern districts where in earlier times labor demands had drawn them. In consequence, when the depression was at its worst an excessive proportion of Negroes found themselves most disadvantageously located. Those who had migrated northward before 1930 as a rule found themselves in the most favorable situation when the depression began.

The Indian population, concentrated in rural regions west of the Mississippi, frequently on very poor lands, and tied to the soil through reservation and land allotment policy, was distinctly unfavorably situated in 1930 with relation to visible economic

---

[12] For an excellent bibliography on Negro migration in the United States see Ross, F. A. and Kennedy, Louise V. *A Bibliography of Negro Migration.* New York: Columbia University Press. 1934. Pp. 251. A migration bibliography is also contained in Work, Monroe N. *A Bibliography of the Negro in Africa and America.* New York: The H. W. Wilson Co. 1928. Pp. xxi+698

For basic statistical data on the American Negro see *Negroes in the United States, 1920-1932,* and *Negro Population in the United States, 1790-1915,* both issued by the U. S. Department of Commerce, Bureau of the Census, Washington, D.C., in 1935 and 1918 respectively.

resources.[13] This condition, however, was offset by unprecedented federal generosity in the allotment of public funds to this minority during the depression. It may be said with confidence that not since the coming of the white man to America has this group been provided for so bountifully. This exceptional depression circumstance, together with the fact that Indian migration is economically unwise if not actually impossible under present government policy, rules this group out of further consideration in a discussion of depression population distribution.

Other than for the Indian, internal migration fluctuations of minorities during the depression should differ neither in method of study nor in actual direction from those of the majority except as minorities may be more or less mobile than the dominant white majority because of their status and history.

Goodrich and his associates reached the conclusion that migration in the decade preceding 1930 shows no "direct correspondence with the measure of depression distress as it does with the measures of predepression standards." They write:

> In the one case, the regions that looked favorable to the imperfect vision of the migrants tend to coincide at least in broad outline with those that were later to appear favored according to the imperfect figures of the statistician. In the other case, the relationship is more complex. The migrants left the safer farming regions in large numbers, though in lesser proportions than they did the sections of more precarious agriculture. . . . Yet nothing in the entire analysis is more striking than the degree to which migration of the twenties was drawing population away from those areas of chronic distress. . . .

---

[13] Indians east of the Mississippi are omitted from consideration because of the poverty of information concerning them. It should be remarked, however, that they afford excellent research opportunities for the social scientist which have been too long neglected. Reference may be made to the fact that Dr. Frank A. Ross of Syracuse University has undertaken extensive study of these relatively unknown Indians.

For the basic statistics of Indian population in 1930 see Truesdell, Dr. Leon E. (Supervisor) *The Indian Population of the United States and Alaska.* Washington, D.C.: U. S. Department of Commerce, Bureau of the Census. 1937. Pp. vi+238

It is therefore the more interesting to discover that just such areas as these made the most noteworthy increases in population when the trends of migration were reversed during the depression years.[14]

Even as temporary refuges . . . there is question enough regarding the places to which so many of these migrants have had to turn. But if we . . . ask whether they have in this movement found suitable areas for permanent location, the answer permits no doubt whatever. Even if the conclusions of the preceding chapter were wholly rejected, and a case made for a general return to the land, it would be impossible to argue for the long-run desirability of a back-to-the-worst-land movement. . . . To an extraordinary degree, the depression migrants have gone to the very regions which past experience has shown to be least capable of providing a decent living. . . .

Broadly speaking, then, migration during prosperity tended to carry people toward the areas which . . . appear more favorable for permanent settlement, and migration during the depression carried them back in the opposite direction.[15]

Whether these broad generalizations, subject to many qualifications with reference to special groups and exceptional local conditions, as their authors point out, have validity in application to the various minorities may not now be said. The repatriation of immigrants already referred to corresponds, of course, in some measure to the native migrant's return from the city back to the farm. Negro migrants to industrial centers may be assumed to have returned in some proportion to rural refuge regions, but in what proportion is not known. Immigrants, their children, and others characterized by strong foreign cultural and family ties, may be expected to have drawn together somewhat into concentrations of their own kind for material and psychological support. The methods employed by Goodrich and his associates in studying internal migration during the depression, such as the analysis of school census returns and agricultural census data, are not feasible for use in determining specific minority group population movements. Either the 1940 census returns must be awaited in the hope that they may be manipulated to throw light on depression migrations, or special local

---

[14] Goodrich, Carter. *Op. cit.* Pp. 505-506
[15] Goodrich, Carter. *Op. cit.* Pp. 516-517

studies must be undertaken utilizing such fragmentary records as those of relief and welfare agencies, or, most reliable of all, direct inquiry of the history of minority individuals.[16]

In addition to the general internal migration trends, attention must also be given to the wanderings of individuals and families following rumors of better conditions here and there about the country, engaging in casual and seasonal labor, searching for more generous relief centers, or just moving about more for the purpose of moving than for any definite material objective. Minorities, with the previously mentioned exceptions of the Indians and those Negroes who did not migrate prior to the depression, are characterized by a low mobility threshold. May it consequently be assumed that they responded more quickly than the rest of the population to vague gossip about places where it was easier for a man to earn a living, or where the authorities were more openhanded with funds for the needy? Did they turn more readily than others to the open road when employment seemed hopeless?

The major sources of information concerning this type of migration lie in the largely untabulated records of relief agencies and the schools. Unfortunately, this material often seems to distinguish with accuracy only between the white and Negro migrants, except perhaps in the Southwest, where the Mexican migrant is a cause of especial concern. Other groups are either not classified at all, or so carelessly that the figures are of little value. Furthermore, it is something of a matter of chance whether one of these migrants comes in contact with a relief

---

[16] For an excellent example of procedure for such inquiry see Kiser, Clyde V. *Sea Island to City*. New York: Columbia University Press. 1932. Pp. 272

Local censuses taken during the depression must not be overlooked as sources of data concerning minority groups. Florida, Kansas, Massachusetts, Rhode Island, and South Dakota regularly take a census of population under the provision of permanent state legislation. A special census was taken in Michigan in 1935, partly by the sampling method. Complete censuses were taken in Chicago, Illinois (1934) and in Cincinnati, Ohio (1935).

agency or school system to be counted, and whether if so, an accurate case history may be obtained. The most that may be promised with certainty is that the records can be made to throw some light on contacts of Negroes and perhaps, locally, of some other minorities with these agencies.[17] The following summary of the results of one study of migrant families with reference to color and nativity justifies quotation:

The color and nativity characteristics of the economic heads of migrant families were sufficiently unlike those of non-migrant families to

TABLE B-2

PER CENT DISTRIBUTION, ACCORDING TO COLOR AND NATIVITY, OF MIGRANT AND RESIDENT RELIEF FAMILIES AND OF FAMILIES IN THE TOTAL POPULATION

COLOR AND NATIVITY	MIGRANT FAMILIES 1935	RESIDENT RELIEF FAMILIES 1933[a]	TOTAL U.S. FAMILIES 1930[b]
All races	100	100.0	100.0
White	90	81.3	89.3
Native-born	83	c	70.1
Foreign-born	7	c	19.2
Negro	7	16.7	9.4
Other	2	2.0	1.3
Not ascertainable	1	—	—

[a] Unemployment Relief Census, No. 1, Federal Emergency Relief Administration, October 1933, p. 7

[b] Abstract of the Fifteenth Census, 1930, p. 405

[c] Not reported

provide another distinction between the two groups. Although approximately nine-tenths of the family heads in both the general and migrant family populations were white, it was found that migrant families included only a small proportion (7 per cent), whereas families in the general population included a relatively large proportion (19.2 per cent) of white family heads who were foreign-born. (See Table B-2.) Similarly,

[17] For type of relief data available see, for example: Webb, John N. *The Transient Unemployed.* Washington, D.C.: Works Progress Administration, Division of Social Research. 1935. Pp. 132; *Migrant Families.* WPA mimeographed reports. January 20 and April 21, 1936; *Statistics of Youth on Relief.* WPA mimeographed report. January 6, 1936; *Negroes on the Road.* State of New Jersey, Emergency Relief Administration. January 1935

a high proportion of white persons, including only a small proportion of foreign-born, has been found among unattached transients.

The relatively small proportion of foreign-born white persons among depression migrants is largely the result of two factors which tend to immobilize the foreign-born white population. Since the end of the period of agricultural expansion, foreign white immigrants have settled in large industrial centers and grouped themselves according to racial or national ties. Such ties act as deterrents to migration, despite the pressures arising from limited economic opportunity and recurring periods of unemployment. In addition, it is probable that local prejudice outside of the highly industrialized States makes migration for needy foreign-born persons more difficult than for the native-born and less likely to provide a solution of their economic problems.[18]

Of equal importance, according to this study, with the difference in the nativity characteristics of migrant and non-migrant family heads is the difference in their distribution according to color or race. Whereas Negroes constituted 9.4 per cent of the heads of families in the general population and 16.7 per cent of those included in the Unemployment Relief Census of October 1933, only 7 per cent of the economic heads of migrant families were Negroes. The marked overrepresentation of Negro families on resident relief rolls in comparison with their numbers in the general population is evidence that they were less able than white families to withstand the rigors of a depression. Yet, despite this evidence of greater economic pressure, Negro families were much less likely to migrate than white families. No doubt custom and prejudice operate to restrict the mobility of Negro families even more effectively than that of the foreign-born white. Migration without adequate resources, whether by highway or railroad, is much more difficult for Negroes, particularly in the South. Moreover, the practicability of migration is further limited by the preference of many employers for white labor.

Other race or color groups were proportionately as numerous among migrant as among resident relief families. The principal

---

[18] Webb, John N. and Bryan, Jack Y. "Migrant Families." *Monthly Report of the Federal Emergency Relief Administration.* Washington, D.C.: U. S. Government Printing Office. February 1 through February 29, 1936. Pp. 21-22

group among migrant families in the "other" classification was composed of Mexican families of migratory workers in the central and far western parts of the country.

This field of minority depression inquiry appears to be one in which the opportunity for good work has been lost by failure to make or preserve adequate records.

In spite of the appreciable number of minority individuals dispersed and footloose because of depression circumstances, it is reasonable to assume that, as in the case of the majority, most persons stayed about where they were in 1930 throughout the hard times that followed. Increased minority population congestion rather than dispersion appears to have taken place. Some migrated to rural regions, but usually to rural regions with which they had some familiarity either through former residence or through friends. Others crowded together even more closely than before in the cities. There was, of course, some dispersion. A small number of Negroes moved into the plains states and the Pacific Coast states in communities where Negroes previously had been almost unknown. Individuals of other less visible groups undoubtedly did the same. Studies of their experiences in such communities would be valuable as instances of the rise of majority consciousness of a new minority in its own back yard, particularly with regard to the development of accepted patterns of relationship.

The more important problem, then, at least from the point of view of numbers involved, has to do with concentration and congestion. Were pressing economic needs met by this type of migration as well as they might have been by greater dispersion? The chances are that those who moved to get more adequate relief were benefited, as were those who moved to get a share of the resources of family and friends. The exceptional number of Negroes, for example, who moved into Harlem during the worst years of the depression probably achieved better material conditions than would have been possible in their home communities in the South. Unplanned desperation migration may not be expected to achieve anything like a perfect balance between population and resources, but purely from the point of view of getting a place to sleep and enough to eat it seems to have worked out in this case.

Subsistence, of course, was the prime motive for this migration, not the prospect of improved social conditions of a brighter future in later years. This means that of necessity other social standards were submerged by the pressure of the need for subsistence. The question of minority internal migration during the depression, then, is not whether it was effective in avoiding starvation, but whether it had unfortunate social consequences which must be guarded against in the next depression.

Essentially this question has to do with social conditions as aggravated by depression migration in minority communities in the city and village. Those who found refuge in the open country undoubtedly encountered adverse conditions similar to those faced by all settlers in poor rural districts, but since minority status was not the predominating factor (except in those regions where farm tenure is linked with race, which will be discussed later) in the troubles of the rural settlers, no further immediate attention need be given them. In urban and even village communities, however, minority status takes on major importance among the factors determining living conditions.

Districts in which minorities may live are limited. Patterns of residential segregation vary from one community to another, but inferior and inadequate housing is the rule even in prosperous times, as must be expected in zones of transition between commercial use and residential desirability, or in back-street and alley segregation. This type of housing is rarely kept in adequate repair. Expenditures are kept down by crowding. Neighborhood facilities for recreation, education and the like, are generally inferior. Has the depression crowded more minority families into such areas? What has been the depression influence on family functioning, on health, and on personal standards because of migration in connection with inadequate housing? Have new districts been opened up to minorities, has there been any tendency for one minority to drive another out of its section, or has there been increased sharing of the same area by various minorities?[19] To what extent have minorities who in prosperous times succeeded in obtaining better housing been forced back into transitional zones? Is it true that their children rebelled against this "return to the Ghetto"? What has been the effect of business retardation on the development of minority residential areas, usually crowded in prosperous times by encroaching business and apartment houses? Have more majority members moved into minority areas, or vice versa, because of depression changes in individual fortunes? What has been the history of property owners' covenants and deed restrictions barring Negroes and Jews? What has been the experience of housing projects, particularly those involving public or philanthropic funds, designed for minority occupancy? The comprehensive question seeks to discover the extent of minority population concentration with its concomitant isolation, congestion, inferior housing and community facilities, health problems, behavior problems, and retardation in the rate of consolidation with the general population.

Perhaps the most interesting, and also the most difficult problem in connection with minority migration and the depression has to do with the social and personal adjustments necessitated by or resulting from changes in location. It is ordinarily assumed

---

[19] In Los Angeles, for example, there seems to have been an increasing tendency for Chinese, Japanese, Mexicans, Filipinos, Negroes, Jews, and Eastern Europeans to move into the same area. Schrieke, B. *Alien Americans.* P. 22

For a description of patterns of Negro residential segregation and urban life in general see Woofter, T. J. Jr. *Negro Problems in Cities.* New York: Doubleday, Doran & Company. 1928. Pp. 284. Especially recommended as a study of urban residential segregation of a minority group is Wirth, Louis. *The Ghetto.* Chicago: University of Chicago Press. 1928. Pp. xvi+306

that the uprooting of a family or individual involves a more or less severe shock to social and personal integration. Experience indicates that community stability is essential to social and personal stability. This assumption, however, presupposes a high degree of stability before migration and unfamiliarity with the new environment. In so far as minority migration in recent years has resulted in overcongestion in relation to available living facilities, it may be assumed to have increased maladjustments. On the other hand, when it is recalled that depression migration was to an appreciable extent a reversal of predepression trends, a desertion of individualistic industrialism and a search for refuge among scenes of earlier familiarity, the problem loses its simplicity. There is little reason to believe that aimless migratory families and transients, persons seeking better relief, or those following false rumors of economic opportunity, thereby achieve a more complete integration unless they chance to be individuals whose personalities are best adapted to the freedom of the open road. It is entirely conceivable, however, that many minority depression migrants found environments to which they were well adjusted.

Are the Mexican, Italian, and other immigrants who returned to their homelands during the depression living in better adjustment with their circumstances than comparable groups of compatriots who remained in the United States? Similarly, what of the Negroes who returned from the North to the South, from city to country, from factory to farm? What has been the sociopsychological effect of return to the ghetto, to Little Italy, and other minority areas of residential concentration by individuals who had escaped to unsegregated districts in more prosperous times? Has there been increased family consolidation as a consequence of increased dependence on family resources? Has community solidarity been increased because of the desirability of returning to friendly neighborhoods for mutual aid? Has the fact that relatives, friends, and neighbors of similar status were found to be valuable depression resources by minority individuals who were forced back after previous physical escape, afforded a degree of peace of mind and social adjustment? In terms of individuals, the answers to these questions must be both "yes" and "no." In terms of group trends they may be either "yes" or "no."

Whatever the answers may be, they must be inferred from a synthesis of the answers to questions raised elsewhere throughout this monograph. There is no one index to personal and social adjustment, nor is there any one method of approach to the problem. Various types of overt social behavior, such as forms of delinquency, and various evidences of personality problems, such as the neuroses and psychoses, must be compared with reference to migrants and non-migrants otherwise reasonably comparable. The problem is a special one properly included in this chapter only by virtue of the need for careful selection of the groups to be compared so that depression migration will be a controlled variable capable of linkage with differences discovered. Negro migrants returned to the South, Mexicans returned to the Southwest or across the border, French Canadians returned to Canada, migrants of any group who have been forced by the depression to lean more heavily on family and minority group resources offer opportunities for studies of any size and of manifold approach.

The discussion thus far has been of the internal migration of individuals free to move where they wish, guided only by unofficial fact, rumor, or personal inclination. During the depression, however, government planning has been an appreciable factor in the flow of population. It is probably true that every government measure related to the depression has had some influence on migration. Among those not purposefully designed either to move people or to decrease mobility may be mentioned international tariff agreements, changes in interest and tax rates, the extension of credit to business and the home owner, the National Industrial Recovery Act, the Agricultural Adjustment

Act, the public works program, and relief agencies. Other measures more directly designed to influence mobility include the Resettlement Administration and its predecessors, the Division of Subsistence Homesteads of the Department of the Interior and the Division of Rural Rehabilitation of FERA, the conservation, irrigation, and land retirement programs, the Tennessee Valley Authority, the Rural Electrification program, and other efforts to bring population distribution into better balance with that of resources. To attempt a complete catalogue of federal activities influencing depression shifts in population, to say nothing of those of state and local governments, would be a task unjustified by its value for present purposes.

It should be possible to examine the work of government agencies whose major objective was directly concerned with making it possible for people to stay where they were, or to improve their lot by moving, with respect to their effect on minority peoples. Were minorities given attention proportionate to their numbers and circumstances, or did they figuratively sit at the second table? Was their social status officially recognized in such matters as the location of resettlement communities, in exclusion from projects, and in the quality and amount of facilities offered? Was account taken of their cultural differences, their unbalanced age and sex distributions, and their problems of race contact and assimilation? Were various minorities as able and as willing to cooperate with the government agencies as fully as other groups? The activities of government agencies are matters of record and it should be no difficult task to extract from the records information on the nature and extent of the consideration given peculiar minority problems in public effort to adjust population and resources during the depression.

It is not likely that in any region of the world migration has succeeded in effecting an optimum distribution of population even if defined in the simplest economic terms. Maladjustment in this respect seems to be increased rather than decreased by the impact of economic crises, especially with reference to future prospects. Whether minority characteristics such as inferior social status, exceptional population composition, differential mobility potentialities, and separate cultural histories help or hinder their rationalized redistribution in time of crisis, is practically unknown. But these matters are none the less important for the national welfare.

Chapter IV

Economic Life

D IVISION of labor is commonly cited as a characteristic of modern economic organization. One form of specialized assignment of tasks in present-day economic production is that which restricts opportunity for work on the basis of the racial or national origin of the individual. This restriction may be founded on the belief in group inheritance of innate occupational aptitudes or handicaps, on the prejudice and self-interest of the dominant majority, on the culture and history of a particular minority, or on the processes of economic competition through the creation of dominance or monopoly. Whatever its foundation and justification, the question of prime concern in connection with the depression is whether national economic crisis tends to reduce or expand minority opportunities for earning a living. Since earnings today are largely in dollars of value only in terms of what is bought with them, knowledge of minority consumption opportunities and practices as well as of cash income is essential.

MINORITIES AND THE ECONOMIC ORDER

The casual observation that the greatest problem of minorities is to gain employment is a gross understatement of the case even if the economic aspects of living alone are under consideration. The remark that minorities are the last hired and the first fired is equally superficial and not entirely accurate. In the face of starvation, desperation may remove all considerations save the need for bare subsistence. This, however, does not eliminate such other economic problems as the need for the maintenance

of a level of living sufficiently high to permit personal and social integration; the need for occupational training and the
full development of productive potentialities; the need for
conditions of labor which will not destroy bodily and mental
health; or the need for the rationalized development of national resources, both material and human. It is consequently
inadequate merely to suggest further economic research which
will afford more detailed information of the type already in
hand on minority unemployment if we are to understand the
interrelationship of the depression and American minority peoples.

The field of economic activity is an extensive one, and minorities participate in all its phases. By far the greatest number of
minority economic problems are essentially identical with those
of anyone else. Thus the Negro cotton planter, the Italian truck
farmer, the Japanese grape grower, and the Indian sheep herder,
face the same uncertainties concerning weather and markets as
their neighbors of any racial or nationality stock. In the same
way, there are few economic problems confronting the minority
laborer, capitalist, or consumer that depend on his group status.
Such common problems are not of present concern; our immediate interest is in economic activities directly linked in their
performance with distinctive minority traits and status. The
selection of problems for presentation must consequently be on
the basis of minority limitations or advantages during the depression growing out of historical experience, characteristic culture patterns, population composition and distribution, and
intergroup beliefs, attitudes and behavior.

Though minority groups may not be assumed to have fared
alike in economic activity throughout the country, one general
question concerns any possible causal relation between minorities and the depression or its intensity, nationally or locally.[1]

---

[1] For a clear exposition of the point of view that the immigrant is decidedly
not a serious contributor to depression unemployment, see Ostrolenk, Bernhard.

A second has to do with the manner in which minorities fared during the depression in so far as their economic condition was influenced by their peculiar characteristics and their social status. A third raises the problem of the extent to which minority economic circumstances were a factor affecting the intensity of intergroup antagonisms during the depression.

Unless one makes the naïve assumption that the amount of unemployment may be determined by subtracting a fixed number of jobs from the total population, and that the situation may be relieved by shipping the surplus people out of the country, the mere excess of available individuals in the United States envisaged as members of minorities, is not a phenomenon of itself to be given prominence as a depression cause. Absolute number, moreover, is not the only matter that needs to be taken into consideration in this connection. More important is the agricultural and industrial expansion which has been facilitated by the presence of millions of poverty-stricken, cheap, tractible, mobile, minority workers on a low level of living who have been constantly available for the occupation of undeveloped land and for filling the labor needs of industry. On the West Coast the Chinese, Japanese, and Filipinos were found most useful as laborers in periods of expansion. Since the World War the Mexican laborer has been a main reliance of employers in a large area of the Southwest. The Negro has been the backbone of Southern agricultural and industrial labor for generations. Since early in the nineteenth century the European immigrant has been depended on to settle vacant lands and to supply industrial labor needs. The Indian, of course, has been regarded as more of a hindrance than a help in economic development, but as a minority he is exceptional in this respect.

Considering minorities as a whole, it thus appears reasonable to assume that from the establishment of this nation they have

"Immigration and Unemployment." *North American Review*. 239: 212-217. No. 3. March 1935

been utilized to speed the development of resources to an extent which from time to time may well have been so rapid as to intensify if not to induce every depression. Their rôle in agricultural expansion has been relatively unimportant in recent decades except in the Southwest, so that the problem of depression influence in this connection may be confined to periods prior to the present century. Minority influence on the intensity of the last depression through the facilitation of rapid economic expansion is therefore probably confined mainly to the effect of the abundant, mobile, and cheap European immigrant, Negro and possibly the Mexican labor supply. The importance of such a minority influence is not easy to determine, since it involves not only the careful description of the industrial employment of the members of minority groups, a relatively simple matter, but also an estimate of how American industry might have developed had there been no minority labor supply, a question practically impossible of satisfactory solution.

Turning to the second question, the relation between minority characteristics as such and minority economic status during the depression, one is immediately faced with the necessity for securing a predepression record of economic achievement as a base for comparison with depression trends. Since immigration research until some time after the World War was predominantly economic and students of the Negro also stressed his material living and working conditions, there is no shortage of general predepression economic data. The trouble is that these data, pointed as much of them are in both government census reports and in private studies toward geographic areas and economic classes, are nevertheless so gross as to be relatively incapable of refinement for the purposes of comparison with specific types of minority groups classified on the basis of cultural differences, economic and social history, and other traits. Yet without relatively detailed comparisons of this nature it is no easy matter to demonstrate the degree to which economic status is a function of minority characteristics in themselves or of more general national and local conditions.

Logic and general observation, of course, lead inevitably to the conclusion that there is a causal relationship between minority economic status and minority characteristics. The proportions of each minority class and caste, and of each of their subclasses and subcastes engaged in agriculture, industry, trade, personal service, and the professions, or unemployed, vary tremendously. These variations must be functions of differences between the various groups in culture, time of arrival in the United States, the existence of previously settled communities of similar minority status to which newcomers are attracted, intergroup antagonisms, and many other factors. Unfortunately, these differences as of normal times have not been analyzed in relation to economic status and, consequently, nothing may be said about their relative influence in depressions without a great amount of preparatory study. The economist in studying immigration has been neither prepared for nor interested in more than casual observations as to the social and cultural factors influencing immigrant economic activity. Students of the Negro until very recently were with few exceptions more interested in the manifestations of race prejudice and the description of the consequences of discrimination than in intensive analyses of basic causal factors. As a result, students of minority economic status in the depression who desire to establish trends must be largely content with descriptive statements, in the customary terms of economic measure, of the wealth and poverty, employment and unemployment, private income and relief assistance of broadly defined minorities in the mass, undifferentiated with regard to specific minority qualities except as they may be inferred from general knowledge.

As a modification of this discouraging outlook, attention should be called to samples of the few predepression studies of minorities or of minority communities which attempt to include both economic activity and distinctive group traits. Among these should be mentioned *The Negro in American Civilization* (New York, 1930) by Charles S. Johnson, *Immigrant Farmers and Their Children* (New York, 1929) by Edmund deS. Brunner, *Greek Immigration to the United States* (New Haven, 1911) by H. P. Fairchild, *The Polish Peasant in Europe and America* (2nd Edition, New York, 1927) by W. I. Thomas and F. Znaniecki, *Japanese in California* (Stanford University, 1933) by E. K. Strong, *Resident Orientals on the American Pacific Coast* (Chicago, 1928) by Eliot G. Mears, *Black Yeomanry* (New York, 1930) by T. J. Woofter, Jr., *Filipino Immigration* (Chicago, 1931) by Bruno Lasker, *The Problem of Indian Administration* (Baltimore, 1928) by Lewis Meriam and Associates, *The Mexican Immigrant* (Chicago, 1930) by Manuel Gamio, and the various monographs under the series titled *Mexican Labor in the United States* (Berkeley, 1928-1931) by Paul S. Taylor. No one of these is adequate for our present purposes, either from the economic point of view or that of the minority characteristics, but all offer the possibility of use as bases for depression comparisons. This list, it may be noted, is representative rather than complete. But even where such predepression studies are unavailable, it may possibly still be worthwhile for students to undertake depression studies of minorities and to investigate the economic status of specific subgroups or communities without any more predepression comparative data than may be obtained from such general sources as may be available.

In connection with the third general question raised above, the hypothesis may be suggested that group conflict varies in intensity in relation to the extent that individuals of two different status groups are dependent on wage employment and other economic facilities subject to competition. A second and interrelated hypothesis deserving further investigation holds that the intensity of intergroup antagonisms varies with the frequency of contacts between minority and majority individuals not in accord with customary practice under an accepted social definition of status relationship.

Such broad hypotheses, of course, may not be tested by any single workable research project, although there is perhaps sufficient evidence already in the literature to promise convincing verification or refutation through summarization and synthesis. Indeed, although no definitive synthesis has yet appeared, there is already a decided presumption in favor of the hypotheses. The depression, however, offers unusual opportunities for the intensive study of the relation between intergroup antagonisms, contacts in socially undefined situations, and economic competition, because of the sharp changes it brought about in all three variables.

A few of these opportunities may be indicated. The curtailment of employment in any industry accustomed to using both minority and majority labor should increase the intergroup competition for the remaining jobs and consequent increased conflict should become evident upon investigation. Serious decrease in general employment facilities in a community in which there have been traditional minority occupations might be expected to increase majority pressure to drive minorities out of these employments with concurrent evidences of increased intergroup conflict. Depression moves to replace majority labor with cheaper minority labor should be another focal point in minority-majority tension. On the other hand, anti-minority feeling should be observably decreased in situations and among individuals where intergroup competition is reduced by depression migration changes. Further, anti-minority antagonisms should not increase as greatly in those areas of the country where minority individuals are a rarity. Old established minorities in communities where they have lived long enough for their situation to be defined and accepted should show less evidence of increased depression antagonism than might be found for other communities of less recent minority invasion. There is no scarcity of situations in which such relationships may be tested.

The problem, of course, is to define any particular research situation in terms of economic competition and intergroup contacts so that it may with reasonable accuracy be compared with other situations, and also to devise reliable indexes of intergroup antagonism. The first part of the problem is complex but feasible, since the use of the customary indexes of employment and economic status may be limited only by their availability, and there are a sufficient number of these available for the present purpose. The second part of the problem is more difficult, since intergroup antagonisms express themselves in innumerable forms, and practically none of the basic work of classification and collection has been reliably done. This means that the individual research worker must fall back on a heterogeneous mass of group conflict data ranging all the way from such concrete items as race riots and lynchings to verbalized expressions of social attitudes. In an uncharted wilderness all paths offer possibilities.

Other than such broad generalizations as the three just suggested for examination—and it should be borne in mind that they are not readily feasible for direct study in their entirety except as large scale expensive projects or through synthesis of already published materials—it seems most practical to discuss separately the problems peculiar to agriculture, to urbanized labor, to business and finance, to the professions, and to the consumer.

AGRICULTURE[2]

Among American minorities, the Indian, the Mexican, the Filipino, the Japanese, most Negroes, and some European immi-

---

[2] More general aspects of social problems arising out of the impact of the depression in agriculture are discussed by Sanderson, Dwight. *Research Memorandum on Rural Life in the Depression.*

grants and their children are of primary concern as rural residents. Partly to save time and space, but largely because no outstanding minority depression problems will be omitted by the procedure, the terms "rural" and "agricultural" will be used almost as if they were synonymous, and no special attention will be given to the village or to rural industry and other non-agricultural rural occupations. The urban Indian is so rare and generally so well assimilated that he will be entirely omitted from discussion. The Mexican in industry, although not unimportant in restricted localities before the depression, will be given no more than passing reference, on the theory that the approach to his problems in urban areas may be inferred from that suggested in connection with other immigrant minorities of high social visibility. The Japanese will be similarly considered as though he were almost entirely in agriculture. The Negro and the European immigrant, however, have entered in such large numbers into both urban and rural occupations that their depression experience must be examined under both classifications. So far as practicable, problems common to more than one minority will be discussed only with reference to one.

One cluster of problems common in varying degree to all minority rural residents is composed of those related to land tenure. These may at first be thought to belong to that group of economic phenomena not of prime importance in the consideration of minorities as such in the depression. Land tenure, in fact, is a focus of problems for all agricultural communities of either minority or majority status. Actually, however, they are fundamental in a discussion of minorities, since in agriculture the form of control over land determines many other aspects of life, and is subject to variations both because of majority attitudes and of minority traits.

Land may be owned outright by the man who works it, or subject to mortgage, it may be rented by the farmer for cash or shares, with or without improvements or various forms of advances to the tenant, or it may be worked by laborers for hire. Which type predominates among a given group of minority agricultural workers is of course partly a matter of economics and of economic history, but to a surprising extent it is also a function of intergroup feeling and of minority history and culture. Perhaps the simplest evidence of this fact is the wide disparity between the predominating forms of land tenure to be found when different minority agricultural groups are compared as, for example, the Mississippi Negro and the New Jersey Italian farmer, or, if we but consider the state of California alone, the Mexican, Japanese, Filipino, and European immigrant farmers. Similar disparity may be observed when other aspects of farm operation and life are studied, such as the size of the unit of operation, the crops raised, farm equipment and housing, money and credit, or levels of rural living. Infinite variety of land tenure may be found among the rural members of any one minority, but each minority has its own distinctive land tenure pattern which is closely related to its special history, characteristics, and social status.

To a gratifying extent these distinctive patterns may be worked out, and have been worked out, from government census materials and special surveys such as those made by various agricultural experiment stations. There is, in fact, so much detailed data available in this field both for depression and predepression times that it will be enough of a task to sort out and rework that pertaining to minorities, while little if any need be added to the basic facts now available concerning minority land tenure and farm operation. One exception must be noted, however, for few facts have been collected separately for some minorities (Jews, for example) and none at all for minority subclasses and subcastes. These require investigation of a special type, so difficult that it may be said that, on the whole, the greatest promise lies in the analysis of material already in hand.

In addition, however, a direct attack should be made on the problems of minority land tenure and farm operation which the existing materials illuminate only through inference. These problems concern the causes and consequences of existing conditions with reference to local natural resources, economic structure, minority characteristics, and intergroup relationships. Outstanding in this respect, Negro land tenure and general rural conditions have been extensively and intelligently investigated both regionally and locally in the South so that the story of the depression experience is about ready to be written even if some details still need to be secured by special research.[3] For the European immigrant and his children, on the other hand, little is available except raw census and survey data. For the other minorities, between these two in importance and social visibility, not only the usual raw data can be had, but also some specific material for the predepression period to simplify special depression studies.[4]

---

[3] Two recent studies of the rural Negro may be cited both for the significance of their content and for their exemplifications of research methods: Raper, Arthur F. *Preface to Peasantry*. Chapel Hill: University of North Carolina Press. 1936. Pp. xiii+423; Johnson, Charles S. *Shadow of the Plantation*. Chicago: University of Chicago Press. 1934. Pp. xxiv+214

Especially recommended as a source from which may be obtained perspective on the Negro in agriculture in relation to southern economy as a whole as well as a source of specific data and bibliographical reference is Odum, Howard W. *Southern Regions of the United States*. Chapel Hill: University of North Carolina Press. 1936. Pp. xi+664

See also the following three research monographs prepared under the Federal Emergency Relief Administration, Division of Research, Statistics and Finance: Beck, P. G. and Forster, M. C. *Six Rural Problem Areas, Relief—Resources—Rehabilitation*. Washington, D.C. 1935. Pp. ix+167; McCormick, Thomas C. *Rural Households, Relief and Non-Relief*. Washington, D.C. 1935. Pp. xiii+141; Woofter, T. J. Jr. *Landlord and Tenant on the Cotton Plantation*. Washington, D.C. 1936. Pp. xxxiii+288

[4] See Young, Donald. *American Minority Peoples*. New York: Harper & Brothers. 1932. Pp. 594-607, for a selected bibliography including references to studies containing such material.

Study of legal limitations on the ownership and leasing of land by aliens proposed or in force during the depression should be especially revealing of rural attitudes toward minority competition. Alien land laws have been notoriously easy to circumvent through various subterfuges with or without the connivance of citizen owners eager to sell. They have not been favored by all elements in the population of the seven states in which they are in effect. An analysis of popular interest in such legislation and of possible depression changes in strictness of administration, either state by state or, since there are so few, all states together, is entirely possible now, but will not long remain so.

Turning to the separate minorities in the open country, and beginning with the Indian, it may be observed that he has had his own peculiar agricultural problems to face during the depression. As in the case of farmers in general, the primary depression influences on the Indian were through the disturbance of the market for his products, through the increased scarcity of cash and credit, and through the necessity for readjustment of consumption habits. In other respects, however, his situation was distinctive. The Indian farmed mainly to supply his own wants and those of the local community market, he was accustomed to little cash and practically no credit, and his consumption level was extremely low before the depression, even in comparison with other minorities. Remembering that there are many tribes represented by the Indians in the United States, each with some unique economic and cultural characteristics, what agricultural research questions present themselves?[5]

---

[5] Clark Wissler, in his "Foreword" to Margaret Mead's *The Changing Culture of an Indian Tribe,* summarizes the economic development of the Indian since the coming of the white man as follows:

"According to popular belief, the Indian has met with little short of disaster at the hands of the whites, his health, family life, and mode of getting a living are all believed to have been smashed by the steam-roller-like advance of white culture. Such statements may be too sweeping, in that attention is fixed upon

As might be expected, they are neither few nor simple. Among those tribes in which the tradition of communal ownership of land still persists, was this factor a source of strength or weakness in the depression? What was the comparative depression experience of those Indians whose land title or control was in the hands of the community, of the government, or of individuals? Did the traditional sex division of labor, differing from that customary in Western civilization, suffer more rapid disintegration or in any manner influence the impact of the depression? Was there any noticeable reversion to more primitive agricultural methods and practices, or did the depression tend to

the most tragic phase of the adjustment instead of upon the whole cycle of contact, for if the history of any American tribe is scanned, it appears that, for the most part, the first period of contact was to the Indian a season of prosperity. The first whites were traders rather than settlers; they brought new and useful objects for which the Indian could exchange furs and food. At once the Indians became producers of surplus goods, they broadened their outlook and many tribes increased in population and power. Later came the encroachments of settlers and diminishing natural resources, leading to a struggle in which the Indians were subdued by force and confined to reservations. Perhaps more than half of these died during this time of stress, while the remnant, in almost total economic and social collapse, entered upon a period of sullen passive resistance, attempting, as far as possible, to rehabilitate in isolation their old aboriginal life. Yet, after a time, adjustments began to be made; a slow increase in population set in and, with varying success, each tribe muddles along as a social and economic dependent of the nation in charge.

"The fundamental situation in this tribe [the anonymous one studied by Miss Mead] is not far to seek. It strives to maintain the old ideal, that food and other necessaries are for immediate consumption and distribution at the hands of him who calls, and at the same time to carry on in the midst of a nation-wide intense economic individualism. To maintain a community in which the accumulation of goods is regarded as anti-social and integrate the same with contemporary white culture is to try to harmonize two incompatible systems. The usual white policy is based upon the concept that under a reservation and land allotment program the tribe may so adjust its culture as to form a block of individual land holders, retaining their social solidarity and at the same time operating in the white economic system as self-supporting producers. Perhaps this is one of the most difficult social problems a people can face, but it does not follow that a solution is impossible." (Pp. vii-ix)

speed the adoption of the white man's ways? In those communities where the custom of communal labor on tasks of importance to the group as a whole still persisted, as in the Southwest, was it in any way a bulwark against the depression? What of such culture patterns of economic importance as the potlatch, the common right to food in the possession of any individual in time of need, or a system of matrilinear inheritance? The existence of many distinct tribes in distinctive agricultural regions is a source of confusion, but it is also responsible for the opportunity for unusually promising comparative studies designed to show the influence of variable factors between communities, and to evaluate such studies with reference to the government regulation of minorities characterized by distinctive cultures.

Study of the efforts on the part of the federal government to aid the Indian is perhaps the best comprehensive approach to an understanding of the problems of the rural Indians during the depression. The extraordinarily large amounts of federal funds spent in behalf of these people during the depression and the domination of Indian Office policies and personnel in their expenditure make investigation of the objectives, procedures, and consequences of governmental economic planning and subsidizing the paramount task. The theory and operation of the Wheeler-Howard Act of the present Roosevelt Administration will require study by many individuals and organizations over many years before its consequences may be appreciated. Embodying, as it does, a shift in emphasis in federal policy, from the previous objectives of tribal disintegration and rapid assimilation toward community self-determination through corporate organization and the full utilization of local material and cultural resources for the common welfare, it is a departure from American procedure in the regulation of minorities of extreme significance. As is so frequently true in the case of governmental shifts in policy in time of emergency, the provisions of the Wheeler-Howard bill were not a product of the depression, nor were they originated to meet depression needs. The depression merely operated to give their sponsors opportunity to put them into operation. How they worked as depression measures will long be a matter of dispute between partisans unable to agree on social objectives which are mutually acceptable.

It is possible, however, for the working of the act to be considered in the light of observable consequences. Since for its provisions to become operative for any particular Indian group it had first to be approved by formal ballot, a study of the votes cast and of the preliminary campaigning and propaganda to swing individual elections affords an excellent opportunity to gain insight into the attitudes of Indian communities, and the extent and bases of divided opinion within each group. In the same connection it would be interesting to examine into the origin and nature of the sharp disagreement between white partisans such as the Indian Office, the American Indian Defense Association, the Indian Rights Association, white business men and neighbors of Indians, and their representatives in the Congress. How did those Indian groups which took advantage of the provisions of the act fare in comparison with those who failed to do so? Was there any measurable improvement in the utilization of land and other resources under the act? To what extent were improvements in the conditions of groups taking advantage of the act the result of exceptional public expenditures and of general improvement in the local economic situation rather than of the act itself? How were social organization and social relationships affected by increased group self-determination? To what extent and under what circumstances was it actually possible to turn over to Indian management the independent regulation of community affairs on the extensive basis contemplated? Was the process of acculturation hastened or was native culture given a new lease on life? Comprehensively stated, how did the Wheeler-Howard Act modify the economic and social behavior of Indian communities operating under its provisions in comparison with each other and in contrast with those who failed to take advantage of it?

The Indian Emergency Conservation Work program is a second form of federal depression activity. With multiple objectives such as the conservation of resources, relief, and individual rehabilitation, its activities under the direct supervision of the Indian Office were planned to take full account of the Indian's cultural differences and of his status as a racial minority element in the population. It was for this reason that its operation was assigned to the office of the Commissioner of Indian Affairs rather than to the authority in control of the parallel work of the Civilian Conservation Corps, also known as the Emergency Conservation Work program. Official records already have established the material value of the work accomplished under this program, such as the construction of dams, of roads, and general forestry activities. More important, at least from the human point of view, is the degree of success achieved by the IECW in organizing its activities so as to cause as little social disorganization as possible and act as a positive influence in personal and social integration. The trained cultural anthropologist with an interest in the applied aspects of his field, and perhaps those sociologists and social psychologists with special competence in the cultural approach to their problems, may be expected to contribute most to our knowledge on this point. Existing techniques for such study are unsatisfactory, but rich material is available in every community where this type of activity was initiated. For the most part, however, such data are not recorded, and must consequently be utilized promptly or not at all.

A third major federal activity in connection with the rural Indian has been the work of the Soil Erosion Service. This program, closely related to that of the IECW, has had a profound influence on the development of Indian life through the development in the Southwest of special plans for areas occupied by this minority which consider natural resources in terms of the region's inhabitants, their wants and needs. The same questions should be asked as to the work of this agency as to that of any other depression agency in contact with the Indian, regardless of the degree to which special conditions applying only to this minority may have been taken into consideration in their operations.

Aid through the support of public works, the conservation of resources, assisted resettlement, federal loans to communities or to individuals for designated purposes, or outright relief in the form of a dole, all have modified their impact on the economic and other activities of the rural Indian because of his minority characteristics. It is the nature of this modification which concerns us.

The expenditure of exceptionally large amounts of public money in aid of the Indian during the depression raises one final question of the utmost importance.[6] Granting that the Indian has been in frightful need, and that his treatment by the white man in the past warrants most generous compensatory consideration today, it may none the less be asked to what extent have the depression expenditures in his behalf tended to be a disrupting influence because of sudden and unearned comparative wealth? In one Southwestern Indian community where community labor on tasks of common value has been a matter of course for generations, it has been observed that even emergency situations are today allowed to continue unattended while applications for government aid take their course. In another, it has been noted that Indians work for the government at two dollars a day on a public project designed to meet depression needs, and pay Mexicans the prevailing wage of one dollar a day to do farm

---

[6] ". . . during the three years ending June 30, 1936 $75,000,000 of federal funds were expended for the benefit of the Indians in addition to the regular annual appropriations for administration, which amounted in the three years to over $66,000,000." Kinney, J. P. *A Continent Lost—A Civilization Won: Indian Land Tenure in America.* Baltimore: The Johns Hopkins Press. 1937. P. 319

work. The personal and community disruption which may result from even a few exceptional situations such as these are such that investigation of their extent and nature is imperative. Furthermore, since it is not expected that present generosity will continue indefinitely, the question may be asked as to what will happen when individuals whose standards of living have been raised and for whom luxuries have taken on the nature of necessities are sooner or later thrown back on their own resources in regions incapable of affording more than a very low subsistence level. The question raised in this paragraph is not one of incompetent administration, favoritism, or political mismanagement. It is, rather, the general one prominent in practically all forms of depression aid concerning the conflict resulting when a society organized on an individualistic, competitive basis is forced by economic emergency to support an extraordinarily large proportion of its population out of public funds. It is a question of special importance for the Indian because of his position between conflicting cultures and because of the circumstance of his residence in large part in areas apparently doomed to perpetual poverty.

The Mexican in agriculture, also largely of Indian ancestry, faces a different situation in the United States. Leaving out of account members of "Spanish" families of many generations' residence in the Southwest and considering only relatively recent Mexican immigrants and their children, the outstanding rural problems have been those related to agricultural wage labor, particularly that of a seasonal nature. Many Mexicans have long held title to their own farms; others have been tenants. The similarity of the problems of Mexican farm owners and renters to those of other minorities is such, however, that no further mention need here be made of them except to suggest that when questions of minority land tenure are under consideration it should not be forgotten that all the questions ordinarily studied in this connection need investigation with relation to the Mexican. Opportunities for farm wage work were a major incentive to recent Mexican immigration, and the conditions of this labor furnish the center of interest in connection with the Mexican in the depression.

The majority of Mexicans who migrated to the United States to work as wage laborers came after good cheap land was exhausted. They were welcomed by employers, but only so long as they constituted a usable labor supply. Competing laborers of other stocks were always suspicious of them. Their culture, a mixture of Indian and Spanish with a multitude of local adaptations, was not entirely strange in that section of the United States bordering on Mexico, but to some extent even there, and always farther north, it was a factor which, together with the distinctive physical characteristics of this group, set them apart as of alien origin. They were anything but stable, crossing and recrossing the border in large numbers, frequently illegally, and in this country following employment opportunities from place to place within relatively restricted regions. Unsettled and without reserves for emergency, the depression struck them with exceptional severity.

Their principal place of residence having been in the open country, the urban regions on whom the brunt of the burden of relief for them fell were resentful of the cost. Under such pressure it is not strange that, as previously mentioned, many returned to Mexico voluntarily, with or without the assistance of relief agencies and others anxious to be rid of them. Others were forced out of the country by deportation and threats. Children, citizens of the United States because of birth in this country, went with them, creating legal problems to plague us later. How many remained it is difficult to estimate. Of these a comparatively large proportion required public relief, given but sullenly by many local authorities. One purpose of the interstate migration barriers erected in the Southwest was to keep out indigent itinerant Mexicans. Local anti-Mexican sentiment increased. The depression situation of the Mexican immigrant family turned out to be the entirely natural consequence of a previous policy of quantitatively unrestricted immigration of a highly visible minority to meet regionally acute but unstable needs for unskilled labor.

How this type of rural labor met the depression, the consequences to agriculture of dependence on cheap, mobile Mexican labor when the depression came, and changes in the manifestations of intergroup antagonisms, are questions of central importance. Recognizing the practicability and desirability of local and specialized studies of Mexicans in some particular area or type of agriculture selected because of the facilities of particular research workers, it is suggested that the most profitable investigations promise to be those so organized as to area and method that use may be made of predepression studies. Fortunately, several such studies were made shortly before the depression and may furnish both bases of reference for comparative purposes and guides to feasible materials and methods. The work of Professor Manuel Gamio, for example, which essays a broad picture of the Mexican immigrant to the United States came but shortly before the depression. The studies of Professor Paul Taylor, also correlated with the beginning of the depression, give detailed accounts of the Mexican laborer in selected areas. With the detailed knowledge made available by Professor Taylor of predepression conditions in sample cotton, sugar beet, and truck raising counties, the task of discovering what changes have come about in these districts is a comparatively simple one, differing mainly from the original undertaking in increased emphasis on public aid to the needy and on the cultural factors involved in the situation.

Another, but much smaller minority group of the mobile type employed seasonally in agriculture is the Filipino. Concentrated on the West Coast, a recent migrant to continental United States, he has been an important element in the labor situation in certain highly specialized types of market farming in California. Unlike the Mexican, the Filipino migrated to this country as an individual without bringing his family. With almost no women or children in the group, the depression impact on the Filipino has naturally been different than in the case of other groups with more nearly normal sex ratios. He has also been a temporary immigrant typically intending to return to the Philippines after accumulating experience and savings sufficient for his needs at home.

A study of this group by Bruno Lasker, published in 1931, mentioned previously in this chapter, covers in comprehensive fashion the problems of the Filipino immigrant, and makes available a reliable picture of his condition in this country prior to the depression while indicating the sources to which one may turn for depression materials. The imposition of a quota during the depression setting the maximum Filipino immigration at 50 for any year—in itself perhaps a partial consequence of the depression—promises the extinction of this minority as of any importance in our population. It is, however, still possible and desirable to utilize the experience of the Filipino immigrant during the depression for research purposes. The practical unimportance of the minority numerically does not affect the validity of conclusions drawn from studies of the experience of its members in the United States.

The Japanese immigrant, numerically unimportant until about the beginning of the present century, also sought work on the West Coast and first found it as a rural laborer. Unlike the Filipino, he brought or later sent for his family, began acquiring farms of his own, showed little desire to return to his native land, and did his best to fit into the American scene as a permanent resident. Accustomed to long hours of hard work on a

low subsistence level, he was found to be a most satisfactory
farm laborer by employers, and a menace by white workers. As
he became increasingly successful in operating farms of his own,
criticism against him became stronger. Characteristics which
might be considered virtues in a native white American—his
willingness and that of his family to work from sunup to sun-
down at back-breaking labor for whatever could be earned, willingness to live on as little as possible in order to save for future
advantage, eagerness to become a worthy part of his new home
community—were emphasized as his vices in the eyes of competitors. There is little evidence of antagonism toward those
Japanese who were content with servants' work, who operated
Oriental import houses, or who in some other manner "stayed
in their places."[7]

Parenthetically, it may be mentioned here for comparative purposes that the Chinese immigrant, who did not bring his family
or make any serious effort to become economically and socially
assimilated, who concentrated increasingly in non-competitive
work, and who usually intended to return sooner or later to
China, has during the present century aroused much less active
antagonism than his fellow-Oriental, the Japanese immigrant.
Peace has apparently been purchased by renouncing those forms
of success which have seemed most desirable in the eyes of the
dominant majority.

The major sin of the rural Japanese, then, appears to have
been his success as a wage worker and as a farmer, success which
was probably exaggerated by the magnifying power of his striking racial visibility. It would seem reasonable to assume that
anti-Japanese sentiment in the rural districts where he was concentrated should have increased noticeably during the depression, just as there was a corresponding increase of active preju-

[7] For a good symposium portraying the predepression circumstances of the
Japanese and Chinese in the United States see the *Survey Graphic*. Vol. IX,
No. 2. May 1926

dice against the highly visible, successful Jew. Actually there is little satisfactory data which supports such an assumption in the case of the Japanese.

Is this because the assumption is false or because insufficient study of the rural Japanese during the depression has been carried on? Has the presence of Mexican and Filipino wage workers in the same region attracted attention away from the Japanese? Has the relative prosperity and self-sufficiency of the Japanese been a significant factor in the situation? Has the presence of a well-assimilated second generation of Japanese had any effect in maintaining interracial peace? May clues to the solution of the problem be found in recent trends in Japanese farm activity, such as the systems of farm labor and land tenure, crop specialization, rising standards of living, general rapid assimilation, geographic distribution and the like?

Considerable information regarding the predepression rural history of the Japanese in this country is available as a result of earlier research. The central problem of their depression experience as a highly visible minority concerns the manner in which, during the crisis period, the rural element was advanced or retarded economically and in intergroup relations, because of inferior group social status, to an extent that is out of line with the degree of assimilation and success achieved in competition. It is reasonable to assume that some other minority with a similar culture and history of achievement in this country, but without high visibility because of distinguishing racial characteristics, would with a record equal to that of the Japanese have lost all but a few vestiges of minority status. It should be possible to obtain an estimate of the effect of physical traits in "freezing" a given status under the emphasis of depression conditions, through the analysis of the comparative agricultural productivity of the Japanese, especially if such matters are taken into account as the crops raised, labor conditions, system of farm operation, operation of racially segregated and mixed marketing cooperatives, occupational trends of the younger generation, and evidences of group antagonisms to be found in overt instances of discrimination and strife and in media of public opinion. The comparison of the depression records of ordinary American rural communities with those having Japanese population elements, as to such points as these, would in most likelihood bring rich rewards. It is probable that such studies would indicate that the Japanese, like other minorities having distinguishable physical traits, have fared well during the depression to the degree they have succeeded in avoiding the appearance of competition with the majority, either by "staying in their places," or by following paths which because of relative physical isolation and group obscurity, permit some measure of success even though they are actually of a competitive nature.

The number of questions which can be asked concerning the experience of rural European immigrant families in the depression is bewildering. This is attributable in part to the fact that the adjective "rural" does not limit its noun by the exclusion of any single type of human activity, but only suggests that many activities may take specialized form because of the locale in which they are found. Since this difficulty can be reduced by arbitrary ad hoc definition, it is probably less serious than those which derive from the vagueness of the term "immigrant" as a concept in social science, even when this term is modified by the adjective "European." A European immigrant is anyone who has come from any part of any European country to any part of this country.

As a consequence of this difficulty in terminology and in the relative absence of collected data assembled under scientifically meaningful classifications, the only feasible research procedure is to rework existing economic materials now available for immigrant rural families as a whole and at the same time make every effort to break them down and add to them by new research so that comparisons may be made between relatively homogeneous immigrant minority subdivisions. The reworking of materials by nationality and mother tongue groupings is feasible only to a limited extent.

It is often said that the "old immigrant" from Northwestern Europe was attracted to the United States by the chance to acquire land, and that he stopped coming in large numbers and was supplanted by the "new immigrant" from Eastern and Southern Europe when his own country became industrialized and when cheap, unskilled industrial labor came to afford the main opportunity for newly-arrived aliens. With this generalization usually went the implication that there was something superior about immigrants who went to the open country and that the farm was the best place for remaking aliens into an American mold. The simple facts are, of course, that immigrants have always concentrated their settlements in those regions of the country which happened at the moment to offer the greatest economic promise; that it was primarily the chance circumstance that emigration from Southern and Eastern Europe did not get into full swing until the cheap land supply in the United States was practically exhausted; that the pressure for emigration from Northwestern Europe decreased about the time of industrial expansion in America; that the major advantage of the open country for assimilation is the comparative isolation of individuals and communities, permitting a long time process of assimilation without acute social discomfort; and that both "old" and "new" immigrants (with the major exception of the Jews) have throughout our history settled both in the open country and in the congested city, the proportional distribution between the two types of location, a function of the time of arrival, being the main distinction.

Nevertheless, the fact remains that the "new" or recent immigrant has established himself mainly in urban regions, and this is particularly true of those nationalities lower down on the scale of alien minority status. It may be worth observing, however, that the immigrant groups predominating in former days, such as the Germans and Irish, although now popularly ranked well up on the social scale were once down near the bottom of the list. The term "shanty Irish," for example, once carried as much stigma as ever did such words as "wop" and "dago." In spite of the general urban-industrial trend, immigration during the decades at the turn of the century has been so large that even the minor fraction engaged in agricultural pursuits is an impressive number.[8]

Immigration as a research subject has in practice been considered either a division of economics or a minor field in social history. Sociologists, however, have constantly claimed title to the subject, and it now seems to be theirs by default, possibly because the decrease in immigration since the World War has materially reduced its national importance. Volumes on immigration by sociologists, however, have as a rule contained much history, economics, and crude statistics, and very little sociology. As a result of the mixed academic history of the field, adequate attention has been paid neither to fact nor analytical methodology in nationality comparisons and contrasts, with the consequence that even today white immigrants from all countries are distinguished for purposes of economic study only in gross statistical groupings based on political boundaries. Language groupings are also available but it is not correct to assume that this one cultural characteristic is an adequate index of group culture and history. Because of the inadequacy of the social data collected, there is almost no feasible alternative to consideration of the European immigrant in American economic life, agricultural or urban, as though the bare fact of recent alien origin in itself overshadowed minority individual and group differences. This is obviously an assumption scientifically inadequate as a

[8] See Brunner, Edmund deS. *Immigrant Farmers and Their Children.* New York: Doubleday, Doran and Company. 1929. Pp. xvii+277

classification basis for the study of the economic activities of millions of otherwise diversified persons. Economic statistics of immigrants, however, are practically unavailable on any other basis of classification than national origin or mother tongue.

The European immigrant farmer may be expected to have had depression experiences differing from those of colored minorities, immigrant or native-born, because of the greater similarity of his cultures, whether north or south European, to that of his majority neighbors, because of his different pattern of distribution in rural regions, and because of his lower social visibility. All three of these factors should have made it easier to meet the impact of the depression, the degree of adjustment achieved varying directly from group to group as they approximated the majority setting. The approximate degree of validity of this proposition may be established by anyone competent to manipulate existing agricultural statistics using national origins as the basis for population classifications. The establishment of detailed relationships between particular culture patterns or degree of social visibility, however, requires individual rural community studies whose feasibility is diminished by unavoidable expense and lack of predepression studies for comparison except in a very few exceptional cases.

In view of the general preference, verbal if not actual, exhibited for immigrants who locate in rural rather than in urban regions, it is especially desirable that more be known concerning the comparative impact of the depression. This is not simply a matter of comparing relief rolls, useful as such comparisons may be. The problem goes deeper than that, and requires information concerning the functioning of the individual, the family and the community in other than the economic process of getting a place to sleep and enough to eat. Contrasting urban and rural immigrants, what happened to their physical and mental health, to their progress in formal education and general cultural assimilation, to their family composition, structure and functioning, to their community relationships?

Considering in further detail only the last section of this multiple question, it may be observed that rural life forces fewer contacts between people than does urban industrialism. Physical distances between individuals are greater. Division of labor is not so specialized. Human relations may be more personal in the country, but they may also be more limited in number by circumstances or individual choice. It is also clear that local types of agriculture and of social organization influence the degree to which these observations are true. Truck farming, for example, far more nearly resembles urban conditions in its typical patterns of organization than does dry farming in the Northwest, while hog raising in Iowa is somewhere in between the two. Significant results should come from a project classifying rural immigrant centers on the basis of necessary intergroup contacts for the purpose of comparing the intensity of intergroup antagonisms. While it is desirable that as many different minorities as possible be studied in this manner, comparison of communities of similar minority composition where the main variable is the number of necessary intergroup contacts seems especially promising.[9] Allowance must be made, as always in such problems, for differences in the time and severity of the impact of the depression between communities. Account must also be taken of such complicating factors as drought, pest plagues, and the fact that there was a practically continuous agricultural depression from about 1921 on, excepting, of course, certain specialized regions such as those concentrating on dairy and truck farm products.

---

[9] For suggestions concerning the research approach to the study of minority rural communities see: Brunner, Edmund deS. *Op. cit.;* Dawson, C. A. *Group Settlement: Ethnic Communities in Western Canada.* Toronto: The Macmillan Company of Canada. 1936. Pp. xx+395

Before passing from the immigrant farmer to the largest characteristically rural minority, the Southern Negro, final attention may be called to the unlikelihood that any generally valid conclusions may be found applicable to families of recent European origin in American agriculture during the depression. Trends valid for some groups will certainly be discovered reversed for others. Because of diversity in population traits ranging from age and sex distribution to degree of cultural assimilation, any generalized trends which may be advanced are practically certain to possess meaning only as fictitious mathematical averages, about as accurate in specific application as a composite photograph of the average immigrant. With this minority, which is in fact an agglomeration of many divergent minorities, it is best to strive for conclusions concerning small definable groups rather than for inclusive universals.

The rural Negro has been a rural inhabitant in his present regional location for generations. The types of agriculture in which he engages have been the same for many years, as have been the systems of land tenure, credit, operational practices, and living conditions. The scheme of his existence has been so stabilized that his position in the economic and social order is regulated by custom so well crystallized that his conduct in his relations with the white man is limited by rules enforced by effective extralegal sanctions. Not that there are no unpunished infractions of the rules, or variations in them from community to community, or changes in their nature as time goes on. Allowing for such variations, the patterns of Negro-white relations in the rural South are nevertheless far more explicit and rigid than those governing any other majority-minority contacts in the United States.

Our concern, then, is with the depression consequences of the rural Negro's farm life under his minority status regulations. Their influence, of course, may not be appreciated without considerable familiarity with the history of the Negro in this country and with his present cultural standards. The historical material is available, but very little is known concerning the divergencies between Negro culture patterns and those of the white man with whom he is in contact. In the large, it is correct to say that the Negro's culture is essentially that of his white neighbor, and that it is essentially Western European in nature. Minor cultural differences, however, may be of the utmost significance in race relations, and it is regrettable that for lack of knowledge on the subject it must be seriously underemphasized in consideration of the economic activities of this minority.

Depression problems in connection with the Negro in agriculture which are feasible for study include the influence of survivals from Africa, slavery, and post-emancipation experiences, of the cash crop system, including the credit practices involved, of land tenure systems, and of white domination in general. Of these, the first and the last are the least tangible, but they are none the less important on that account.

Contact of the Negro population in the United States with European civilization extends back only some three centuries. Many colored family lines first came to this continent well after the beginning of the nineteenth century. Although tribal cultures quickly disintegrated after forced migration to this country, it is reasonable to assume that some vestiges have remained down to the present time, and that the cultural transition involved in the move from Africa to America has not yet been perfected. African economic patterns were far from the same as Southern economic patterns in many fundamental respects, ranging from mechanical techniques to concepts of property. Much as the European migrant to the American farm was required to adjust his practices and ideas to his new situation, the problem was infinitely more extensive for the Negro transported suddenly from his tribal cultures to a cultural setting stemming from Europe.

Once in the United States, the Negro began the process of adjustment to the American scene in which he occupied the lowest status whether free or slave, agricultural worker or artisan. For most, the necessary adjustment was to slavery, a slavery in many respects unlike that with which he had been familiar in Africa and involving practically complete reorganization of life in terms of work, family relations, religion, government, and personal standards and obligations. After this process of reorganization had made considerable headway, emancipation, its consequences and concomitants following the Civil War, made necessary the initiation of a new cycle of adjustment involving basic changes in obligations and responsibilities.

That the transition from Africa to America, followed by two incomplete cycles of adjustment in periods of slavery and of freedom should not have left some imprint on the Negro of today certain to influence his condition during the depression is unthinkable. The African background, of course, is probably of significance primarily because of its destruction. Some lingering positive cultural traits may well be found to be influencing the economic behavior of the Negro of the present generation, but the present state of knowledge in this field does not justify study narrowed down to the investigation of its interrelationships with depression experience. The record of the period of slavery, however, is sufficiently rich to warrant investigation of the question whether a people who received general emancipation but a few generations ago by virtue of that fact encounter depression experiences distinguishable from those of others.

The entire problem of the importance of the Negro's historical and cultural background in relation to the depression background is tenuous, not because of any lack of importance or of complete lack of source materials, but because of neglect, the underdevelopment of methodology, and the absence of predepression studies. A few specific questions, however, may be raised as samples of a much larger possible number. Does the

Negro have a concept of, and an attitude toward, property in any respects unique because of his African origin, his transportation to America, and his adaptation to the Southern slave economy? More specifically, is the possession of property more of a means to an end than an end in itself than for the white man of older European tradition? Is there any basis in reality for the old story about the Negro who refused to run an errand for a quarter because he already had a quarter? Is there any truth to the common allegation that the slave economy is responsible for a somewhat general lack of respect among domestics for employers' property rights in leftover food? Is there an exceptional tendency among Negro families for the woman to be the more economically dependable member of the household, an alleged survival from the slave practice of giving family rations to the woman rather than to the man? What about attitudes and behavior with regard to such matters as saving, consumption standards, debt, economic forethought, economic initiative, and work habits? Is there any tendency for Negro labor groups to be more or less homogeneous than white? Has the Negro been trained to expect a personal relationship with his employer which makes strange his employment by an impersonal corporation? What elements in his background have been unfavorable to cooperation between fellow workers, as in union organizations? Has there been developed in him a tendency toward individualism in economic activity capable of detection through examination of his experience in collective bargaining, of the patronage of Negro businesses, of agricultural activity, of investment and banking practices, or of any other activity in which cooperation may be practiced?

The relation between the answers to such questions and depression experience is obvious. It is conceivable, for example, that there may be Negro tendencies in economic standards and practices which, entirely apart from the direct consequences of his generally low economic status, may have acted as special handicaps in the depression by working against savings, economic forethought and cooperation. At the same time, other pre-Civil War heritages may well have given him certain advantages in meeting adversity with exceptional ease in comparison, shall we say, with the ordinary New Yorker, depending on the truth in the assertion that incomplete acculturation and slave adaptations have attached in his mind less importance to the need for property and economic security as such, to the economically man-centered family, or to the maintenance of economic self-sufficiency independent of public aid. It is understood, of course, that in all such questions, there is no assumption of individual uniformity, but that it is the Negro as a group who should be compared with other groups, not colored individuals with white individuals.

In addition to the problems presented by the pre-Civil War history of the Negro, there must also be taken into account his experience since emancipation. His material, social, and personal facilities for coping with the depression no doubt may be traced more directly to his post- than to his pre-emancipation history as the most inferior caste group in America. Of particular importance, for example, is the history of the reconstruction period. With the Southern economic system disrupted by war and defeat, the staggering task of reorganization must have left at least some imprints on succeeding generations. There come to mind the failures and disappointments of freedmen unprepared for freedom, the hostilities and oppressions of impoverished whites fearful of Negro domination, the blunderings of the Freedmen's Bureau in its efforts at economic, political, and social rehabilitation, the disillusionments caused by incompetently sentimental and downright thieving "friends of the Negro," and the shift in the Southern politically dominant white class from the pre-War favored few to the masses. Historical data on this period is abundant. It needs only to be reworded in terms of problems of today.

The closer the story of the Negro is brought to the present decade the more it loses its distinctive qualities as a research field requiring emphasis on the historical and anthropological techniques and the more it becomes instead an area for the sociological, psychological, and economic study of caste phenomena. Inasmuch as the Negro in agriculture since the Reconstruction has undergone no comparably serious transition, his more recent history will be passed over with no more mention than the hardly necessary suggestion that any study of his rural experiences in the depression naturally requires recognition of at least the more immediate historical background.

To understand what happened to the rural Negro during the depression would be to understand what happened to the entire rural South and sections of the Southwest. Such comprehensive knowledge, if it is ever to be achieved, must be pieced together from tens and hundreds of independent studies, the majority of which will be concerned with other aspects of regional development than race relations. The task in hand, however, is a more restricted one and may be limited to selected outstanding foci of depression change in which the Negro's status as a minority played an important rôle.

It is customary in considering the agricultural Negro to stress land tenure, the cash crop system in raising cotton and tobacco, seasonal field work for hire and other supplementary income wage work, credit facilities, regional and subregional resources, and training and education for intelligent farming in all its aspects. Such items are obviously of importance to white as well as to colored farmers; it merely happens that the course of history has placed most Negro agriculturists in the section of the United States where money crops have been depended on with disastrous consequences, where days' wages are exceptionally low, where personal and crop financing are so organized as to have exceptionally pernicious aspects, where human and natural resources have been grossly abused, and where both general education and occupational skills have lagged in development. Our present concern, however, is not with general regional problems.

"The first consideration of the Negro farmer," in the words of Woofter, "involves his dependence on the larger movements involving the whole agricultural situation. The general agencies for rural improvement—cooperative marketing, credits for land buying, credits for production, agencies stimulating more economic production, and agencies for the improvement of rural community life—need to be made to function for the Negro farmer as well as for the white farmer.

"The way in which the Negro fits this southern agricultural situation is summed up by the statement that southern agriculture is greatly dependent upon the Negro and the rural Negro is entirely dependent upon southern agriculture. . . .

"Up to 1910 the colored farmers had made progress not only in the number of farms which they cultivated, but also in climbing the tenant ladder from the position of dependent laborer to that of semi-dependent half-share tenant, and on to a position of third and fourth share tenant, independent renter of land, and farm owner. The number of owners had increased in 1910 until 210,000 Negroes owned their land. While there were 161,000 Negro owners in the Southeast in 1910, this number decreased to 145,900 by 1925, indicating a surprising proportion who are losing heart and moving to the city."[10]

This quotation suggests the need for analysis of the manner and extent of depression influence in facilitating or retarding the Negro's integration into southern agriculture. Leaving out of account general problems of southern rural inadequacies because of their general rather than minority character, there remains the question of how the Negro in agriculture underwent experiences different in degree or kind because he was a Negro. How did his functioning as a farmer differ from that of other

---

[10] Woofter, T. J. Jr. *Races and Ethnic Groups in American Life.* New York: McGraw-Hill Book Co. 1933. Pp. 101f.

farmers? It is reasonable to suppose that Negroes, constituting the lowest caste in the population, encountered the greatest discrimination and suffered the greatest difficulties in attempting to cope with the depression. The accuracy of this supposition is susceptible of checking by references to the comparative tendencies in Negro and white land tenure, rural employment and wages, size, quality, equipment and length of operation of farms operated, crop data, and the like. Such data, however, tell far from the whole story.

Reference has been made to the fact that the rural Negro has for generations lived his life under more clearly defined and more strictly enforced status regulations than are applied in any other American minority-majority relationship. Negro-white rules of intergroup conduct in the South vary tremendously from place to place, from time to time, and in the rigidity of their application, but in some degree and form they are always in force, governing the behavior of both races, and never leaving any doubt about the importance of the gulf between the two castes. No other minority in the United States lives in so well-defined a situation. Inferior social status need not be and in the United States usually is not accompanied by any generally accepted detailed social definition of that status, as the Negro himself discovers when he moves out of the South to find himself at a constant loss in trying to understand his privileges and restrictions. The influence of the depression on the complex customs which describe the Negro's "place" in the rural South is by all odds the most important focal question which can be raised in this section.

Did the depression tend to blur or sharpen southern rural race distinctions? Has the range of socially proper activities for the Negro been expanded or contracted, and is there more or less community certainty concerning the exact boundaries of this range? To no small extent agricultural census and other Government farm survey data may supply bases of inference in this connection. The problem, however, is not the simple one of comparing Negro and white farm trends on the assumption that if the Negro averages for the various agricultural indexes fell faster during the depression than those of his white neighbors, increasing rigidity and restriction of permissible Negro activity has therefore been established. Nor would disproportionately rising Negro agricultural indexes establish the opposite.

The test lies rather in the extent of overlapping of the ranges of Negro and white activity and achievement, and in the trend in intergroup cooperation. This may be illustrated by reference to farm credit practices, so crucial in cash crop agriculture.

Private farm credit in the South may be obtained from landlords interested in their tenants' crops, from banks on real estate mortgages and occasionally on chattel mortgages, from fertilizer companies interested in selling their wares, and from merchants willing to carry their customers until crops are harvested and sold. Among these sources of loans, the only type really belonging in the finance business, the bank, is the one of least importance in fact. The others because of the nature of their main business have conflicting interests in their customer's borrowings in that banking caution and policies essential to sound loans are in conflict with the desire for profits from other dealings with the clients. Unwise consumption, bad debts, high interest rates and downright chicanery are natural consequences of such a situation.

In addition to these private credit sources, there should also be mentioned the federal credit agencies. However, in spite of the national government's efforts to avoid racial discrimination, these agencies have been of relative unimportance to the Negro. In part this has been the result of the Negro's inability to offer the required security and of his distrust and ignorance of the available facilities. The extent to which he has been prevented from making use of these public credit agencies because of community feeling that it was not in keeping with his status to do so would make an interesting subject for the study of local sabotage of national depression measures. A special problem in this connection grows out of the fact that borrowers from Federal Land Banks must be members of loan associations from which Negroes have been excluded when organized by white people and which have been found practically impossible of organization among Negroes.

Negro credit resources, of course, have always been inferior to those available to the rest of the population. In connection with the depression, the first question is naturally whether this difference was materially increased or decreased. Beyond this, however, is the question of greater significance in southern race relations concerning whether under the stress of exceptional economic hardship, the dominant majority showed any increased tendency to permit Negroes to take advantage of any credit facilities for which they could qualify as individuals apart from their caste status. Or was the reverse what actually happened? Throughout the South, for example, there has been general white agreement that Negroes as bank customers could rarely be profitable, and should probably be discouraged anyway as out of place. Negroes, on the other hand, have been generally distrustful of banks in any form, preferring a more personal credit relationship. There are scattered reports that the depression has encouraged southern bankers to pay more attention to the Negro as a source of business and profit. To the extent to which this is true it means a significantly wider horizon for the southern Negro through a change in the definition of his acceptable sphere of activity, even though the average Negro credit facilities may have slumped disproportionately in the same period. Whether or not the disrupting influence of the depression has modified the earlier rules governing Negro farm credit, as through increased federal activity in the field and through desperation need for business of any sort, is a question which may be settled most readily by regional and community studies.

Other points at which long-established interracial code rules might be examined with reference to the depression behavior of the rural Negro include marketing practices, the conditions of tenancy ranging from the form of contract to the supervision of labor on crops, mobility, federal policies in relief, the Resettlement Administration, the Tennessee Valley Authority and other depression measures, and the use of collective bargaining by Negro and mixed organizations, particularly the Southern Tenant Farmers' Union. Such a list could be extended and particularized almost without limit. There is no need, however, for the detailed study of every last item with reference to the depression. Only an absurd perfectionist would ask for a map showing each tiny rise and fall in the surface, each little rivulet, every habitation and dim footpath. A relatively small number of well-selected foci of investigation can furnish sufficiently precise data on the comparative trends of Negro and southern white agricultural workers to establish with adequate certainty the influence of the depression on both the material welfare of the colored rural resident and on the intergroup code under which he lives.

Chapter V

Economic Life (*Continued*)

BEFORE considering the economic life of urbanized minority peoples reference may again be made to the fact that village and other non-farming rural minority groups are arbitrarily omitted from discussion. To no small degree this omission is compensated for by the circumstance that for the greater part American village life parallels open country life both in material fluctuations in prosperity and in behavior. Mining and forestry regions, of course, are outstanding exceptions to this rule. It seems unlikely that any decentralization of industry will soon destroy the close kinship of village and farm, since such decentralization as there is appears to be predominantly suburban rather than truly rural. Nevertheless, it must be confessed that the omission is in large part a confession of ignorance concerning both minority and majority village life. Books have been written without end differentiating urban and rural sociology, agricultural and industrial economics, but the village and the suburb, the country artisan and the suburban farmer, remain practically terra incognita.[1]

INDUSTRIALIZATION

On the basis of data collected at the very beginning of the depression and earlier, T. J. Woofter, Jr. has concluded that "The status of the European foreigner and the Negro seems to

---

[1] The report of the Research Committee on Urbanism of the National Resources Committee, now in the final stages of preparation, may be cited because of its inclusion of recent data on the suburb and village.

be that of progress in industry in spite of difficulties. The Mexicans show signs of beginning in the cycle of heavy industry where their predecessors have begun. The migrated Indians are so small in number that they are a negligible factor. With the Orientals the vocational problem of the second generation seems to be the most hopeless. . . . By their American birth and education they have lost touch with the land of their parents, by their color they are debarred from many contacts in the land of their birth.

"Second only to the problem of the children of Oriental immigrants is the vocational handicap of the Negro in the South. . . . This is evident in sporadic attempts of white groups such as barbers to drive Negroes out by municipal ordinance and in the licensing of electricians, plumbers, and other skilled tradesmen and in the barring of Negroes from public employment on such work as construction, street cleaning, and garbage removal."[2]

After pointing out these special difficulties confronting the separate major minority groupings, Dr. Woofter continues with a summary of other difficulties "which apply more or less to all groups in industry varying in degree largely with the length of the time of their contacts with the industry," as presented by Herman Feldman in his *Racial Factors in American Industry*. These include (1) the necessity for living down a "tradition of disparagement," (2) handicaps to the full utilization of occupational skills because of prejudice, (3) the antagonism of other workers, particularly in times of unemployment and labor disturbances, (4) limitations on the employment of minority workers, and (5) lack of confidence in minority workers' occupational capacities.[3]

These difficulties are manifestations of economic competition

---

[2] Woofter, T. J. Jr. *Races and Ethnic Groups in American Life.* Recent Social Trends Monographs. New York: McGraw-Hill Book Co. 1933. Pp. 142f.

[3] *Ibid.* Pp. 143f.

between population elements differentiated by characteristics of racial or national origin. Set apart by their social visibility, minority workers suffer discrimination in employment as they are believed to threaten the economic welfare of the dominant majority workers or as their vocational qualities, actual or fictitious, are assumed to render them unfit for certain types of work. If the basis of their visibility is enduring because of racial inheritance, as is particularly the case with Orientals and Negroes, discrimination itself also tends to be exceptionally enduring; if it is relatively ephemeral because of cultural origin, as in the case of most European immigrants, discrimination tends to be temporary. In any event, employment opportunities for minorities tend to expand in times of prosperity and contract in times of depression.

The analysis of the situation of minority workers in industry just previous to the depression by Dr. Woofter must for our present purposes be supplemented in two main respects. First, there is need for more emphasis than he found it possible to give on subgroupings within the larger American races and ethnic groups. Jews, for example, are not given separate consideration. The necessity for such subclassification has been discussed in our introductory chapter, and need not be given further space here. Second, cultural differences between races and ethnic groups and subgroups are among the most important factors in the occupational circumstances of minority peoples, although given no prominence in this connection by Dr. Woofter. This circumstance may no doubt be explained by the mandate under which Dr. Woofter worked, since in the planning of the work of the President's Research Committee on Social Trends it was stated that "To safeguard the conclusions against bias, the researches were restricted to the analysis of objective data" with the full knowledge that "Since the available data do not cover all phases of the many subjects studied, it was often impossible to answer questions of keen interest."[4] Within the definition of the task implied in these quotations, it was naturally quite impossible to give full recognition to desirable subclassifications of minority peoples or to take account of the significance of their cultures in industrial development.

It is clear, of course, that the industrial progress which was being made by all minorities prior to the depression was severely checked by the economic catastrophe of the present decade. The same may be said, however, of the economic progress which was being made by the entire population. Our problem now is to consider the ways in which minorities in industrialized regions, because they were minorities, underwent experiences in relation to the depression which were unique either in degree or in kind.[5]

Employer-employee relationships may be taken as the first focus of inquiry in this connection. Employers as such are interested in their workers as necessary parts of a productive machine. Their major motive in paying wages is to make a profit. This being the case, it is to be expected that in time of depres-

---

[4] *Ibid.* P. vi

[5] Attention is called to the *Report to the National Resources Committee on the Rôle of the Urban Community in the National Economy.* Washington, D.C.: Urbanism Committee, United States Government Printing Office. 1937

This report treats among other topics the status and rôle of the Negro and the immigrant in contemporary urban life, the influence of minority groups upon the urbanization of the United States and the conditions and problems of social life in American cities.

In addition to the summary report above-mentioned, the National Resources Committee has completed a series of monographs on selected aspects of urbanism of which the following are of interest in connection with minority groups: Urban Population Changes in the United States, Social Welfare, Education, Public Health, Public Safety, Recreation, The Religious Life of Urban Communities, Voluntary Associations in the United States, Urban Housing, Opposing Theories of Rural and Urban Ways of Life, and Talent and Achievement. The Urbanism Committee of the National Resources Committee expects to publish several of these studies during the coming year. Meanwhile, the manuscripts will be on file and available for consultation in the library of the National Resources Committee.

sion as at any other time, their attitude toward the employment of minority workers will be a function of their experience and beliefs concerning the possibility of employing them at a wage, under working conditions and with an expectancy concerning output which will compare favorably with the balance of costs and profits believed possible with majority laborers. The dominant variable in this connection is that during a depression the labor supply is abundant and the employer may consequently exercise a finer choice between potential employees, while during more prosperous periods there is pressure for the employment of almost any worker available. Are there circumstances which affect the exercise of choice between potential employees during the depression to the advantage or disadvantage of minorities?

Although no doubt a net advantage or disadvantage could be determined for all minority peoples or for any one minority in the United States, little is to be gained by attacking the problem on such a broad front. In actuality, there are instances in which minority workers have been favored during the depression as well as instances in which they have been exceptionally handicapped in securing and retaining employment, with the latter type probably predominating. Minority workers are on the whole more easily handled than workers of old American stock, they will work under less satisfactory conditions with less effective protest, and they are accustomed to lower living and wage levels. Their exploitation, or, in less critical terms, their management for profit under intensive competition, may for such reasons be both easier and less of a strain on the employer's humanitarianism. Furthermore, special industrial qualities and skills may be available to an employer only in minority workers. In some districts, also, none but minority workers may be available for hire, and community, industrial or plant custom may favor their employment in particular jobs and discourage the introduction of old American white stock.

On the other hand, the tractability of all labor is increased at least during the early stages of a depression and minorities thus have one of their main employment advantages diminished. At the same time, influences come to bear on employers to hire white people desperately in need of work rather than colored, citizens rather than aliens, descendants of old Americans rather than the children of immigrants. Propaganda to this effect appears in the newspapers, is talked on the streets, shows up in the activities and resolutions of societies and organizations with patriotic interests, and is not foreign to the employer and his managers, themselves likely to be of old white stock. Beliefs in the superiority of majority workers come to the fore and support a policy of discrimination against minority workers. For many it is a matter of both patriotism and profit to keep work from minorities until better provision is made for the others.

Relief records and statistics naturally occur as one of the first sources to turn to for evidence as to what really happened to minority employment in industry during the depression. They have, however, a number of inherent defects and may be used only with the greatest of caution. It is not enough to say that if the racial and national origin and customary occupation of persons on relief are known, deductions concerning minority industrial unemployment may be made. There are, in the first place, no predepression relief statistics of a comparable nature, and there is no certain way to relate relief occupational data to previous Bureau of the Census occupational data, although an approximation is possible. The quality of relief records varies tremendously from place to place and from year to year. General rules and local practices in placing persons on the relief rolls have not been uniform and there is every reason to assume that the proportion of minority names on the rolls is not related with any certainty to the proportion of minority unemployed. Relief data, whether federal or local, may be used with greatest accuracy in the analysis of what they actually are supposed to represent, and that is relief given to a definite number of individuals. These individuals may or may not be proportionally representative of any class in the total population. In any event, minority peoples are rarely distinguished in the records with any accuracy, if at all, unless they happen to be colored.[6]

It consequently seems wiser to turn to records of employment rather than to records of unemployment as represented by relief

[6] The occupational characteristics of minorities on the public unemployment relief rolls should offer some opportunity for the study of the differential economic impact of the depression. Only the Negro minority, however, was differentiated in the March 1935 census of 4,157,813 households containing one or more workers, and the same is true of earlier occupational studies. Furthermore, even such data for the Negro, excellent though they are, are severely limited for research purposes by the primacy of relief policy and administration in the motivation for their collection. For example, the March 1935 occupational census was limited to a population defined as follows: "Only persons 16 through 64 years of age, inclusive, working or seeking work, who were members of households which received relief under the General Relief Program jointly undertaken by the States and the Federal Emergency Relief Administration, were enumerated for this census. This included workers in the specified age group in all resident households, consisting of families, single persons, or local homeless persons, who received aid through direct relief or through the Federal Emergency Relief Administration work program. It should be noted that workers of households which participated only in the following special programs are excluded from this tabulation: (1) Transient; (2) Emergency Education; (3) College Student Aid; (4) Rural Rehabilitation; (5) Drought Relief; and (6) Surplus Commodities." *Workers on Relief in the United States, March 1935: A Census of Usual Occupations.* Washington, D.C.: Works Progress Administration, Division of Social Research. 1937. P. 1f.

See also Hauser, Philip M. "Workers on the Public Unemployment Relief Rolls in the United States, March 1935." *Monthly Report of the Federal Emergency Relief Administration.* April 1 through April 30, 1936. Washington, D.C.: U. S. Government Printing Office. Pp. 1-29. Another similar census was taken on January 15, 1936.

In spite of its limitations, however, such material is still too valuable, particularly in the absence of more satisfactory data, to permit its neglect in the study of the Negro and the depression. It is a happy circumstance that predepression Negro occupational data from nonrelief sources is also available in abundance. See, for illustration, Edwards, Alba M. "The Negro as a Factor in the Nation's Labor Force." *Journal of the American Statistical Association.* 31: 529-540. No. 195. September 1936

data. The estimating of unemployment in the nation by any technique is still a hazardous process, as is witnessed by the varying results achieved by experts. To attempt to classify the unemployed by minority status starting with existing inclusive national estimates in the hope that they may be broken down race by race and nationality by nationality seems utterly unfeasible except for the Negro. It would also seem to be hardly worth the effort if it were possible, since such gross comparisons can tell little more than is already known from general observation. Without entering into a discussion of the merits of the various methods of estimating unemployment, a field of specialization in itself, it may be suggested that the student of minority-majority relations requires more detailed and specific data than the totals of the employed and the unemployed.

Starting with the assumption that minorities contain high proportions of marginal workers and that the employment differentials to their disfavor tend to become more acute in time of depression, inquiry concerning the actual facts in this respect needs to be made region by region, group by group, industry by industry, plant by plant, and job by job. It is not at all likely that any economic generalization concerning minorities with even approximately one hundred per cent accuracy can be found. What is the significance in depression of the fact that minorities at all times contribute a larger proportion of the working masses than of the total population? How have the unique geographic and occupational distribution of minorities handicapped or aided these peoples with relation to the differential impact of the depression as between regions and industries? What changes have there been in the present decade in the ratio of persons of minority status per worker in various industries and occupations? To what extent, under what conditions and with what effects did traditionally minority jobs change into majority jobs? What was the ratio of minority workers discharged to majority workers discharged in specific plants? Were minority workers used to replace majority workers, or workers of some other minority, in an effort to cut production costs? What happened to hours of labor and wages as between workers of different status groups? In addition to industrial discrimination based directly on employer preferences, what may be learned from specific instances of outside anti-minority pressures, particularly as evidenced by local nativistic expressions, demonstrations, and policies?

Turning more to definite minority cultural qualities, search should be made for traits of depression importance. Were some minority individuals given extra security because of occupational traditions and skills? Recognizing that immigrants commonly shift occupations upon arrival in the United States, was it of any appreciable advantage to them to have a second string to their bow because of previous occupational training abroad? Did their occupational mobility in this country give them any advantage through increased flexibility in employment? Was the urbanized Oriental because of his occupational specialization able to weather the depression better than if he had been less concentrated in what have come to be considered traditional "race jobs?" Was there any increase in the practice of playing one minority against another during the depression by taking advantage of cultural differences for the benefit of employers? Illustrative cases of this practice may be found involving the playing of Mexicans against Negroes in Texas, of French Canadians against the Irish in New England, or in the use of one minority to break cooperative labor bargaining by another or by majority workers in various sections of the country. In plants employing large numbers of minority workers, does analysis show that this is a consequence merely of availability or rather of planned exploitation of workers who because of status and culture differentials afford peculiar opportunities for cheap production?

Another set of problems of importance in the present connection concerns what happens to minority workers displaced during the depression in comparison with displaced majority workers. For example, the Negro for generations has had some security in employment to compensate to a degree for his exclusion from most of the better occupations, because of powerful traditions that certain tasks were "nigger jobs." To some extent these restricted jobs were being invaded by white workers before the depression set in, but there is reason to believe that the depression speeded the process enormously. Some traditional Negro occupations practically vanished during the depression, as in the case of hotel employment in resorts such as Atlantic City and Miami. Where did the displaced Negroes go, and how did they live following the disappearance of their customary opportunities for employment? Similar examples for study, but with much less emphasis on traditional limitations in employment, may be found in any industrial community, such as the mill towns of New England, the mining towns of both the anthracite and bituminous coal regions, centers of the iron and steel industry, and other manufacturing areas.

Too much emphasis cannot be placed on the need for starting the investigation of problems of minority employer-employee relationships with the records of individual plants, or at least with workable groupings of plants. It is a practical impossibility to begin with the displaced worker as found on the government relief rolls of any type, for there is no way of determining the sampling value of such data. Studies of the individuals in an entire community are feasible if the communities are small enough and if ample funds are available. Individual plants, however, may be found in all sizes to suit available research facilities; their records are in many instances reasonably full and accurate, and may be made significant by proper definition of the research problem. It is understood, of course, that in many cases they may be closed to the student, but employer cooperation for research is sufficiently common to make this problem relatively unimportant. To cite but one illustration of a multitude of possibilities, reference may be made to the willingness of the receivers of the Amoskeag Mills to turn over the entire records of the company for research purposes—records which contain data on the employment of immigrants and their children which could be made to throw real light on the experience and rôle of several minorities in the textile industry beyond the expectancy from any other source of investigation. Other similar opportunities are not lacking.

The experience of employment agencies, both public and private, offers another type of data concerning minorities in industry. The factors influencing differential registration at such agencies as between groups are so complex that the sample of any minority cannot be assumed to be representative. Nevertheless, it should at least be possible to utilize the information available to them in the study of employer attitudes toward various minorities during the depression and perhaps also of the employability of minority applicants in comparison with others. A related source of similar information are both help wanted and employment wanted advertisements.

A second focus of inquiry concerning minorities in industry during the depression lies in the field of worker competition and cooperation.[7] On all other fronts of economic contact between minority and majority there is an appreciable and understandable bargaining basis for intergroup cooperation in terms of mutual benefit. In the long run employers do hire minority workers if they see their way clear to making a profit out of the transaction. Business men will buy from or sell to individuals of any minority status if the deal seems advantageous. Economic transactions for

[7] For a comprehensive discussion of the basic research problems in the field of competitive and cooperative behavior see May, Mark A. and Doob, Leonard W. *Competition and Cooperation.* New York: Social Science Research Council. Bulletin No. 25. 1937. Pp. 191

gain tend to burst quickly the bounds of race and nationality. It is less clear, however, that competitors within an economic class realize normally any strong motive of mutual interest for co-operation. Among workers, the prevailing tradition teaches that the more fellow workers who can be eliminated as competitors for jobs, the better.

It seems profitless to engage in the ancient dispute as to whether minorities in the United States have pushed labor of superior status out of employment or up into superior jobs. No doubt the pushing has been in both directions. Our concern here is with the depression, and the problem is whether in exceptionally hard times minorities supply especially large proportions of marginal workers who by their very existence protect to some degree the security of majority workers, or whether their inferior status and its concomitants make them a serious threat to other workers. Beyond this it is enough here to point out that white labor of old American extraction believes that its employment opportunities are improved by the elimination of minority competition by such devices as the repatriation of immigrants, the restriction of government employment to citizens by law, the encouragement of anti-minority discrimination by private employers, and by restrictions on union membership.

As a matter of research convenience, the attitude and behavior of majority labor toward minorities may be approached first from the point of view of labor as a whole and second from that of organized labor. The main reason for dividing the discussion in this manner is the fact that research data bearing on the first category are relatively diffuse and intangible; that of the second category are comparatively well defined and exceptionally accessible.

Historically, native white labor has been consistently antagonistic toward minorities. It is not without point that all minorities of racial or nationality origin in the United States were brought to or encouraged to come to this country by the employing classes and in spite of the grumblings and outright opposition of wage earners. Indeed, the growth of restrictive immigration legislation coincides remarkably with the rise of the wage earner as a political power. Furthermore, the most intense race prejudice and nativistic feelings have commonly been between worker and worker. This being the case, it is to be expected that the depression intensified the conflict between minority and majority labor.

In attempting to check the accuracy of this expectation we are hampered by the fact that labor as a whole, as distinguished from organized labor, has no official or centralized means for expressing itself. It is consequently necessary to resort to scattered sources of information difficult of coordination and of interpretation. The general technique which consequently recommends itself is the somewhat dubious one which might be described as historical journalism, a procedure which can be made to yield satisfactory results in the hands of competent individuals. The synthesis which it is hoped may be achieved by this procedure, however, can be facilitated by intensive particularized studies of specific incidents indicative of the working man's attitude toward minorities.

Special situations for study exist without end. Race riots and labor disturbances need to be examined to determine the racial and national origin of the participants, their employment and general status, the immediate and background circumstances which led to actual conflict, the terms of settlement, and so forth. Votes of the people and of their representatives in office may be analyzed to determine the influence of racial and nativistic doctrines. Bills introduced, laws enacted, and administrative regulations issued for the protection of "American Labor" can be studied. Nativistic trends in the news are subject to analysis. Local patterns governing the association of majority and minority individuals should show changes explainable in terms of depression circumstances. Increased minority consciousness and solidarity should be evident if there has been an increase in minority restrictions and oppression. Evidences of increased discrimination should be most extensive in regions of greatest minority competition for work. Limited studies of such specific subjects may be made as scientific as the existing techniques of social research permit in any social field. More inclusive investigations of the relations between unorganized labor and minority workers during the depression, however, must probably remain on a journalistic basis.

The key problem in the depression influence on the relations between majority labor, both organized and unorganized, and minority workers has to do with the extent to which economic class consciousness and solidarity was increased in relation to racial and nationality consciousness and solidarity. Just as farm labor and industrial labor seem to have been brought to greater recognition of their common interests (witness their vote for Roosevelt's re-election in 1936), so it seems that wage workers of the economic classes hardest hit by the depression were made more conscious of the need for concerted action to protect employment and conditions of employment. In other words, native white workers in the stress of economic emergency accompanied by an oversupply of labor found reason to look on minority workers more as fellow workers and less as members of inferior social castes and classes. At the same time, there seems also to have been an opposing tendency toward increased antagonism between minority and majority workers because of sharper competition for employment. The coexistence of these two opposing tendencies, paradoxical as it seems, may be accounted for by the fact that worker cooperation regardless of racial or nationality status was a strategic move dictated by emergency circumstances of the depression labor-capital struggle as a means of reducing the advantage to capital of an abundant labor supply, while at the same time the abundance of labor fostered rivalry between groups within its own ranks. It is not impossible to have open conflict between two companies of a regiment while both are engaged in a war against a common enemy, although lowered efficiency in battle may be expected as a consequence.

The experience of the Negro with reference to organized labor offers perhaps the best opportunity for examining this problem. As summarized by C. L. Franklin for Manhattan, ". . . practices vary from acceptance of Negro workers into membership on an equal basis with white workers, as in the International Ladies' Garment Workers' Union, to a complete exclusion of Negro workers by constitutional provision as in the Masters, Mates and Pilots of America, the railroad Brotherhoods and others. Between those two extremes are the unions that put Negro workers in separate locals or in auxiliary bodies responsible to white unions, those that neither discourage nor encourage Negro workers to join their ranks and those organized independently by Negro workers."[8]

As Spero and Harris have pointed out, "Since the Civil War this black minority, by the very fact of the discrimination practiced against it, has been in a position to do great damage to the majority which prescribed it. The recent northward migrations, which brought hundreds of thousands of Negro workers into the industrial centers, dramatically forced the realization of this fact upon the white wage earners."[9] Unions which have been secure from any threat of effective Negro competition with remarkable consistence have been unwilling to grant him the

---

[8] Franklin, Charles Lionel. *The Negro Labor Unionist of New York.* New York: Columbia University Press. 1936. Pp. 266

[9] Spero, Sterling D. and Harris, Abram L. *The Black Worker.* New York: Columbia University Press. 1931. P. vii. This volume furnishes an excellent summary and interpretation of the Negro in relation to the labor movement in the United States which is more than adequate as a base for depression studies. Other works which may be consulted in this connection include: Feldman, Herman. *Racial Factors in American Industry.* New York: Harper & Brothers. 1931. Pp. xiv+318; Reid, Ira DeA. (Director) *Negro Membership in American Labor Unions.* New York. 1930. Pp. 175; Wesley, Charles H. *Negro Labor in the United States.* New York: Vanguard Press, Inc. 1927. Pp. xiii+343

membership which he required for advancement in the hierarchy of industrial jobs. Since the Negro has been able to compete with workers with any appreciable degree of success mainly at the lower unskilled and semi-skilled levels, with relatively rare excursions into the more highly skilled trades, he has had the most success with the trade unions whose members are also in the levels of lower skills and with the industrial unions. Effective white organization, as in the case of the railroad Brotherhoods, a situation affording security on an artificial monopoly basis no less safe than that derived from superior occupational skills, has also been a strong barrier to Negro advancement. Thus the colored labor reserve of the United States has made headway with organized labor at its weak points where neither superior skills nor strategic priority of unionization were such as to enable the maintenance of white monopoly in defense of economic advantage and of social status.

The negligible Negro union membership prior to the depression does not seem to have been increased greatly until the establishment of the National Recovery Administration. Perhaps it was necessary for some time to elapse before the impact of the employment crisis could produce recognition by white labor of the need for the alignment of both white and black workers in an economic class conflict. Franklin suggests with reference to "the gains of Negro industrial workers in labor unions under the NRA," that "their new position was the outcome of two factors, (1) the more friendly attitude of white workers toward the acceptance of Negro workers into their unions and (2) the new attitude of Negro workers themselves toward taking the risk involved in the early stages of unionization of workers. In reference to the former, it was pointed out that late in 1933 and early in 1934, unions, realizing that the time was ripe for great organizational work because of the protection intended by Section 7A of the National Industrial Recovery Act, began organizing all workers in shops. In many cases large numbers of Negroes were employed in these shops, and for the first time they were considered by white workers as fellow workers rather than as inferior Negro workers. It was pointed out further that there was apparently a shift in the attitude of both white and Negro workers from a race consciousness to a class consciousness. . . . Added to this new favorable attitude of white workers was the willingness of Negro workers to fall in line. Since Section 7A was to offer protection against losing one's job because of union activity, the greatest obstacle in the way of organizing Negro workers, the fear of losing their hard-earned jobs, was partly removed; consequently, they felt the spirit of the time and fell in line with the other workers. . . . On the other hand, in unions controlling work that did not come within the purview of the NIRA—unions of some of the branches of the building trades and the transportation and communication workers, for example—the same apathetic and in many cases hostile attitude of the white members toward Negro members continued to prevail. . . ."[10]

The Negro unionization gains in New York City are quantitatively represented by Mr. Franklin's finding in 1935, "that of the 242,794 members in the unions surveyed, 39,574, or 9.3 per cent, were Negroes. This proportion represents a substantial improvement over the last estimate made in 1928. At that time 3.8 per cent of the organized workers of New York were Negro. . . . Interesting is the further observation that Negroes form a greater proportion of the organized workers in unskilled labor, such as transportation and communication work and domestic and personal service, the percentages for these being 24.8 and 22.5 respectively. On the other hand, Negro membership in unions of the highly skilled workers is negligible, being less than one-half of one per cent in the paper manufacturing, publishing and printing industries, 1.6 per cent in the leather industries, 2.7 in the building trades, etc. Another conclusion is that Negroes

---

[10] Franklin, Charles Lionel. *Op. cit.* Pp. 260f.

constitute a higher proportion in the membership of independent unions than in affiliates of the American Federation of Labor."[11]

Concerning the manner in which Negroes became members of Manhattan unions, Mr. Franklin lists six methods and may be quoted as follows: "(1) being charter members, (2) making direct application to local unions, (3) transferring membership from locals outside of New York, (4) being employed in a shop when it is organized by a local, (5) forming auxiliary units to white locals and (6) being made members through the special organizational programs for Negro workers sponsored by some locals. During the early post-NRA period, the first, fourth and sixth methods were most widely used, while in prior years the second, third and fifth were used, the second and third being early methods by which Negroes gained admittance to the unions."[12]

Although Mr. Franklin's study is restricted to the Negro in Manhattan and emphasizes the NRA and post-NRA periods rather than the entire depression period, it nevertheless has much more general significance than the definition of the project might suggest. Similar studies are needed in other cities. In making such additional studies, it is not necessary that an entire city be covered. Studies of the activities of individual unions in a community may be dictated by the exigencies of time and money, and certainly should not be avoided because of any fear of lack of significance. More emphasis than has been common in the past should be given the industrial union because of the Negro's concentration in unskilled and semi-skilled occupations. Further attention also needs to be given Negro traits of personality and culture in relation to organization problems, although it is not to be expected that any lasting barriers of this nature will be found standing in the way of his unionization. The relation between

---

[11] Franklin, Charles Lionel. *Op. cit.* P. 263
[12] Franklin, Charles Lionel. *Op. cit.* P. 264

color and other physical differences within the Negro group and depression employment is also of interest.

The rôle of the Negro as a strikebreaker in the depression requires particular study. In this connection Mr. Franklin's observations concerning Manhattan are suggestive: "The strike activity of Negro union members during and immediately following the NRA period was strikingly different from that of previous years. They were no longer the weak union members who refused to walk out with their fellow unionists. On the contrary, they were the loyal union members. In this connection it was also observed that the rôle of the Negro worker as a strikebreaker has about come to an end in Manhattan because the major cause for such activity, exclusion from some labor unions and limitations on membership in others, is gradually being removed."[13] The generalizations in this quotation seem to require further research support, not so much with reference to what actually happened in Manhattan following the establishment of the NRA, but rather with reference to the interpretation of cause and the prophecy concerning the future. It is, however, a not unlikely hypothesis that the depression by increasing class consciousness generally among wage earners may have reduced the willingness of Negroes, and also of poorly organized recent immigrant laborers, to work as strikebreakers.

The immigrant, unlike the Negro, has been closely associated with organized labor since its very beginning.[14] It was, however, the immigrant from northern and western Europe who played a leading part in the early phases of the American labor movement. His successors from southern and eastern Europe were not accepted freely into union membership until after the adjustment of disputes and difficulties which are remarkable in their re-

---

[13] Franklin, Charles Lionel. *Op. cit.* P. 266

[14] See Leiserson, William M. *Adjusting Immigrant and Industry.* New York: Harper & Brothers. 1924. Chapter IX

semblance to those which developed when the Negro later entered industry on a large scale.

There is evidence, however, that nativistic tendencies of some unions were encouraged by the depression, and it is not illogical that such should be the case. Some unions, especially the more aristocratic which have held firm control of the occupations they represent, have long discriminated against aliens as well as against other minorities by constitution and in practice. It is natural for any union, even though its own membership be heavily alien in origin, to be skeptical of the wisdom of admitting more aliens to the country or of conceding aliens already admitted equal opportunity with citizens for employment. It is also natural that whatever depression increase in discrimination of this kind occurred should have been directed primarily against the more recent immigrant groups. The depression influence in this respect is capable of determination by the examination of membership practices, including changes in constitutional provisions, general regulations, and actual admissions, and of official policies regarding the employment of aliens and the admission of immigrants to the United States.

The immigrant, as has been suggested, has reached a more advanced stage of labor organization than the Negro. Specific nationality groups have become adjusted to the American labor movement approximately in proportion to their length of residence in the United States. Due allowance, of course, must be made for such factors in organization as their industrial history in this country and the nature of their native cultures and home experience with relation to cooperative bargaining by labor. In view of their relatively advanced stage of labor organization in the United States, it would be well worthwhile to have specific historical studies of the experience of various European immigrant groups with unions in previous depressions so framed that they would throw the most possible light on union action with reference to minorities during the depression of the present decade.

Minority business and banking enterprises are inseparably interwoven. The financial institutions, however, are much more dependent on minority business and other support than is the case with business organizations. For present purposes distinction may be made between those industrial, commercial, and financial institutions under minority control which serve primarily minority needs and those which compete for the trade of all comers.

With reference to the latter, the question is whether the depression caused a more serious loss of business than was the case with similar organizations under minority control. To be specific, did the single fact of minority ownership and direction materially handicap during the depression more than previously the operation of distinctively Jewish banking, manufacturing, and selling concerns, Negro restaurants and other service establishments catering to white trade, or any other group of the thousands of minority enterprises differing from their competitors because of the racial or national origin of their proprietors? To the extent that the organization and management of these enterprises was inferior as a consequence of operation by individuals of handicapping minority status, the impact of the depression may be expected to have been exceptionally severe. Also to the extent that some of them were essentially luxury enterprises capitalizing majority interest in the exotic, such as the Oriental shops for selling Oriental goods to white people and Negro cabarets for white entertainment, it may be anticipated that an exceptional depression loss of business will be found. It seems much less likely, however, that any great number of majority business men and consumers transferred their custom to majority institutions because of anti-minority prejudice emphasized by the depression contrary to their economic advantage. In other words, the hypothesis offered for examination is that however the depression may have increased minority-majority antagonisms, it did not lead to noteworthy boycotting of minority business and finance involving a majority economic sacrifice.

In this connection it is interesting to observe that the one important boycott involving a minority during the depression was that of the Jews against German goods, and in this case the depression in the United States seems to have been at most a remote influence. In Germany itself, however, the boycotting of Jewish business seems to have been linked in origin with the German depression. Why no similar movement developed in the United States is a problem deserving more attention than it has thus far received.

Little is known concerning the history of minority business and banking as a result of research except for the Negro and for immigrant banking. In truth, remarkably little is known even in the excepted instances. Again dependence must be largely on a priori reasoning. No doubt minority business and banking depending on minority custom suffered exceptionally during the depression because of the impact of the depression on minority consumers. This is a supposition which may be checked by anyone familiar with the sources and methods of business and banking research provided he also have some knowledge of the peculiar economic patterns of the minorities concerned. Technically more difficult to investigate but of no less importance is the possibility that the depression has stimulated increased dependence within minorities on intragroup economic resources.

Minority enterprise dependent on intragroup support has been based on the possibility of capitalizing special needs (e. g., the Jewish need for kosher foods), on the demand for services not obtainable freely from majority sources (e.g., the demand for banking services or for recreational facilities), on the desire for group achievement as a matter of solidarity and pride (e.g., the desire to support a fellow minority business man), and on the need of majority firms for minority outlets and representatives in minority communities. The mere geographical location of a business in a minority community, of course, also is an important factor in this connection. It will be noticed that all these factors with the exception of that of geographical location may be classed as uneconomic in the sense that they may interfere with the efficient distribution of goods and services. Were it not for their existence minority enterprises dependent on minority customers would exist only as a consequence of group population concentrations. The problem raised at the conclusion of the preceding paragraph concerns the degree to which the depression has reinforced or weakened these uneconomic, or at least noneconomic, factors.

It is probable that the solution of this problem might establish a depression strengthening of the desire and need for intragroup minority enterprises and at the same time show a weakening of such enterprises. Minorities were not well served by majority enterprises during the depression in spite of a noticeable tendency to give greater welcome to their business. Perhaps minority enterprises served them no better except in the way of employment.[15] Nevertheless, it is understandable that the feeling should have been encouraged that things would have been better had the economic system not been so completely in control of the majority. On the other hand, such minority enterprises as existed were generally not in a favorable situation to meet a national economic crisis.

The story of the Negro bank in the depression and before has been recounted by Abram Harris in adequate detail and with exceptional understanding.[16] The record of failures is appalling.

[15] For an illustration of the possibility of studying marketing problems with reference to a particular minority group see Edwards, Paul K. *The Southern Urban Negro as a Consumer.* New York: Prentice-Hall. 1932. Pp. xxiv+323

[16] Harris, Abram L. *The Negro as Capitalist.* Monograph No. 2. Philadelphia: American Academy Political and Social Science. 1936. Pp. xii+205

Apart from incompetence and downright dishonesty in management, it is clear that these banks could not avoid an extraordinary mortality in a crisis as a consequence of the economic history and status of the people they served and of their unavoidably limited functions and field of operation. Without attempting to cover all of the factors contributing to the weakness of Negro banks, the following revealing statement by Dr. Harris may be quoted in partial explanation of the situation:

The general lack of diversification of the earning assets of the Negro bank can be ascribed to two conditions. The first is the qualitative and quantitative character of Negro business. The second is the fact that the Negro bank is a small bank and like all small banks is handicapped in securing diversified borrowers.

We have already commented on the fact that in 1929 the 70,000 enterprises owned and operated by Negroes were mainly service undertakings. In retail trade, for example, there were 25,701 concerns. . . . These retail stores had 28,243 proprietors but employed only 12,561 other persons. Their stock on hand was merely $101,146,043. The chief concerns were restaurants, which numbered 15,000. Next to restaurants came the grocery stores, which numbered 8,450.

All these concerns—except the restaurants, beauty parlors, barber shops and similar service enterprises that are engaged in business that the whites do not want—must compete with larger and more efficient white enterprises. This is especially true of the grocery and general merchandising stores. In these lines of business the large chain stores and many independent ones have no great difficulty underselling their black competitors. The Negro business man is a small shopkeeper who lives on the margin of commercial advantage barely earning the wages of management. As such his demand for commercial credit and his need for long-term financing of an industrial character are almost non-existent. Although loans collateralled by stocks and bonds have been superseding the strictly commercial loans in the banks of the country as a whole during the past decade, the character of Negro business prevents it from commanding funds on the basis of industrial stocks and bonds, as well as from obtaining credit on a purely commercial basis. This lack of significant industrial and commercial undertakings and the preponderance of small shops in the Negro business world force the Negro bank to find an outlet for its funds in church and fraternal lodge loans, in the development of theatres, in amusements, and in real estate. By far the greater part of the Negro bank's loans to individuals are made to small-salaried persons and wage-earners for consumptive purposes with the integrity of the borrower as the only security.

In thus limiting the scope and liquidity of the Negro bank's investments and loans, the character of Negro business becomes the fundamental factor in its instability and economic weaknesses. While a few of the Negro banks studied would not have failed had they been conducted by judicious and experienced officers, most of them would have failed even if they had had expert management. Lack of experience and technical bank training, dishonesty, fraud, and speculation, are all too prevalent among Negro banks in relation to their size and the amount of business done by them, but they are not primary causes of their failure and weakness. Given sound and honest management, the Negro bank would still face one fundamental and perhaps insuperable obstacle to successful operation, namely, the inherent characteristics of Negro enterprise.

The second cause of the undiversified character of the portfolio of the Negro bank is the fact that it is a small bank. This cause is inseparable from the first. The Negro bank is small because Negro business is. Thus the reason usually given for the need of Negro banks is the inability of the Negro business man, a small merchant and trader by virtue of economic conditions, to obtain credit at the large white banks. But the justification of the Negro bank is but a special phase of the wider defense of the small bank generally.[17]

Limitations of time, of facilities, and of data did not permit Dr. Harris to study the records of all Negro banks or of that other group of Negro financial institutions, the Negro insurance companies.[18] Nor was his analysis carried past the first years of the depression. The product of his research under these limitations, however, is an excellent demonstration that it is not always, if ever, necessary to cover every nook and cranny and collect every last item of information concerning an area of investigation in order to obtain an adequate objective understanding of a problem. It is to be hoped, of course, that the experience of the Negro insurance companies during the depression may be further analyzed, that at least some of the banks not included in Dr. Harris' study will be investigated by others, and that Negro banking

---

[17] Harris, Abram L. *Op. cit.* Pp. 172f.

[18] For an account of Negro insurance companies see Trent, W. J. Jr. *Development of Negro Life Insurance Enterprises.* A master's thesis submitted to the faculty of the Graduate School of Business Administration of the University of Pennsylvania. Philadelphia. 1932. Pp. 62

activities following the date when his investigations closed will be studied. Such studies have been made comparatively simple by his pioneer work. They are not, however, essential for reasonably adequate knowledge of the way in which the depression affected Negro credit and finance. The need is for an equally revealing study of Negro business with perhaps particular emphasis on such enterprises as real estate, restaurants, stores, beauty parlors, and the like.

There is a parallel need for study of the experience of the immigrant and his children in business, and in finance as well. There is, however, little hope that anything but case studies of the foreign-born and of the first American-born generation may be made. The various nationality groups are scattered and diverse. Records of industry, commerce, and trade are rarely classified on the basis of citizenship and parentage of owner and operator. Furthermore, in view of the rapid assimilation and loss of social visibility of white peoples of alien origin, and of the recent decrease in immigration, there is little pressure of public interest to encourage such study, valuable as it would be for both social and scientific purposes. An exception should probably be made of the Jew, for in his case alone among white minorities public interest as manifested in anti-Semitic feeling is perhaps strong enough to lead to investigation of his rôle in business and banking. By a coincidence it happens that this is the one important minority of more than ephemeral special status concerning which there are no reliable statistics whatever. There is, however, no inherent reason why economic studies should not be made of any minority of whatever origin if there is sufficient incentive to the collection of source data.[19]

---

[19] Witness, for example, the manner in which "The Editors of Fortune Magazine" were able promptly and effectively to answer with objective data the charge that the Jews in the United States controlled a grossly disproportionate share of American economic activity. See their *Jews in America*. New York: Random House. 1936. Pp. 104

The immigrant bank is a sufficiently unique economic institution to warrant more detailed investigation than it has received. A product of the unassimilated immigrant's need for a wide variety of financial services not offered by any majority institution, its rôle in its original form is not a lasting one. Professor M. R. Davie's summarization of its origin and functioning may be quoted because of its excellence as a descriptive statement and because it must suggest to the reader a number of depression problems.

Recent immigrants needing assistance in financial and other matters have naturally turned to leaders in their own community, frequently the steamship agent, but often the boarding boss, labor agent, saloon keeper, grocer or butcher; in short, to someone in business or other position of prominence who is more or less established and has some degree of education. To these individuals they intrust their funds accumulated by weekly savings. Before long the leader or agent has a nucleus for a banking b·siness and his assumption of banking functions quickly follows. The banks vary from regular private and incorporated banks of the American type to the most casual sort of arrangement.

The banking functions performed by these institutions are chiefly those of deposits and foreign exchange though some include loans and money exchange. Their functions in foreign exchange are restricted to the transmission of money abroad. . . . Since the immigrant bank is usually conducted as an adjunct to some other business or employment, the receipt of deposits is directly contributory to the personal interests of the proprietors. Immigrant banks are rarely commercial or savings institutions. Deposits are usually left for temporary safe-keeping rather than as interest-bearing savings accounts. Such deposits are not subject to check and thus there is seldom need of clearing arrangements. Beyond an understanding that deposits are subject to demand at any time, no consideration is given nor limitation implied as to their use. So far as his depositors are concerned, the immigrant banker is at liberty to use their funds to suit himself. The most objectionable use to which deposits are usually put is that of direct investment in the proprietor's own business. Many immigrant banks especially in the smaller towns where the principal profits arise from the sale of steamship tickets redeposit the funds intrusted to them in national or state banks, and thus derive interest on thousands of dollars which have been deposited with them but upon which they are making no returns.

· · · · · · · · · · · · · · ·

Many of the services connected with immigrant banks are, of course, not banking functions at all, and that is one reason why the immigrant has not turned to American banks to satisfy his needs. Even in the case of strictly banking functions, the immigrant needs various facilities and services, such as to have his language spoken, letters written, and information given, which American banks have been very slow to develop. . .
Ignorant of American customs, unable to use the English language and finding little encouragement to overcome their hesitance, the immigrants turn to the bankers of their own nationality as the only ones readily able to perform the services they need.[20]

Minority business and banking in so far as it is a response to the limitations of prejudice and of inferior and social status rather than an attempt to compete for success and profit against all comers and for any one's trade encountered the depression in an economically unsound position. It is probable that the disadvantages of this position were but slightly offset by support growing out of group consciousness and solidarity. A similar situation seems to exist in connection with immigrant building and loan associations and real estate enterprises. The degree to which depression inspired intragroup cooperation, fostered intragroup business and banking, or failed to do so because of more powerful opposing influences, is the central problem in the present connection.

A similar problem exists in connection with the minority professional classes. Have minorities turned to or away from preachers, doctors, lawyers, teachers, and other professional men of their own group status? Further, since the professions have long been the easiest means for achieving high status within minorities as well as for gaining exceptional recognition and privileges from the majority, it may be asked whether there was any increased emphasis on the desirability of such occupations as might well be anticipated. A third question, more ready of solution than the other two, concerns the depression attitude of

---

[20] Davie, Maurice R. *World Immigration*. New York: The Macmillan Company. 1936. Pp. 479-482

majority professional people and organizations toward their minority colleagues. Did organizations and institutions under majority control, such as the American Medical Association, the American Bar Association, the National Education Association, the churches, the hospitals, medical schools, and so forth, evidence any increased nativistic or anti-minority spirit as a consequence of decreased economic opportunities in their fields?

Closely related to all economic problems which have been raised are innumerable questions concerning the influence of the depression on minority consumption. Consumption, however, is a neglected division of economics as a discipline and, with the exception of a few studies of standards of living and fragmentary references to cultural differences in living habits, the minority consumer is an unexplored subject for research.[21] For want of better basic knowledge and theory than is now available it is necessary to restrict problems raised concerning the minority consumer and depression to questions which may be approached through the analysis of income limitations, of varying culture patterns, of the influence attendant upon inferior class and caste status, of actual depression expenditures for items which can still be determined after the passage of two or three years or more, such as housing and automobile ownership, and of other scraps of information which happen to be available.

Minorities are characterized by relatively low living planes, both because of low income and because of the old world heri-

---

[21] For a comprehensive statement of the theory of consumption see Zimmerman, Carle C. *Consumption and Standards of Living*. New York: D. Van Nostrand Company. 1936. Pp. xvi+602. For annotated references to factual studies of minority standards of living see Williams, Faith M. and Zimmerman, Carle C. *Studies of Family Living in the United States and Other Countries*. Washington, D.C.: U. S. Department of Agriculture. Miscellaneous Publi ation No. 223. December 1935. Depression problems of the consumer are considered in a separate monograph in this series: Vaile, Roland S. *Research Memorandum on Social Aspects of Consumption in the Depression*.

tage. It is offered as a hypothesis that predepression low living levels made it easier to effect material, personal, and family adjustments to depression circumstances than was the case with the majority population accustomed to higher living levels. Thus, a surprising number of Indians and Negroes receiving federal aid were able to raise their standard of living. Reference may be made in support of this observation to the appreciable number of Negroes who moved from the South to northern cities during the depression to get on relief, and to the government funds expended in southwestern Indian areas which even in prosperous times could not do more than keep their populations barely alive. It is likely that few immigrants, and certainly very few of their children, found their living improved by public aid, but it is probable that their necessary depression adjustments were less sharp and critical than those required of the majority population as a whole.

Clues to the depression impact of minority consumption may be found in differential rents paid and in arrears in family income, in loans secured, in savings and savings dissipation, in housing congestion, in loss of homes, of furniture, of insurance, of clothes, in diet, in health records, and so on.[22] What did actually happen to minority family income during the depression? What were the living costs in regions of minority concentration? What proportion of minority family income was needed for rent in relation to that paid by the general population? What was the

---

[22] Johnson, Charles S. *Negro Housing*. Report of the Committee on Negro Housing. Washington, D.C.: The President's Conference on Home Building and Home Ownership. 1932. Pp. xiv+282, is the best available summary of the subject and contains a bibliography. The treatment of Negro rural housing in this book is far from satisfactory, undoubtedly as a consequence of the unavailability of satisfactory research studies of this aspect of the housing problem. Rural minority housing as a whole has been neglected as a field for research.

Abbott, Edith. *The Tenements of Chicago, 1908-1935*. Chicago: University of Chicago Press. 1936. Pp. xx+505, discusses in considerable detail the housing situation of the various minority peoples in Chicago and is suggestive of many depression problems in this connection.

relation of minority food consumption habits to their ability to weather the depression? What was the result of the fact that some groups, such as the Mexican, were not accustomed to saving, while other groups, such as the Jew, were culturally conditioned to saving? Can anything be learned from study of differential standards of spending? Were there any significant consequences of the fact that minority trade is welcomed in new quarters during hard times, as by certain stores, restaurants, colleges, clubs, the Pullman Company, and other agencies and organizations ordinarily disdainful of Negro, Jewish, Mexican, or some other minority money? Were the communal production and consumption customs of some Indian tribes of any help in the depression? How did Negro individualism and family and community structure affect consumption during the depression? To what extent were minorities represented in the various self-help cooperatives which came into being as depression phenomena? What was the effect on minorities, such as the Indian and the Negro, unaccustomed to regular money incomes, of receiving dependable incomes from relief or public works? It is not expected that all questions such as these may be answered definitively, but it is from improved understanding of them that the story of minority consumption during the depression must be constructed.[23]

In conclusion to our economic discussion attention may be called to the depression emphasis on minority economic separatism. Reference has already been made to the majority tendency

---

[23] At the time of writing an exceptionally well planned study of urban consumer purchases giving some attention to the foreign-born as well as to the Negro, was under way as a Works Progress Administration project with the cooperation of the Bureau of Labor Statistics, the National Resources Committee, the Central Statistical Board, and the Bureau of Home Economics. This study promises significant data concerning minority consumption in urban centers, the exact nature and extent of which cannot now be stated, but unfortunately lacks a predepression basis for comparison.

to blame at least part of the severity of the depression on the presence of minorities in the United States. There seems to be increased antagonism to the newer immigrant stocks, aliens tend to be regarded as economic sinners, Jews apparently become economic scapegoats, and Negroes are regarded as a drag on the welfare of the country. Considering the strength which such views obtained in earlier depression periods of our history and abroad, particularly in Germany, it is surprising that they were not stronger in the depression of the present decade. Certainly they fell far short of any real demand for a "purging" of our population. Nativistic economic separatism might well have been expected to go much farther than it did.

Minority economic separatism might also have been expected to make greater depression headway than it did. While there may have been similar tendencies among other minorities, only the Indian and the Negro have given real evidence of a move in the direction of greater intragroup economic independence. In the case of the Indian, the sympathy of the white man and government direction and aid gave material reality to the movement; the Negro economic separatist movement has progressed but little beyond the stage of being an idea in the minds of a relatively small band.

The Wheeler-Howard Act may be regarded as an effort to give the Indian an opportunity with full government support to develop economically as independently as our national economy will permit of white control and domination. A pooling of both material and human resources is permitted which makes possible a degree of economic self-determination comparable to that enjoyed by tribes on the early reservations in extent and perhaps better secured. Government support through guidance and finance is made available. It is beside the point to say that the essence of self-determination is reduced by the great degree of government initiative and aid involved. Nor does it matter that the self-determination extends beyond the economic to the political and social; without such extension the economic privilege would be of necessity severely curtailed.

As previously mentioned, the Wheeler-Howard program in a sense may be said to be not at all a depression phenomenon. Its essential ideas and provisions were proposed and advocated long before the depression began. In another and very real sense, however, it is distinctly a product of the depression. It was the depression which set the national stage for its acceptance, which swept into power a political party and men who found its objectives compatable with their philosophy of the government of minorities, and which made possible the appropriation of the millions of public funds as part of the emergency program for its support. It will be instructive to observe the history of the consequent inevitable conflict between the forces favoring and those antagonistic to separatism in this experiment under the most auspicious circumstances conceivable.

Negro economic separatism also has a predepression as well as a depression history. To quote Dr. Harris again:

While the Negro's hope of creating an independent black economy dates back to pre-Civil War days, the differential disadvantages suffered by the Negro masses as compared with the white since the depression of 1929 have caused the ideal to gain renewed popularity. One of the groups advocating it follows the individualistic economics and optimistic naïveté of Booker T. Washington. It would therefore develop the black economy upon a strictly competitive and private profit basis. Another group would have it develop through the mobilization of the purchasing power of the black masses; on the one hand, by organizing the masses into producers and consumers cooperatives and on the other, by using the boycott to force white concerns that have a large Negro market to employ Negroes in clerical and executive positions. The leadership of this second group is being rapidly assumed by Dr. W. E. B. Du Bois who has practically abandoned as futile the movement for Negro rights and civil liberty which he so militantly led for a quarter of a century.

It is impossible to draw any great distinction between these two groups. They shade imperceptibly into each other. Their common ideology is middle class. Neither group, of course, sees that the limits of a separate economy are precariously narrow within the confines of the present industrial system. How the independent black economy is to develop and

function in the face of persistent industrial integration, business com-
binations, the centralization of capital control and the concentration of
wealth none of the advocates of the plan can explain. Du Bois, while
admitting the difficulty of establishing his segregated coöperative economy believes that through self-sacrifice and enterprise the plan is highly
feasible. At all events, he maintains that the experiment must be tried
if the Negro workers and farmers are to survive until the inevitable
'social revolution.' As long as capitalism remains, however, it is reasonably certain that the main arteries of commerce, industry, credit and
finance will be controlled by white capitalists. Under the circumstances,
the great mass of black and white men will continue dependent upon
these capitalists for their livelihood, and the small Negro business man
and the small white capitalist will continue subordinate to these larger
financial and industrial interests. Thus it is obvious that the independent
black economy whether it develops upon the basis of private profit or
of coöperation cannot be the means of achieving the Negro's economic
salvation.[24]

Dr. Harris' observations concerning the feasibility of a separate black economy might well be given broader scope to cover
minority economic separatism in general. The depression has
given new life to the old idea, perhaps first observable in this
country in the Indian reservation, that the economic activities
and welfare of minority and majority may be at least in part dissociated, somewhat as the fingers of the hand or siamese twins
are partly dissociated, for the benefit of one or both groups. The
idea has been so tenacious of life in spite of repeated historical
demonstration of its impossibility of achievement that its current manifestations under depression stimulation deserve the
most detailed observation and analysis.

---

[24] Harris, Abram L. *Op. cit.* Pp. ixf.

Chapter VI

Government and Politics

THE modern state recognizes little that is absolutely private in the lives of its citizens and less in the lives of its alien guests. Practically every aspect of existence from recreation to the earning of the daily bread is touched by the hand of government, a hand whose weight does not fall evenly on all classes. It would thus logically be proper to give consideration to a multitude of minority problems under a heading of minority-state relations. Such a catch-all procedure, however, would not be technically feasible, and the present discussion will consequently be limited to questions of minority life in which the rôle of the state is preponderant. These include matters of national spirit, political participation, public aid in time of economic stress, and crime and violence.

NATIONAL UNITY

Throughout the history of the United States there seems to have been a direct correlation between the peaks of nativist spirit and the valleys of exceptional economic difficulty. Not only has there been evidence of a pronounced degree of inverse correlation between the strength of political movements with the objective of preserving America for the Americans and the height of general prosperity, but there also have been similar correlations within internal regions whose economic history has not entirely paralleled that of the country as a whole. Nativist movements of national significance include the rise of the Native American Party in the 1830's, the Know-Nothing Order in the 1850's, the American Protective Association in the last two decades of the nineteenth century, and the modern Ku Klux Klan following the World War.[1] These major movements achieved remarkable successes, if on the whole local and temporary, in view of the flimsy nature of their anti-minority slogans; successes which by geographic location might probably be shown to have a relation to the intensity of hard times in areas of noteworthy minority population. Less widespread minor nativist movements, such as those directed against Chinese, Japanese, and Filipinos on the West Coast, Italians in Louisiana, and the French Canadians in New England, show no serious departure from the rule.

Much has been written concerning such movements, but most of it is historical description paying little or no attention to the possibility of generalization in terms of minorities in depression. This is understandable in view of the past training and tradition of historians and the general skepticism of the possibility of historical science in contrast with what have been cautiously called historical studies. Both reliable secondary and primary source materials are still available in abundance, and well known, for the analysis of the problems involved; the lack is of research personnel trained for and interested in the task.[2]

[1] See Stephenson, G. M. *A History of American Immigration.* Boston: Ginn and Company. 1926. *Passim*

[2] For various types of historical immigration material available see: Abbott, Edith. *Historical Aspects of the Immigration Problem.* Chicago: The University of Chicago Press. 1926. Pp. xx+881; Abbott, Edith. *Immigration: Select Documents and Case Records.* Chicago: The University of Chicago Press. 1924. Pp. xxii+809

In connection with consideration of the use of the historical method in the study of minority phenomena, attention may be called to the possible use of archival material for the quantitative study of population as illustrated in: Sutherland, Stella H. *Population Distribution in Colonial America.* New York: Columbia University Press. 1936. Pp. xxxii+353; Greene, E. B. and Harrington, V. D. *American Population Before the Federal Census of 1790.* New York: Columbia University Press. 1932. Pp. xxii+228

Since the stimulation and training of research personnel require years of time, it is indeed fortunate that satisfactory materials are in no immediate danger of becoming rare. The danger is not of their destruction except in trifling proportion but rather of their misuse by students not equipped for historical research. For example, it has become increasingly evident to sociologists specializing in race relations that historical comparisons with current analyses are indispensable both for purposes of perspective and as checks on accuracy of causal interpretation. They have consequently dabbled in historical research, and with feeble results because of casual interest and lack of adequate technique. It is indeed a question whether the necessarily specialized, intensive training required for historical research will permit many sociologists in race relations to be more than dabblers in historical method; the far simpler procedure is for a few historians to supplement their technical training with sufficient knowledge of the whole field of minority problems to make their work contribute its maximum to an understanding of the problems involved.

Comparisons of contemporary with historical instances of tides of nativism should not be confined to cases found in the experience of the United States. Not to go back into earlier times, attention may be called to Italian Fascist behavior toward minorities of alien origin, or of Nazi treatment of Jews, Poles, and Catholics in Germany. There is no scarcity of comparable situations on any of the continents, and all have their contribution to offer to the understanding of nativism.

In this connection it would be desirable to have more definite knowledge of the relation between nativism as a program for reserving the benefits of a land largely for the use of its "native" majority population element, and nationalism. In the *Encyclopaedia of the Social Sciences* Max Hildebert Boehm takes the position that:

Nationalism in its broader meaning refers to the attitude which ascribes to national individuality a high place in the hierarchy of values. In this sense it is a natural and indispensable condition and accompanying phenomenon of all national movements. In so far as the political life of the national state is governed by national forces there is hardly ever any sharp distinction between patriotism and nationalism. On the other hand, the term nationalism also connotes a tendency to place a particularly excessive, exaggerated and exclusive emphasis on the value of the nation at the expense of other values, which leads to a vain and importunate overestimation of one's own nation and thus to a detraction of others. Nationalism of this sort stands in the same relation to national feeling as does chauvinism to genuine patriotism. Although it represents but one aspect of national movements, this narrower kind of nationalism espoused by miltant groups and often by mass parties, exercises an enormous political influence.[3]

The high value placed upon unification within the state by nationalism, whether it be conceived as a political or as a cultural ideal, seems likely to lead to the limitation of the activities, rights, and privileges of minorities judged to be incompetent or unwilling to participate fully in the movement. Suggestive of such a tendency is the following quotation from Carlton J. H. Hayes:

In Europe the newest national states almost instantly [following the World War] passed from liberal pronouncements to illiberal conduct and speedily vied with older national states in establishing nationalist tariffs, armies, schools, and other agencies of propaganda and in discriminating socially if not legally against dissident minorities. In connection with this last statement it should be remarked that while the new map of Europe conformed in general to the principle of nationality, the population in some parts of the continent was so mixed in nationality or a particular region was so insistently demanded by one of the victors for commercial or strategic considerations that all the new national states (and some of the old) embraced minorities of alien nationality. To those states the temptation of 'nationalizing' their minorities was strong, while states like Germany and Hungary were at least equally tempted to regard the populations and areas which they had lost as 'irredentas' which must be regained as soon as possible. Agitation for the recovery of 'irredentas' and movements for the 'nationalizing' of minorities are alike dangerous to internal and international peace.

[3] *Encyclopaedia of the Social Sciences.* 11:231. 1933

Then too, taking advantage of economic distress and of the enhanced nationalism of the post-war period, demagogues and dictators have risen to positions of influence or power in several European countries and have used their position to preach or enforce an ever more intensive and exclusive nationalism. The most striking illustrations of this have been the conversion of Mussolini from socialism to nationalism and the establishment and maintenance of his Fascist regime in Italy and the ascension to power of Hitler and the Nazi movement in Germany with their hostility to Jews, Poles, the French, Catholics and any other groups at home or abroad who are assumed to belie or belittle German nationalism. Somewhat similar phenomena have attended post-war dictatorships in Poland, Lithuania, Hungary and Jugoslavia and, on widely different intellectual levels, the propaganda of the Ku Klux Klan in the United States and the Action Française in France.[4]

The emphasis thus far in this section has been on the need for comparative research dealing with nativist anti-minority political patterns during economic crises, a field peculiarly promising of fruitful results bearing directly on the relations of government and minority. Study of the same problem during the last depression in the United States promises even better returns since the greater abundance of documentary materials and the possible direct testimony of participants make possible the assembling of more complete data by the social scientists and the use of a wider variety of techniques.[5]

The problem, in essence, is to determine any relationship which may exist between the degree and possible peculiar characteristics of a depression and the development of nativism in various forms. Specific subordinate questions and sources of evidence are legion. Case histories of societies, clubs, political parties, and other associations, with nativistic elements in their programs need quick reporting if they are not to be largely lost or allowed to dry down to bare documentary bones in the passage of time. Legislative proposals and enactments with "America

---

[4] *Ibid.* P. 247

[5] An exceptional journalistic account of nationalistic anti-alien agitation during the depression may be found in "Aliens and Alien-Baiters" by Adamic, Louis. *Harpers Magazine.* 1038:561-574. November 1936

for the Americans" objectives require less haste in study.[6] What was the legislative trend in such matters as special requirements for or the actual prohibition of licenses for hunting and fishing, or for practicing various professions and skilled trades? Were there any changes in the restrictions on land ownership by aliens? Was there any tightening up in the enforcement of laws applying especially to aliens? What was the strength of the agitation for prohibiting some forms of or all public relief to aliens? To what extent was the amount of actual relief given to minority unemployed different from that obtained by members of the majority group? Did public employment offices offer the same opportunities to all? What was the extent of discrimination against minority employees and applicants for work in private industry and on public projects in comparison with previous years? Why did deportations increase so heavily? To what extent were voluntary repatriations of aliens publicly encouraged and subsidized?[7] What modifications were there in naturalization regulations and procedure? What can be inferred concerning changes in public opinion regarding minorities from study of the press and as measured by attitude tests? What information

---

[6] Although much has been written about legislation restricting the activities of the various minority peoples in the United States, it is still surprisingly difficult to obtain an accurate and integrated view of such discriminatory legislation. Many volumes concerned with one minority or another include fragmentary accounts of legislative discriminations, but no one is satisfactory in this connection with respect to freedom from bias, completeness, legal reliability, and social interpretation. For an indication of the type of material available for such studies see Stephenson, G. T. *Race Distinctions in American Law.* New York: D. Appleton & Company. 1910. Pp. xiv+338; Guild, J. P. *Black Laws of Virginia.* Richmond: Whittet & Shepperson. 1936. Pp. 249; Krieger, Heinrich. *Das Rassenrecht in den Vereinigten Staaten.* Berlin: Junker and Dünnhaupt. 1936. Pp. 361

[7] A Department of Labor regulation provides that: "Any alien who has fallen into distress or is in need of public aid from causes arising subsequent to entry and is desirous of being removed to his native country may, on order of the Commissioner of Immigration and Naturalization, at any time within three years after entry, be so removed at Government expense."—From a mimeographed letter to all state emergency relief administrations from the Administrator of the Federal Emergency Relief Administration, dated January 12, 1934

may be obtained from analysis of voting records in contests where a minority issue was involved?

It will be observed that of the subordinate questions just raised, practically all may be subsumed under some other category of minority-majority relations possibly more sharply defined than the subject of nativism, and that no attempt at completeness has been made. Nevertheless it should not be inferred on this account that special study of nativism as such is not needed, that the subject is either one of little merit for research or of such simplicity that when enough basic data has been collected the parts will fall together of themselves. Any single minority problem requires contributions from all over the field, but that of nativism is especially a task of synthesis requiring a technique and philosophy of interpretation for which the historian is peculiarly fitted. The unique potential qualifications of the historian for contributing to the understanding of the political aspects of nativism through documentary research and synthesis, alone would justify setting it apart as a field for study.[8]

A parallel question to that concerning the development of majority nativism in time of depression asks about the relation between general economic hardship and minority reactions in terms of political thought and action looking toward group unity and preservation. Are majority appeals to national or racial unity as a means for battling starvation accompanied by similar increased emphasis on minority symbols of group action?

---

[8] It may well be possible to add to our understanding of any relation between the strength of anti-minority agitation through the study of the biographical data available concerning outstanding minority defenders and leaders of the majority attacks. This suggestion is made because there are many biographies and autobiographies of such persons already published, and material is extant for the preparation of others in every period of American history. The assumption is made that social trends may be uncovered and interpreted through the lives of symbolic leaders as well as through impersonal statistics. The latter approach, of course, is the more reliable one for periods covered by proper statistical tables; the former has the advantage of being feasible for any period and place in modern history.

Although there is good evidence, evidence which is reasonably convincing without having been worked into proper shape by social scientists, that majority nativism in the United States has become an increasingly powerful political factor since 1929, the corresponding minority picture is a confused blur. It does seem clear, however, that there has been no more than a slight tendency for minorities to fight their case politically with a united front, yet it would be valuable to know to just what extent Negroes and Jews, say in New York City, or Chinese, Japanese, and Filipinos on the West Coast, have banded together, if at all, because of their common plight. In spite of the common belief to the contrary, it seems that little success has been achieved by the few minority leaders who have advocated such cooperation. Minority groups have too little in common except their treatment by the majority, and too many points of serious difference, to permit their standing shoulder to shoulder except in sporadic instances, particularly since it is possible to derive some psychic satisfaction out of the presence of other peoples in the same boat and on a lower deck.

A probable hypothesis is that the harder minorities are pressed to get a living, the more they tend to emphasize defensively their minority qualities and traditions. On the other hand, it seems from purely general observation that such an hypothesis can stand only when oppressed individuals find it impossible to pass over into and identify themselves with the majority. Certainly there are tendencies toward both escape from and defensive retreat deeper into minority status. In either case, the possibility of an effective political program for even a single minority is minimized.

Instead of attempting to gain protection through the ballot, a procedure not adapted to the use of numerical minorities unless they happen to hold the balance of power between two major factions, those who can neither escape from minority status nor endure it without compensating adjustments give some evidence of a tendency to resort to compensatory idealized tradition. As a guess, this tendency operated but weakly during the past six years, but its study would furnish an excellent point of beginning for the analysis of minority depression behavior corresponding to majority nativism.

As a first source of tangible evidence, investigation of minority clubs should be made. These would include all varieties of organizations from the purely social to the political. There are literally thousands of such organizations, some of which exist but briefly and have no more conscious purpose than the support of an occasional dance, while others have histories running well into the past century and serve all conceivable functions, including the political. While all may contribute to the answer to our question, since our immediate interest is in minority attitudes toward the state, those of nationalistic import are of prime concern. Other sources of information include all which contain or reflect political opinion, particularly with reference to national or group allegiance, such as minority newspapers, naturalization records, and voting practices.

The theory is widely held that hardpressed minority peoples are fertile soil for the growth of what, for want of a better term, may be called Zionistic tendencies. Without entering into a discussion of Jewish Zionism as such, or attempting to distinguish between political, religious, cultural, and other Zionistic variants, the tendency may be thought of as increasing reliance on glorified history and wishful group myths as a means for easing a present situation and for establishing as a goal a return to a golden age. What happened to Jewish Zionism during the depression? Did the depression give extra life to homeland culture patterns among immigrants, and perhaps serve as a factor leading to the repatriation of many? What of the ideal of the "new Negro," with its glorification of African traditions, which seems not to have prospered during the depression? Did the oral and printed use of foreign languages gain or lose as a symbol of group identity? Whether the answers to such questions support the theory of Zionist tendency or not is fundamental to the interpretation of minorities in relation to problems of nationalism, nativism, or any matter of state unity.

NATURALIZATION

Questions concerning citizenship and the depression naturally fall into two classes—those centering about the method of obtaining citizenship and those connected with the utilization of the rights and duties of citizenship. Inasmuch as persons born in the United States and under its jurisdiction acquire citizenship by virtue of those facts, questions of the first class are limited to aliens eligible for naturalization, defined by law as free white persons or Africans or persons of African descent.

The citizenship status of the foreign-born has been reported for males 21 years of age or over since the Census of 1890; for both sexes and all ages, since the Census of 1920.[9] Of the 14,204,149 foreign-born in the United States in 1930, 7,919,536 had been naturalized, 1,266,419 held their first papers, 4,518,341 were aliens without first papers, and 499,853 were of unknown citizenship status. These figures include both the white and colored foreign-born population, but separate tabulations are available from 1900 to 1930 inclusive. Mexicans, although largely of Indian blood, have been treated as white under the naturalization laws.[10]

---

[9] For more detailed information concerning naturalization see Davie, Maurice R. *World Immigration*. New York: The Macmillan Company. 1936. Ch. XIV; Razovsky, Cecilia. *Handicaps in Naturalization*. New York: National Council on Naturalization and Citizenship. 1932. Pp. 27; Schibsby, Marian. *Handbook for Immigrants to the United States*. New York: Foreign Language Information Service. 1927. Pp. 180

[10] For official statistics see *Fifteenth Census of the United States: 1930. Population*. General Report Statistics by Subjects. Vol. II. Chapter VIII. "Citizenship of the Foreign-born." Pp. 399-492; also, annual reports of the Commissioner of Immigration and Naturalization for the period since June 10, 1933, prior to which date the Bureau of Immigration and the Bureau of Naturalization were separate services.

General statistics of citizenship, whether prepared by the Bureau of the Census or by the Immigration and Naturalization Service, have little research use except as suggestive background and for broad classification purposes because of the impossibility of interpreting their meaning in the absence of essential supplementary detail concerning individuals. Strict warning must be given against their use as evidence of assimilation. It is a common practice to refer to the fact that the foreign-born of certain nationalities show a higher naturalization rate than others and to conclude therefrom that they may consequently be said to become an integral part of the American people more easily and rapidly. If due allowances are made for relative average length of group residence in the United States, for urban-rural and geographical distribution, for changes in legislation and regulations, and for other pertinent factors, such allowances reduce the magnitude of naturalization rate differentials materially, and it is still true that the only fact clearly reported in such statistics is legal citizenship status.[11]

It is, however, not a difficult matter to gain access to basic citizenship data in the records of courts having naturalization jurisdiction, of welfare agencies in general, and of the large group of organizations especially interested in immigrant aid. Records of these agencies include much more socially significant material than the bare facts of citizenship, color, country of birth, location of residence, and the few other items ordinarily utilized because of their ready availability. What is more, they can on occasion be checked and supplemented by direct contact

---

[11] See Bernstein, Ruth Z. *Differences in Rate of Naturalization of Immigrant Groups.* New York: National Council on Naturalization and Citizenship. 1936. Pp. 9. Mimeo. This paper is a preliminary report on a more inclusive project in the field.

For other examples of studies of differential naturalization rates see Gavit, John Palmer. *Americans by Choice.* New York: Harper & Brothers. 1922. Pp. xxiv+449; Carpenter, Niles. *Immigrants and Their Children.* Census Monographs, No. VII. Washington, D.C.: Government Printing Office. 1927. Pp. 250-267; Bernard, William S. "Cultural Determinants of Naturalization." *American Sociological Review.* 1:943-953 No. 6. December 1936

with the foreign-born themselves. Without individual histories obtained from such sources, or a very wide range of detailed statistical data susceptible of coordination, it is wisest to limit observations to changes in legal citizenship status as such and avoid guesses concerning their meaning in personal and cultural terms.

The records show sharp decrease not explainable in terms of declining immigration in the number of declarations of intention, petitions for citizenship, and certificates of naturalization issued between 1929 and 1930, with something of a rise in the years following but in no case back to the 1929 level.[12] At first glance this seems clearly to be a depression phenomenon, but the problem is not so simple. A confusing but undoubtedly overemphasized factor in the decrease is the increase in naturalization fees from five dollars to twenty dollars which was put into effect July 1, 1929. It is unlikely, however, that the depression failed to play other than the major rôle in the change in naturalization trends unless we are convinced that a fifteen dollar increase in charges was sufficient to offset in tens of thousands of cases all incentive toward formal adoption as a citizen of the United States. Halving of the fees later in the depression was not materially reflected in the tables. More light is needed on such subjects as just who were the individuals who were deterred from proceeding with the steps toward citizenship, what were their characteristics with regard to country of origin, length and place of residence in the United States, occupational and economic status, education, and degree of assimilation. Was there any change in external incentives for naturalization, as in the popular attitude toward foreigners, the attitudes of judges and other public officials, or less pressure from employers because of fewer jobs? What does experience in previous hard times tell us? So little is known about the factors encouraging or

---

[12] *Annual Report of the Secretary of Labor for the Fiscal Year Ended June 30, 1935.* P. 92

inhibiting naturalization other than that they appear to be but slightly related to variations in original alien cultures that no explanation can have depth of meaning without further intensive work.

The information needed here may be classified as bearing on factors discouraging legal change of citizenship and those giving extra incentive during depression to such a shift. The former, of course, cover the whole range of anti-alien sentiment and action, and minority reactions against oppressions. The latter include threats and fears of alien discrimination intensified by national calamity, and hope of escape by a shift in group identification.

It is understandable that some aliens should lose interest in American citizenship in proportion as they find themselves objects of suspicion and dislike, a loss of interest shading into discouragement or hatred of the United States and its people so strong as to lead to repatriation in many cases. But how many were so affected, which ones, and under what circumstances? In addition to the pressure of public opinion as such, there are also discouraging forces of a more tangible nature. Have there been changes in legislation, administrative policies and procedures, and personnel in the government service? Although these questions need further study, it may be observed that in general the government has been more encouraging toward aliens interested in naturalization during the depression than immediately before, at least since 1932, and has shown growing humanitarianism in handling the problems involved.[13] Legislation proposed in the press, in political speeches and platforms, and bills actually

---

[13] See, for example, the general order of Commissioner D. W. MacCormack to all districts of the Immigration and Naturalization Service, dated January 1, 1936, on the results of the central office study of educational and other requirements for naturalization and containing a revised program for the guidance of the Service. This order is reprinted in Schibsby, Marian. *Educational Requirements for Naturalization.* New York: National Council on Naturalization and Citizenship. 1936. Pp. 19-29

introduced but failing of passage offer another source of data. Inquiry might also be made as to whether there is evidence that citizenship by naturalization as contrasted with birthright citizenship has undergone any change in practical recognition since the beginning of the depression. It would be interesting to have a comparison of depression with predepression judicial decisions in naturalization cases, including denials and cancellations of citizenship as well as interpretations of the law.[14]

Paradoxically, in time of depression there is compulsion as well as discouragement of naturalization, and the same factors may operate in both directions. In time of strife retreat or advance may recommend itself under various circumstances to various people. How is it that some aliens seek American citizenship when the handicaps of minority status are raised, while others cling more tightly to their foreign allegiance, and still others apparently do not find the matter related to the legal status of their loyalties? The usual immigrant group differentials, such as in tradition and culture, period of residence in the United States, geographic and occupational distribution, and the like, may enter into the question, but so do problems of individual personality. Apart from minority group or individual characteristics, there must also be considered the direction of definite external pressures.

Some employers, for example, tighten their restrictions on the hiring of aliens when the labor supply becomes overabundant. Schools show increased preference for citizens as teachers. Public employment, a relatively more important source of income in the depression than previously, has a policy of citizen preference. Relief in cash, services, goods, or work is the more begrudged the alien as it is needed by the citizen, and has been

---

[14] For an indication of diversity in judicial decisions see Fields, Harold. "Conflicts in Naturalization Decisions." *Temple Law Quarterly.* Vol. X, No. 3. May 1936. Also obtainable as a reprint from the National Council on Naturalization and Citizenship in bulletin form.

both restricted and denied him. The threat of deportation has loomed larger in talk and fact during the depression. Such observations, while fairly reliable, are too general for scientific purposes. They would be classed by most persons in direct contact with immigrants during the depression as practically axiomatic, but their substantiation and more exact definition is demanded.

The questions raised concerning naturalization as affected by the depression are not isolated questions; all are closely interlocked, and each has its contribution to make to the larger, overall question of a possible relation between the depression in its economic, social, and psychological aspects and legal recognition of minority change in state allegiance.

Possible changes in naturalization rates as a result of depression influences on minority status quo have not been suggested. The unimportance of this type of inquiry is not assumed. For illustration, it is a matter of real importance whether the hypothesis that naturalization speeds later assimilation is correct, whether citizenship by adoption has been an effective weapon in minority hands in fighting the depression, or whether motives involved in the various attitudes of both minorities and majority toward naturalization have found any degree of justification in the course of events. Many of the research problems of this nature are not now feasible; some will be answered naturally as a consequence of other studies; a few, notably the three just cited as illustrations, need and are feasible for separate attack.

THE BALLOT

Minorities in possession of the ballot through naturalization or by right of birth theoretically should be in a more strategic position in a general depression than those without the franchise. If this be true, there should be evidence of effective minority voting for group objectives in the years since 1929 by naturalized immigrants, American-born children of European immigrants, and Negroes, where they are not barred from the polls. On the other hand, it should also be possible to show weakness in the position of those groups with restricted franchise, such as the Chinese, Japanese, Filipinos, communities of unnaturalized European aliens, and some restricted Indians who may be denied the ballot as in Arizona because of their government wardship. The problem is confused at the start, however, because citizenship, a matter determined by the federal government, does not coincide with the franchise, a matter subject within generous limits to state government. Varying pressures by local public opinion, officials, and minority incentives add to the confusion. In the absence of research evidence, the hypothesis may be offered that the franchise is not generally an effective depression weapon, but that because of special circumstances it may possess temporary and local values.

Argument of this hypothesis requires first full knowledge of the degree of respect accorded the franchise of citizen minorities by the dominant majority when interests conflict in time of crisis. Worldwide as well as American experience broadly surveyed suggests that the tendency under such circumstances is for those in power to sacrifice frankly or to rationalize previous democratic political theories. Minorities obviously can be outvoted except in areas of local concentration. Further, if minority votes are inconvenient it is commonly not difficult to effect group disfranchisement by property qualifications, educational tests, fraud, and outright intimidation. State voting laws, primary regulations, party practices, and judicial decisions during the depression can be made to furnish the basis for study of the respect granted minority franchise rights. Disregard for the rules of the game generally increases with the heat of the contest and the importance of the stakes. Rules are particularly in danger when the stronger contestant is also the referee.

On occasion the majority has found it more useful to manipulate minority votes than to block their registry. A mass of ballots which can be handled with relative ease because of concentration, poverty, ignorance, or an appeal to tradition and emotion has long been known as a boon to politicians, but whether such votes have been of greater or less value to political machines during the depression than before is a difficult question. Minority votes are also subject to manipulative efforts when their swing in one direction or another would determine the outcome in a contest between two majority factions. This, too, is a process which might be expected to have been influenced by the depression.

The long history of minority ballot manipulation calls attention to the importance of preparation for the use of the ballot. Cultural standards differentiating minorities and the handicaps consequent to minority status are a priori evidence of inexpertness in the use of the ballot and make disfranchisement and manipulation relatively simple. Further, disregarding majority interference, they also tend of themselves to weaken voting effectiveness. Attention has been called previously to the general failure to induce various minority groups to stand together in adversity. It has proved similarly difficult to mass the votes of members of a single minority for the common advantage except locally where special circumstances have perhaps been of greater importance than minority cause. On the whole, minority voting is patterned closely after the practice of the region except where such votes are not wanted by the majority, as in the case of the Negro in the South. It could hardly be supposed that positive use of the franchise by the inexperienced and inexpert would spring up suddenly under the stimulus of the depression. Yet there are sufficient sporadic local instances of intelligent minority balloting in recent years to warrant study of the depression as an influence in this direction.

Briefly put, what is needed is information concerning changes in the nature and degree of minority political participation as a result of the depression, growing out of either external pressures or of group limitations. Did minorities furnish more or fewer candidates for public office, and what success did they have at the polls? This is a matter of public record. Did the Negro, the Oriental, the immigrant, become involved in political issues as a result of the depression, and if so, under what circumstances and with what consequences? Again the basic data are a matter of public record, and may be readily supplemented from other sources as necessary. Of foremost value, however, are the actual voting records of various political units from the precinct on up. Individual votes, of course, are not available except by interview and questionnaire methods. There are, however, innumerable voting districts with minority populations so solid that with no more than ordinary precautions the voting behavior of any group may be analyzed with almost perfect reliability.[15] Interpreted in the light of special local conditions and supplemented by life histories of politicians and plain citizens, series of voting statistics can be made to furnish the facts needed to understand any relation which may exist between the depression and minority political participation.

Questions should also be raised concerning the relation between the exercise of the franchise and the distribution of government benefits intended to mitigate the depression's effects. The political practice of parcelling out public improvements and services where they may be expected to bring the most votes to the party in power has never been rare. Pavings, sewers, street lights, school buildings, parks, jobs, relief, police protection, and so forth, are tried and proved inducements to "vote right," grudgingly bestowed on communities of non-voters or "safe" voters. To the extent that the Negro has remained traditionally Republican he has required no persuasion to vote the Republican ticket; in centers such as New York and Chicago he has

---

[15] For examples of studies of minority political behavior see Gosnell, Harold F. *Negro Politicians*. Chicago: University of Chicago Press. 1935. Pp. xxxi+404; Lewinson, Paul. *Race, Class, and Party*. New York: Oxford University Press. 1932. Pp. x+302

needed tempting into the Democratic camp. For example, Negroes did not swing toward the Democratic Party in Chicago until 1932.[16] Was there any connection between this swing and political reward? Historically the European immigrant, tractable because of his transition status, has been a strong foundation of the urban political machine. Since the cityward migration of the Negro following the restriction of immigration he has been found useful to the city politician in the North, at a small price. Bids for the political support of the Negro vote, the German-American vote, and all other so-called hyphenated American votes are an incident in every election from local to national in scale. But what of those regions where the Negro vote does not matter? And what of those minority individuals who cannot vote, or those who vote so steadfastly on tradition that it does not pay politically to offer rewards? With the decrease in the importance of personal resources and private charity in combating want, and the parallel depression increase of reliance on the government for assistance to the unemployed and destitute, the linkage between votes and public aid moves into the rank of prime importance.

In this connection and as a postscript warning against too ready generalization, there may be recalled the item that the Indian has been dealt with far more generously during the depression than ever before in spite of his negligible votes. This, however, has been a matter of national policy; local regions of Indian concentration have not lavished their time and money on the aboriginal.[17]

---

[16] Gosnell, Harold F. "Relation of the Press to Voting in Chicago." *Journalism Quarterly*. P. 131. June 1936

[17] Thus: "The relationship of the Federal Government to the Indians is determined by treaties, acts of Congress, Comptrollers' decisions, customs, and humanitarian considerations. A number of States and communities have shown a disposition to allow Indians to share in the services which are maintained for other groups of the population. However, during the present economic depression, when local resources are overtaxed for relief purposes, there has developed a tendency on the part of many State and local governments to transfer responsibility

PUBLIC WELFARE

Although the Indian is the only minority whose relief services have been almost completely taken over by the federal government, a centralizing tendency during the depression has affected the lives and government relationships of all minorities. Increased federal support of the needy has also meant an increasing attitude of reliance on Washington, a significant change if only because of the greater likelihood of impersonality and mutual unfamiliarity between source of aid and recipient.

Paralleling the shift from local to federal public benefits has been a shift from private philanthropy to public aid. In the past every minority has had a multitude of private agencies especially interested in the problems of its needy, and with exceptional facilities and understanding in giving assistance. The larger and more centralized the aid-giving organization, the greater the difficulty in recognizing, sympathetically understanding and intelligently handling the problems of minorities—this is a safe generalization, particularly with reference to a transitional period. What actually happened to minorities as a result of increasing centralization of relief administration is known only vaguely through inference. Certainly in the earlier stages of the depression there was much ineffective relief work because of the unavailability of, or failure to use, relief workers of

---

for Indian relief measures to the Federal Government. There has also developed a disposition on the part of the Federal authorities to extend benefits to persons not heretofore regarded as truly ward Indians. In effect the number of Indians who depend on the federal government for the fulfillment of their social and economic needs is increasing rather than decreasing." Mountin, Joseph W. and Townsend, J. G. *Observations on Indian Health Problems and Facilities.* Public Health Bulletin No. 223, U. S. Treasury Department, Public Health Service. Washington, D.C.: Government Printing Office. February 1936. P. 4

A thorough account of the relations between the Federal Government and the Indian may be found in: Schmeckebier, Laurence F. *The Office of Indian Affairs.* Baltimore: The Johns Hopkins Press. 1927. Pp. xiv+591. See also Meriam, Lewis and Associates. *The Problem of Indian Administration.* Baltimore: The Johns Hopkins Press. 1928. Pp. xxii+872

minority status. It is also known that the use of Negro relief workers, officials, and local committee members in the depression emergency in some cases improved efficiency in dealing with Negro destitute; the same was true in scattered cases of other minorities. Study of relief records, particularly case records where available, with reference to the effect of governmental centralization of relief and the relative advantages of minority in comparison with other workers is required to remove such questions from the realm of speculation.

According to the Director of Research and Statistics of the Federal Emergency Relief Administration, the Unemployment Relief Census conducted under the direction of his office during October 1933 gave "for the first time, reliable facts relating to the families receiving relief . . ."[18] This census distinguished the "color or race" of persons in relief families. In doing this, it classified persons as white, Negro, or of "other races," the last division including predominantly Mexicans in all states except Oklahoma where the Indians predominated. Apparently as a matter of political policy, and perhaps also because of statistical difficulties involved, no satisfactory effort has been made by the government to secure basic relief data concerning white minorities either in the Unemployment Relief Census or otherwise. Such data must consequently be obtained by the private investigator on his own initiative by sampling rather than complete enumeration procedures.[19]

---

[18] *Unemployment Relief Census, October, 1933.* Report Number One, Federal Emergency Relief Administration. Washington, D.C.: U. S. Government Printing Office. 1934. P. iii

[19] The poverty of information concerning depression unemployment and relief in relation to minority peoples may be illustrated by citing an exceptionally fine state report, that by Haber, William and Stanchfield, Paul L. *Unemployment, Relief and Economic Security.* Lansing, Michigan: State of Michigan, Second Report of the State Emergency Welfare Relief Commission. March 1936. Pp. xi+ 329. This report devotes a few pages to Negro-white comparisons, but neglects adequate treatment of even the colored minority element in the Michigan population, to say nothing of the minorities of recent alien origin. See also in the

According to the 1933 Unemployment Relief Census, "In more than 2,500,000 of the relief families, the head of the family was white, in nearly 600,000, Negro, and in only 56,000 was the head of any other race than the white or Negro. When classified in terms of the color or race of the head of the family, the number of whites on relief in 1933 represented 81.3 per cent of the total relief group, Negroes 16.7 per cent, and other races 2 per cent, as compared with 88.6 per cent whites, 9.7 per cent Negroes, and 1.7 per cent other races in the total population in 1930. Both Negroes and other races on relief were highly concentrated in certain sections of the country. Twenty-four States (including the District of Columbia), which in 1930 had 97 per cent of all the Negro population in the country, contributed in October, 1933, 96 per cent of the Negro relief persons; similarly six States having 85 per cent of all the population of 'other races' in 1930 contributed 88 per cent of all the relief persons of 'other races.' "[20] Since the materials on "race or color" collected in this census may be studied in relation to such other social data as geographical distribution, age, sex, size, and composition of family, and urban-rural distribution, it constitutes a mine of research information in spite of the limitations to which attention is called in the report itself, necessarily inherent in such an emergency survey.[21]

present series: White, R. Clyde, and Mary K. *Research Memorandum on Social Aspects of Relief Policies in the Depression;* and Chapin, F. Stuart and Queen, Stuart A. *Research Memorandum on Social Work in the Depression.*

[20] *Unemployment Relief Census.* Report Number One. October 1933. P. 7

[21] *Ibid.* Pp. 17ff.

Two later reports on the same census should also be consulted: Report Number Two, "Urban and Rural Areas"; Report Number Three, "Family Composition"; Reports One and Two were printed by the U. S. Government Printing Office, Washington, D.C., in 1934; Report Number Three was apparently prepared for distribution in the same year directly by the Federal Emergency Relief Administration by a more economical process than printing.

See also *Urban Workers on Relief.* Works Progress Administration, Division of Social Research. Part I: Palmer, Gladys L. and Wood, Katherine D. "The

A search of the literature has revealed innumerable articles and reports on practically all minorities of racial and national origin and relief during the depression. It is not unfair, however, to characterize these writings as being motivated mainly by a desire to increase or curtail the share of government benefits not being spent on "100 per cent American stock."[22] Minority discrimination in actuality, fear, or threat seems to be the exclusive concern of one set of statisticians and writers; waste of national resources on the unworthy, the interest of another set. Occasionally there is encountered a dispassionate discussion of the pros and cons of the question. By and large, such writings may be disregarded by the research student except as they reflect public opinion.

Discrimination against minorities in the distribution of public aid has, of course, been commonplace during the depression, with the treatment of the Indian by the federal government being the only general exception. The problem of why there should have been such extensive discrimination is the whole problem of minority-majority relations, and not one subject to special research limited to relief data. It is, however, entirely proper to utilize relief sources for more limited purposes. Further, although little is to be gained by collections of instances

Occupational Characteristics of Workers on Relief in Urban Areas, May, 1934." Washington, D.C. 1936. Pp. xxvii+203; Part II: Wood, Katherine D. "The Occupational Characteristics of Workers on Relief in 79 Cities, May, 1934." Washington, D.C.: U. S. Government Printing Office. 1937. Pp. xx+301; also Hauser, Philip M. *Workers on Relief in the United States, March, 1935: A Census of Usual Occupations.* (abridged edition) Washington, D.C.: Works Progress Administration, Division of Social Research. 1937. Pp. v+133

[22] A fact commonly overlooked by advocates of discrimination in employment and relief against aliens and in favor of citizens is the large number of citizens in the immediate families of, and consequently dependent upon aliens for support. One estimate indicates that "the families of the almost five million aliens in the United States include approximately seven million American spouses and children." Fagen, Melvin M. *The Families of Aliens.* New York: National Council on Naturalization and Citizenship. 1937. P. 3

of differential treatment accorded minorities during the depression by public or private agencies or agents charged with administering aid unless the purpose is to use such instances in an appeal for action, any case of discrimination may prove to be an excellent point in which to sink the scientific pick.

For example, only by the study of relief as administered in definite regions and communities may one hope to learn the comparative effects of a single standard relief policy for all groups regardless of racial or national origin as against one of considered discrimination. No account need here be taken of discrimination growing out of general prejudice or caprice. Is there, however, any sound basis for a policy of equality or discrimination in terms of relative verifiable effects? In a community of customary racial division of labor, does a uniform dole or a fixed wage in work relief disrupt industry, encourage wasteful extravagance, undermine minority stability, or block distribution of benefits to minority members through the sabotage of an aroused majority? Can minority lower planes of living be interpreted to warrant differential relief payments under any practical definition of social welfare? In view of special living conditions, food habits, and cultural standards which may define as necessities objects generally regarded as luxuries, is a flat relief income with standard limitations on permitted purchases satisfactory under any scale of values other than a minimum subsistence level? Such questions apply not only to minorities; they are part and parcel of the problem of all relief standards. It so happens that they have been brought to the fore by the depression and that they can be attacked with special facility in majority-minority comparisons.

Relief data, in addition to their utility as sources for the study of the consequences of depression relief policy and administration, also possess unusual value in the analysis of other aspects of minority-majority relations. Confining our illustrations to the Negro as the only large minority group ordinarily separately reported in the official statistics, there may be pointed out the possibility of gaining insight through study of the uses and abuses of federal benefits into landlord-tenant relations, farm and home ownership, wage work in agriculture, industry and personal service, family life, education, and what not. The following samples of titles of bulletins issued by the Division of Reseach, Statistics and Finance of the Federal Emergency Relief Administration suggest the broad possibilities through this approach: *The Rural Negro on Relief, February, 1935; Industries and Occupations of Male Heads of Rural Relief and Non-Relief Households, October, 1935; Some Types of Unemployability in Rural Relief Cases, February, 1935; Rural Youth On Relief, February, 193̄; Statistics of Youth on Relief; Migrant Families; Landlord-Tenant Relations and Relief in Alabama; Comparison of Relief and Rehabilitation Cases in Rural Areas, October, 1934; Relief Administered to Workers in the Tobacco Industry in Winston-Salem, Durham, and Richmond During November, 1934; Monthly Earnings of Rural Relief Households at the Time of Closing Cases.* In all of these bulletins Negro and white are to some extent differentiated.[23] They constitute but a small sample of innumerable bulletins issued. Unfortunately, largely because of the emergency nature of the work and the administrative purposes to be served, the data in them have little research value except suggestions for further work. Considerable use can be made of the records of the FERA, its subsidiary and its coordinate depression agencies.[24] But it is suspected that

---

[23] For a brief statement concerning the disproportionate number of Negroes on relief, including a list of possible explanations of the disproportion which for the most part require further research before full acceptance, see Smith, Alfred Edgar. "The Negro and Relief," *Monthly Report of the Federal Emergency Relief Administration.* March 1 through March 31, 1936. Washington, D.C.: U. S. Government Printing Office. Pp. 10-17

[24] Of special interest are the Emergency Conservation Work (Civilian Conservation Corps), the Resettlement Administration and its forerunners such as the Division of Subsistence Homesteads, and the Works Progress Administration and its forerunners and agencies for removal of persons from relief rolls to work on public projects and in private employment. For a listing of federal agencies in connection with relief, together with brief statements of objectives and descriptions

the best results may be obtained not from the breakdown or synthesis of emergency agency statistics but rather from small, intensive individual studies inspired by them.

The Indian, however, may turn out to be an exceptional case in this respect. If so, it will be because there is a permanent bureau, the Office of Indian Affairs, charged with the duty of looking after his welfare. *Indians at Work,* an illustrated "news sheet for Indians and the Indian Service," started under the present administration, containing all possible variety of items concerning Indians but devoted primarily to the Indian Emergency Conservation Work, repays reading by explanation of legislative and administrative policy and reference to suggestive case material. It makes no pretense at being scientifically useful, and is naturally biased in favor of the present Administration's policies. The research clues which it unwittingly furnishes, however, are invaluable. Although the only major study of the Indian during the depression prepared by the Indian Office now available is the report on "Indian Land Tenure, Economic Status, and Population Trends," issued as Part X of the *Supplementary Report of the Land Planning Committee to the National Resources Board,* the announced purpose of the Commissioner to foster social research concerning his wards justifies the expectation of full cooperation with qualified research workers. Results thus far, in terms of usable research data and scientific studies undertaken, are meagre. Trained social scientists, particularly anthropologists, have been consulted and employed by the Indian Office more than during any previous period.

The program and influences of the Socio-Economic Division of the Soil Conservation Service and the activities under the Indian Emergency Conservation Work program should be especially profitable for research in the social aspects of the depres-

of organization and activities see, *United States Government Manual,* issued in loose-leaf form and revised currently by the National Emergency Council, Washington, D.C. This *Manual* also contains an appendix on recently abolished, transferred, or terminated executive agencies and functions.

sion since they have had profound effects on every phase of the life of this minority. The peculiar advantage of studying the work of these two agencies is their emphasis on recognition of Indian cultural variations in the administering of government aid. Although it seems obvious that public aid needs to be co-ordinated with minority culture variants, only in the sentimentalized case of the Indian has there been any noteworthy public effect at such coordination. It would be most valuable to know whether such theoretically intelligent policies achieved measurably superior results in comparison with routine aid to Italians, Mexicans, Negroes, and others in terms of personal, family, and community functional integrity. For further comparison, the work of selected private organizations for the aid of special groups, such as orthodox Jews and some immigrant Catholic parishes, which takes into account cultural differentials, would also be significant.

To summarize the depression relief situation with reference to research possibilities, it may be repeated that the outstanding minority problems flow from the trend to federal from local and private sources and administration, that official statistics, reports and records are most readily usable in the study of Indians and Negroes, that official sources are discouragingly reticent concerning white minorities on relief and that in no case are the public records adequate for more than the most simple numerical manipulation of superficial data. Prompt supplementary investigation is required for the investigation of the relation between minority relief and group status, cultural standards, personal adjustments, and community welfare.[25]

It may be ventured as a conclusion from the available literature that relief practice has exercised a strong influence toward maintaining the minority status quo, and in many instances the

[25] For a good, summary account of welfare activities in California, affecting Indians and immigrants see: Cahn, Frances and Bary, Valeska. *Welfare Activities of Federal, State, and Local Governments in California, 1850-1934.* Berkeley: University of California Press. 1936. Pp. xxiv+422

stronger term "freezing" could be used. To quote from an article having special reference to the Negro in the South, "Even in the administration of Federal relief, the Civil Works program, the AAA, etc., there has been, particularly in the lower South, a tendency to perpetuate the existing inequalities."[26] It would be interesting to know the extent to which such a generalization applies to the effect of relief on all minority-majority relations in exceptionally hard times.

RADICALISM

The charge of excessive minority radicalism has been exceptionally strong during the depression. As a rule the cultures which aliens bring with them to the United States have been less conducive to the growth of radicalism than the individualistic traditions of this country. The American-born children of immigrants seem to be more receptive of radical ideas than their parents, possibly because of their marginal status, but facts are lacking. The Indian and the Negro have been notoriously poor material for "red" organizers. Nevertheless there is an interesting speculation concerning the extent to which minority peoples turn to the hope of improvement of their condition, made difficult in depression by their status, by intellectual and overt acceptance of programs directed toward the overthrow of the existing economic and political system.

That radical organizers have thought such a tendency conceivable is evidenced by their special efforts to convert the Negro and the European immigrant groups. Thus far these efforts seem to have met with indifferent success so far as numbers are concerned. Such conversions as are evident are apparently mainly of younger urbanized intellectual leaders, as among Negroes, and mostly on an intellectual level, a result of hopelessness of finding either a way out of or of adjustment to the status quo.

[26] Johnson, Guy B. "Does the South Owe the Negro a New Deal?" *Social Forces.* Vol. 13, No. 1. October 1934

Locally radicalism has made sporadic advances among minorities, not because of the appeal of radicalism itself but because organizers offered a means of fighting a particular unbearable condition, as in sections of some sweated urban industries and among certain groups of hard hit colored tenant farmers in the South. There is also reason to believe that some of the apparent success of radical leaders in encouraging minority violence has in fact been a form of profiteering in race riots and other disturbances among minorities which were cleverly adopted as propagandistic evidence of strength, as seems to have been the case of the Harlem riot on March 19, 1935. Oppressed minorities seem generally uninterested in adding the stamp of radicalism to their other handicaps.[27]

All this, however, must be clearly marked as speculation; the most simple, essential facts necessary for sound analysis are not known. What efforts have been made by radicals to proselyte minorities; what groups, individuals, and situations have been considered "hot spots" for organization; how many radical workers have there been and how much money has been spent? What of the relative effectiveness of appeals to the intellect and through leadership in action? What groups have been most or least fertile soil, and what individuals? Flagwavers have talked and written much on the subject; students have said little and done less research. Perhaps the numerical unimportance of minority radicalism has had much to do with its neglect as a subject for research along with the unpopularity and secretiveness of the movement. Whatever the reasons for previous research neglect, study of particular radical organizations and of local situations in which the movement has taken hold is feasible, the more so because of their smallness. Analysis of radical votes cast does not seem promising because of the confusion

---

[27] For an example of the application of Marxist-Leninist theory in the interpretation of an American minority group see Allen, James S. *The Negro Question in the United States*. New York: International Publishers. 1936. Pp. 224

of motives, such as the desire to cast a protest vote as a mere gesture or the opposing incentive to avoid wasting a vote on a candidate with no chance of election, influencing the tallies for communists and other radicals.

CRIME AND CRIMINALS[28]

It is a common thesis not restricted to laymen that the blocking of socially approved paths to success as during a period of national economic adversity tends to increase the number of individuals who seek their ends through criminal actions. Without stopping to examine the degree of validity of this plausible theory, which in its general application falls in the province of the monograph in this series on crime and the depression, the question may be raised whether or not it has any special application to the problem of minorities in the depression.

Such special application would seem likely, since minorities are among the hardest hit by the depression and their cultural as well as material sources of encouragement to stay within the law are at least not the same as, if not weaker than, those of the native white majority. It is a popular belief that if all persons of recent alien origin and all colored inhabitants of the United States were eliminated from the country a much greater proportion of the total crime than the percentage these people constitute in the total population would be simultaneously eliminated. The prevalence of such folk beliefs warrants the formulation of hypotheses feasible of research attack designed to test their reliability.

Tentatively, it is suggested that the effects of the depression on the amount and types of minority crime varied primarily as specific minorities were characterized by variations in demography, culture, and economic and social status in contrast with the parallel characteristics of the majority. In other words, it is

---

[28] For a more general discussion of criminal activity in the depression see, in this series Sellin, Thorsten. *Research Memorandum on Crime in the Depression.*

proposed that the study of minority crime in the depression should stress the same types of factors influencing criminal behavior as would be the case in the study of majority crime, the distinctions being largely matters of degree and the need for special consideration in the selection and training of personnel for work with unique culture groups. Similar differences in degree are found in the composition of countless subclasses of old American stocks and within minorities themselves.

On a priori grounds, it is doubtful whether more than a minor proportion of minority crime properly may be said to be minority phenomena, and of this small proportion only a fraction is likely to be of depression origin. As a practical matter and in view of the highly specialized nature of the field of criminology, the problem consequently seems to be one on which the main attack will have to be made with the tools of the criminologist supplemented and guided by those of minority specialists. To illustrate by analogy, the fact that persons of minority status get married is not a peculiarity of minorities, and study of the causes and consequences of this behavior is for the most part in the province of those trained in family rather than in minority research; only such problems as those connected with minority-majority differentials in the number of persons who marry, their age, occupation, and other individual characteristics, type of ceremony used, and so forth, come within the special competence of students of minority peoples. In the case of crime, it is extremely difficult if not impossible to establish adequately the extent and nature of such differentials because of the secretive nature of criminal acts, the absence of reliable records, and the shortcomings of general criminology.

A crime is a violation of the criminal law; a criminal, legally speaking, is a person who has been convicted of a violation of the criminal law. The criminal law is a body of regulations voted by legislators, usually approved by the executive authority, and interpreted by the courts, and covers offenses ranging from traffic violations to murder. Obviously neither crimes nor criminals are subjects for scientific causational investigation as such, since the concepts possess no unity capable of logical addition or comparison, but are products of capricious temporary definition under which have been gathered together in popular language a collection of behavior items with but one common element; failure to observe a legal command with a penal sanction.[29]

Statistics are plentiful in the field of crime, and almost meaningless in a study of minority violations of the penal law. There are readily available tables of the populations of state and federal prisons and reformatories, of city and county jails, of institutional commitments, of court convictions, of arrests, of crimes known to the police, and in most of them there is some separate classification of minorities of racial or national origin.[30] Classifications of European immigrants are untrustworthy, Jews are sometimes tabulated as a separate nationality and sometimes not referred to at all, the first American-born generation prisoners

[29] Similar criticism properly may be levied against practically all of the common concepts used as statistical units in the social sciences adopted from lay terminology; consider, for example, such terms as race, family, lynching, poverty, migrant, and so forth. Such words may be useful as vague delimitations of areas of interest, and some may be redefined for scientific purposes, as the economists have redefined rent and capital, but they have no research value in social science as units of statistical comparison and analysis without being broken down to the point of loss of original identity.

[30] See for examples, *Prisoners in State and Federal Prisons and Reformatories.* 1927. Pp. iii+127; *Ibid.* 1931 and 1932. Pp. ii+72; *County and City Jails.* 1933. Pp. iv+149; *Juvenile Delinquents in Public Institutions.* 1933. Pp. iv+62; *Crime and Mental Disease or Deficiency.* 1933. Pp. ii+25. These five reports were prepared by the Bureau of the Census. See also *Uniform Crime Reports.* Bureau of Investigation, Department of Justice. Monthly from August 1930 until December 1931, and quarterly since then; Flexner, B., Oppenheimer, R. and Lenroot, K. F. *The Child, the Family and the Court.* Children's Bureau, Department of Labor, Bureau Publication No. 193 (revised edition). 1933; National Commission on Law Observance and Enforcement. *Report on Crime and Criminal Justice in Relation to the Foreign-Born.* 1931. Pp. 416 (all references above printed at the Government Printing Office, Washington, D.C.). Federal Offenders, 1933-1934, *Bureau of Prisons, U. S. Department of Justice.* Fort Leavenworth, Kansas: Federal Prisons Industries, Inc., Press. 1935. Pp. ix+283

may be counted as native Americans or as of foreign nationality, and so on. There is frequent incentive for the prisoner to conceal his origin, and only rare interest among officials in the matter. Arrests, indictments, convictions, severity of sentence, probation, and parole are biased by minority status. Crimes known to the police unaccompanied by arrests at best give weak testimony about the race or nationality of the offender. Criminal statistics fail worst of all because only a minor portion of the total number of criminal offenses ever enters the records in any form.

At best, statistical tabulations may be said to indicate apparent criminality, and there is every reason to believe that statistically apparent criminality bears not even approximately fixed relationship to actual criminality as between minority and majority groups, or between any other social classes. Because of the popular impression that minorities supply more than their quota of criminal behavior, it is possibly justifiable to point out that such statistics as are available indicate proportionately less immigrant than native white criminality, tell nothing about the criminality of the first American-born generation except that their rate is probably somewhat higher than that of their parents, and give the Negro an extraordinarily high rate in comparison with any other group. Mexican criminality rates are generally above the average for the entire population. Native Indian and the Oriental statistics are so faulty that it is best to say nothing at all even about apparent criminality.[31] These observations refer solely to statistically apparent criminality, and bear no necessary relation to actual criminality. They also make no allowance for such criminologically important population variables as age and sex distribution, urban-rural, regional and other classifications according to residence, education, or eco-

[31] For a statistical analysis of Oriental crime covering the period from 1900 to 1927, see Beach, Walter G. *Oriental Crime in California.* Stanford University, California: Stanford University Press. 1932. Pp. 98

An outstanding opportunity for research is offered by the existence of Courts of Indian Offenses, a source of criminological material practically untouched.

nomic status, nor do they take into account the wide range of cultural variations involved.

With this brief background it is clear that no inferences concerning the influence of the depression on minority criminality may be drawn from the official tables even though series of many governmental units run back before 1929. The charting of any one or all of such series combined to show gross numerical fluctuations would be most misleading. Possible statistical refinements taking into account the fact that crime by its very nature is unevenly distributed in various population classes which are themselves unevenly distributed among minorities, can be made to improve the picture, but not to make it anything like an approximation of actual criminal behavior. The best that can be done by the reworking of existing official figures is to make them reflect more accurately government contacts with minority criminals.

At this point it becomes obvious that lack of knowledge of the extent of real criminality and of criminal causation in general discourages all present statistical prospect of doing more than measure with reasonable accuracy the superficial item of minority contacts with the police, the courts, and penal institutions either before or during the depression, and of contrasting them numerically with comparable majority population groups. With the exercise of care not to draw conclusions concerning comparative group real criminality not supported by the data, such procedure should produce results of considerable administrative and some scientific value. Variations in minority contacts with the law have real significance in their own right in study of the social aspects of the depression.

Discouragement with the prospects of definitive treatment of this area should not, however, lead to an abandonment of the field after bringing as near to perfection as feasible the records of apparent criminality. Because of their differentiating characteristics, racial and national minorities offer unique opportunities for studies of real criminality with general as well as special implications. They furnish, for example, readymade workable population groups with contrasting traits of significance in criminal causation. It should be fruitful to inquire why the amount and predominating types of crime vary from group to group. Most important of all, by providing delimitable populations with a wide variety of demographic characteristics, cultures, and social and economic status differentials, they afford a rare chance to gain an understanding of these elements in crime causation with or without reference to the depression.

From this broad field of research problems, two, in themselves of no mean proportions, may be selected for special mention because of their especially significant relation to the impact of the depression on minorities. Reference is made to the question of the influence of inferior status as such on individual behavior with respect to the law and to that concerning the consequences of coexistent conflicting cultural standards on the observance of legal sanctions.

Inferior status may be conducive to crime, but it may also have an influence in the opposite direction. It may, for example, give greater freedom from legal surveillance through majority indifference so long as minority offenses do not directly affect majority members, but it may also evoke especially strict control of conduct injurious to majority individuals. Subjectively, it may encourage criminality by weakening group restraints, by arousing defiance of law and order, and by discouraging hope of achievement through sanctioned channels, and it may also stimulate group consciousness and solidarity on a defensively high plane of law observance. In any given case much depends on the traditions of the group, the separate personal histories and personalities of its individual members, and on the nature and severity of the class or caste distinctions. Clearly, any unusual economic crisis may be expected to be a powerful influence under these circumstances, particularly if it sharpens lines of group cleavage. Reasonable as it may sound, all this is abstract inference supported by no satisfactory pointed evidence.

Since official statistics of crime and criminals measure contacts with the law they may at least be used to determine any modification in minority surveillance and severity of treatment in depression, their greatest defect for this purpose being the common failure satisfactorily to classify minority groups in the tabulations. Beyond this, since they bear no fixed relationship to uncounted legal offenses either in amount or kind, they must be used with extreme care. Direct study of minority communities and of individual life histories seem to promise more reliable and causally significant results than comparisons of existing statistics even though it does not lend itself to prompt broad generalization. When this approach is adopted it is important for time-saving and other purposes to select communities already subjected to survey: For example, Muncie, Indiana, described in *Middletown* and in *Middletown in Transition* by Robert S. and Helen M. Lynd; Chicago, on which there is an enormous mass of detailed social data gathered under the leadership of the University of Chicago Division of Social Sciences; New Haven, a city where excellent basic data are available as a result of activities of the Institute of Human Relations of Yale University; Newburyport, Massachusetts, and Natchez, Mississippi, areas studied by W. Lloyd Warner; Indianola, Mississippi, studied by Hortense Powdermaker and by John Dollard, and many others.[32] Minority subgroups of individuals are always available within such communities where the background has at least to some extent been prepared by previous surveys. The problem then is to select or devise research procedures feasible for the area of investigation, the objective in mind, and the facilities at hand. The choice is infinite between extremes patterned after broad crime surveys or individual histories such

---

[32] For further suggestions of districts where some preliminary data are available, particularly if specialized rather than broad survey material is required, see Eaton, Allen H. and Harrison, Shelby M. *A Bibliography of Social Surveys.* New York: Russell Sage Foundation. 1930. Pp. xlviii+467

as *The Jack Roller* by Clifford Shaw, between a multiple inter-disciplinary approach and specialized techniques such as an attitude test. The scope and procedure of any project are deter-mined by a multitude of factors and should not be influenced by any generalized suggestion unless the purpose is stultified research. The purpose here is to suggest and stimulate research bearing on the hypothesis that there is a relation, single or multi-ple, between depression crime and minority inferior status.

The person subject to the influences of two conflicting cul-tures is generally assumed to be under weaker personal compul-sions to govern his behavior in accordance with the standards of either culture than the man exposed only to one. Starting with this likely assumption, it follows that the men whose intellect and emotions are the battleground of conflicting cultures should evidence a notably high tendency to yield to criminal tempta-tion under the pressure of economic hardship, other factors such as opportunity and external restrictions being equal. In-dians and immigrants and their children are the notoriously out-standing culture conflict groups in the United States. Negro cul-ture patterns, although very much like those of the white man in the same neighborhood, are easily distinct enough to offer sharp conflict. Granting these points, a rise in minority crimi-nality during the depression should be observable unless, as is entirely conceivable, there were counteracting influences associ-ated with minority status. Again we find ourselves dealing with indirect inferences rather than with direct evidence.

The point of attack on culture conflict and depression crime must to a large extent be the same communities and individuals suggested in connection with the problem of inferior status and depression crime, but the method must be fundamentally al-tered to permit taking advantage of the contributions of cultural anthropology. Psychology, psychiatry, and sociology, of course, have major contributions to make in the case of both problems. With regard to anthropology, it is not so much the techniques developed in that field as the concepts which here need to be taken into account. Culture conflict is itself an anthropological concept, although one which is not yet recognized as a legitimate member of the family by all anthropologists. The meaning in use of such terms as culture, acculturation, culture pattern, culture complex, culture area, culture trait, material culture, and the data and hypotheses centering about them, cannot be learned by memorizing definitions or reading selected textbooks; it requires training in anthropological theory and field work. Unfortunately such training is not enough by itself, for it is equally essential that there must be working understanding of the concepts and techniques bearing on personality and behavior. Anthropology is here stressed not so much because of any inherent priority in importance as because of the historical accident that specialists in that field have shown a promising if superficial tendency to utilize the contributions of neighboring disciplines in the study of socio-psychological problems. It is to be hoped that psychologists and sociologists may increase their effectiveness in the culture-conflict field by extending their interdisciplinary training. What is wanted is an understanding of the behavior of the person as a community member under the impact of conflicting cultures and as influenced by the depression.

Without slighting the fruitful possibilities of studies of adults and of entire communities, it may be emphasized that the opportunity of observing young children and adolescents growing up as marginal individuals caught between the culture of their parents and their parents' circle and the culture of an outside majority group of more enviable status seems of extraordinary promise. Immigrant parents, for example, grown to maturity abroad, are likely to have had their native cultural standards of behavior so thoroughly ingrained that the more stable personalities at least are not prone to be confused to the point of a serious break. This is supported by the remarkably low crime rate for adult immigrants from socially stabilized foreign communities. Their children brought up in this country, including both those born in the United States and those brought in as immigrants at a very early age, become familiar with two sets of frequently conflicting behavior standards simultaneously and from competing auth⌐ritative sources. It is to be expected that some of these second generation children will fail to build personal resistances to criminality strong enough to stand the strain of depression confusion and hardship. Such records as exist suggest their greater criminality than their parents', and possibly than that of the native white population of native parentage, even in normal times. Since crime statistics universally fail to distinguish accurately the second generation criminals, and usually make no attempt to do so, and since juvenile delinquency statistics are a notoriously bad index of juvenile delinquency in fact, specially collected data on a sample scale and life histories offer the only ways out of this particular morass of ignorance unless one is willing to rely on long distance theorizing.

COERCIVE MOB BEHAVIOR

It is not enough to consider only crimes by minorities during the depression; crimes against their members are equally significant. These latter may for convenience be divided according to the twofold classification of offenses by individuals against minority persons without the specific approval of the majority group, and offenses by mobs supported in their action by strong public opinion. In the second class comes that type of behavior ordinarily known as lynching.

If the depression increased the severity of group conflict, as is generally conceded, it is a reasonable assumption that purely individual crimes against minority individuals for gain, personal motive, or as expression of group prejudice should both increase and be penalized with increased leniency. Under such circumstances, there should also be a demonstrable correlation between intergroup crimes, a tendency to regard them somewhat more lightly than before the depression or than intra-majority offenses, and the proportional size of the minority population element involved and other possible indexes of the severity of group competition. The testing of this hypothesis and its corollaries is a task requiring ordinary statistical competence and considerable time and patience. It is surprising that a number of such studies covering selected communities have not appeared. Perhaps the difficulty again is lack of faith in the reliability of crime statistics, but in this case their inadequacies are not so serious. Analysis of crimes by persons of minority status reported to the police and the subsequent disposition of the cases, supplemented by personal canvass of selected minority populations for unreported offenses and details of evidence concerning the suspected or proven perpetrators, should be sufficient to settle the issue beyond reasonable doubt. There is no problem of finding all manner of indexes of the intensity of group conflict in any community with which the results of such analysis could be related.

Studies of mob force directed against minority peoples with one recent exception have been restricted to behavior threatening or accomplishing the death of a victim.[33] The death of a person at the hands of a mob is of importance to the victim, his community, and the entire nation from a practical point of view, but it is a matter of slight significance in the study of mob behavior as a socio-psychological phenomenon. It is a matter of local tra-

---

[33] See for examples, Raper, Arthur F. *The Tragedy of Lynching.* Chapel Hill: University of North Carolina Press. 1933. Pp. viii+499; Chadbourn, J. H. *Lynching and the Law.* Chapel Hill: University of North Carolina Press. 1933. Pp. xi+221; White, Walter. *Rope and Faggot.* New York: Alfred A. Knopf. 1929. Pp. xiii+272, 14; Cutler, James E. *Lynch-Law.* New York: Longmans, Green & Company. 1905. Pp. xiv+287

The exception referred to, the only comprehensive study of "lynching" known to the author which approaches the problem from the point of view of the social processes and social actions involved and avoids dependence on fatal lynchings for data, is Hoot, John Weldon. *Lynch-Law, the Practice of Illegal Popular Co-ercion.* Unpublished Ph.D. thesis. Philadelphia: University of Pennsylvania. 1935. Pp. 288

dition and chance whether a mob decides to kill, mutilate, flog, tar and feather, ride on a rail, destroy property, or otherwise exercise its will. Selection of any one type of punitive action as the basis for inclusion or exclusion in the statistics of mob behavior will distort conclusions concerning its nature, causes, influences, and possible means of repression.[34]

Death, however, is a fact ascertained and counted with relative ease, and has come to be the focus of interest in studies of minority coercion by mobs. Unofficial statistics of death by lynching have been kept by the *Chicago Tribune* from 1882 through 1917, and are supplemented by similar records collected by the Department of Records and Research, Tuskegee Institute, and the National Association for the Advancement of Colored People for more recent years. These records give a reasonably accurate picture of lynchings as defined in terms of death. Negroes predominate as the victims. The number of lynching deaths for the five predepression and five depression years totalled 17 in 1925, 30 in 1926, 16 in 1927, 11 in 1928, 10 in 1929, 21 in 1930, 13 in 1931, 8 in 1932, 28 in 1933, 15 in 1934, and 20 or a few more, depending on the disposition of some doubtful cases, in 1935. Threatened lynch killings, naturally somewhat difficult to estimate, seem to have increased in total during the depression over the immediately previous period.[35] Actually the number of accomplished and threatened lynch killings combined is much too small in proportion to the total populations involved to justify any generalization concerning the depression influence, although in specific instances a relationship between hard times and mob murder might be established by painstaking investigation. Year to year fluctuations in number offer slight if any opportunity for the discovery of a trend.

---

[34] *Cf.* the article by Coker, Francis W. "Lynching." *Encyclopaedia of the Social Sciences.* 9:639-643. 1933

[35] See *The Mob Still Rides.* Atlanta, Ga.: Commission on Interracial Cooperation. Undated. Pp. 4, 7

Discarding murderous attempt, successful or otherwise, on the lives of the subjects of mob wrath as a possible statistical base for the establishment of a depression trend both because of the small number of items of count and because of the necessarily biased results of such procedure, the alternative possibility of promise is to locate cases of coercive mob behavior directed against minority individuals by search of newspaper files (local rather than metropolitan newspapers should be used) and by direct community inquiry. For this purpose the item of inquiry must be defined in terms of the socio-psychological behavior involved instead of in terms of the consequences to the victim. The essential elements in such a definition would be (a) the coercion of one or more persons of minority status, (b) by mob action (c) strongly supported by public opinion in the larger population group to which the mob belongs. Distinctions will not always be sharp, but they never are in classifications of human behavior, and the relatively few borderland cases in which it will be difficult to decide on inclusion or exclusion will not weaken the value of the material. Subtypes will have to be developed as the material is worked up. In no case should newspaper accounts be relied on without substantiation through field investigation or correspondence. In all instances the community background and population composition must be considered parts of the case as essential as the composition of the mob and the circumstances of its action.

As cases of this nature become available one by one, community by community, for analysis and synthesis, lynching deaths will assume their proper rôle in the understanding of mob coercion of Negroes. At the same time other minorities, now neglected as subjects of inquiry in this field, will probably be found to be not infrequently under similar compulsions. It will then be possible to study the influence of the depression on such behavior.

Chapter VII

Selected Problems of Cultural Disparity

AS PREVIOUSLY emphasized, in so far as the influence of the depression on the lives of minority members has *paralleled* that on the lives of majority members, it is by definition of no present concern. Our immediate interest is in the differential aspects of the problem which may be attributed in some measure to distinctive characteristics of minority groups. These characteristics may be subsumed under three headings, namely: biological, cultural, and group status.

Concerning the first of these, the biological, we know that sex ratios and age distributions vary from group to group because of social circumstances and with repercussions on social organization, and that there are marked anthropometric differences as yet uncorrelated with social potentialities except as they contribute to social visibility. Beyond this there seems to be no possibility of establishing a direct linkage between biological group traits and depression phenomena. Group status may be viewed as a social consequence of more basic factors in group conflict, although of course it is itself in turn an important factor in the social process. It may be suggested that population distribution should be added as a fourth heading to the three mentioned, but this appeared to be unnecessary, if not illogical, in view of the fact that the idiosyncrasies of minority dispersion in the United States may be explained largely in terms of culture, history, and status. In this chapter the emphasis will be on the rôle of cultural differences between population groups.

The problems brought together for discussion in this chapter have been selected arbitrarily in the sense that they do not exhaust the range of possibilities and that only practical rather than inherent considerations prevented separate and lengthier analysis of each. In another sense the selection of these problems for brief examination in the concluding chapter is logically justified by the need for stressing the relatively neglected cultural approach. Previous chapters have paid attention to this approach in other connections which makes feasible brief treatment here.

HEALTH[1]

Sickness and death are not to be feared equally by all persons. The very poor have more to fear than the very rich, the ignorant than the educated, minorities of racial or recent alien origin than the majority of old white stock. The black, red, yellow, and brown peoples of the United States are mowed down before the white, the alien before the native.

The consistent history of unfavorable minority morbidity and mortality rates in this country has been interpreted particularly with reference to colored peoples, as a matter of inherited racial weakness. Were this interpretation correct to a significant degree, a fatalistic attitude of waiting for selection to weed out weak minority stock could be justified. In such case the depression might be viewed as a merciful if not happy speeding up of the process of selection through its consequences of abnormally low income, malnutrition, bad housing, and the like. In actuality, however, it is becoming increasingly clear that exceptional minority morbidity and mortality rates are much more a consequence of social circumstances than of racial susceptibilities and immunities, and that whatever minority handicaps of disease resistance exist may be offset by improving medical and hygienic knowledge.

---

[1] For more general treatment see, in the present series, Collins, Selwyn D. and Tibbitts, Clark. *Research Memorandum on Social Aspects of Health in the Depression.*

The predepression record shows significant differences in health between the majority and minority groups unfavorable to the latter in rough relation to their class and caste status.[2] This statement should be taken as no more than a crude approximation, for there is no good measure of degrees of difference between the various levels of group social status. The record also shows important differences as between groups with regard to the incidence of various diseases and their fatality, to infant mortality and mortality of other age groups, to the vitality of the two sexes, and to changes in the morbidity and mortality rates of minority migrants, which may go up or down following a change of residence. Rates for any minority may be found to vary widely with relation to such social factors as occupation, economic status, education, and place of residence. Minority rates most nearly approximate those for the country as a whole when the groups under consideration most nearly approximate majority standards of culture and physical facilities. It seems generally true that American minority peoples increase their freedom from serious illness and their length of life as they are successful in the process of assimilation and national integration.

To the extent that this observation is true, it may be assumed that the influence of the depression on minority health as such will be found to be a function of the influence of the depression on the process of assimilation and national integration. Since for some individuals and groups this process was aided, while for others it was retarded, no depression health trend applicable to all minorities is to be expected.

The Indian health situation may be used as an illustration of

[2] Main dependence for the mortality and morbidity records of American minorities has been on government statistics and on life insurance company reports. For an excellent summary of the range of government vital statistics see Dunn, Halbert L. *Vital Statistics Collected by the Government;* Dublin, Louis I. "The American People." *The Annals of The American Academy of Political and Social Science.* Philadelphia. 188:340-350. November 1936

the manner in which minority characteristics and status affect morbidity and mortality. Apart from the circumstance that there are no Indian urban congregations of importance, there is probably no health problem derived from the peculiar conditions of immigrant and colored minorities which does not have its counterpart in the American Indian population. This may be attributed to the wide diversity of original tribal cultures, the limitless variety of post-Columbian tribal experiences, and the present dispersion of the Indian population of the United States.

There is considerable evidence substantiating the popular belief that the pre-Columbian Indian was a man of remarkable vitality as expressed by physical endurance, freedom from disease, and longevity. These facts now are of historical interest only; the Indian of today has all the diseases and physical disabilities found in the general population. Moreover, the adverse economic position of the Indian forces him to live on a bare subsistence level amidst environmental conditions which bring about a lowered state of health and predisposition to particular diseases.

While a definite attempt is now being made to secure reports of births, deaths, together with communicable diseases and other illnesses, the data available are still very inadequate. Despite the absence of exact figures on vital statistics, certain general information is on hand which can be considered sufficiently reliable to furnish a basis for making the following general statements regarding the incidence of certain types of illness.

The three outstanding disease problems among the Indians today are tuberculosis, trachoma, and intestinal disorders of infancy. Venereal diseases are known to be very prevalent among certain groups, but the incidence of these diseases in the total Indian population has not been determined with any high degree of certainty. The acute infectious diseases of childhood, notably measles and whooping cough, are attended by a high mortality. This excessive mortality is attributed to respiratory complications believed to result from exposure and inadequate nursing care. The high infant mortality has not been studied sufficiently, but it is said to be contributed, in the order of importance, by diarrheal conditions, acute respiratory infections, birth injuries, and tuberculosis. Skin diseases, particularly impetigo and ringworm are extremely common among children and a source of considerable complaint from the school authorities. Dental caries varies with the different tribes, but generally speaking, it is at least equal to and perhaps exceeds that found in the lower economic groups of the white population. Exceptions to this general rule may be found among certain groups: the Pima, Apache, and particularly the Navajo tribes are remarkably free of dental caries. Disorders of the gums are exceedingly common throughout the Indian population.

The diet of most tribes is not balanced and is deficient in many respects. Such articles as milk and fresh vegetables are used very seldom or not at all. Generally speaking, carbohydrates and fats are proportionately in excess of other elements in the diet although the Navajos subsist on meat almost exclusively. Not infrequently the total quantity of food available is below the requirements of the tribe. Malnutrition is reported by agency physicians to be fairly common among the children; on the other hand overweight due to the excessive carbohydrate diet may be seen quite frequently in adults. Deficiency diseases, such as pellagra, scurvy and rickets, are not reported as often as might be expected. It is possible that these conditions may not be diagnosed in the mild stages.

Environmental conditions in and around the Indian homes are prejudicial to health and social development. The house itself may be built of clay, reeds, stones, or logs found in the immediate vicinity, or it may be a simple cabin constructed of wrought lumber. These primitive abodes do not afford reasonable protection from the elements. Overcrowding is extremely common with two or more generations often living in the same household. There is scarcely any separation of ordinary functions such as cooking, living, and sleeping; privacy is out of the question. Water for drinking purposes may be obtained from wells, springs, streams, or irrigation ditches and often is polluted with domestic sewage. In much of the Indian country, the supply of water is very limited and must be transported some distance, thus personal and household cleanliness is rendered difficult even if the Indian were so inclined. The Indian agencies, the institutions, and a few of the villages have central water supplies of known sanitary quality. The great majority of Indian homes use a surface type of privy or, as so frequently happens, they have no methods of excreta disposal. Improvement of the Indian's physical surroundings remains a problem to be solved if diseases associated with defective environment are to be controlled.

Anyone interested in improving the health of Indians cannot overlook the extreme poverty of the Indians as a race. This subject, though closely related to health, was not studied during the survey since the solution of economic problems is not within the scope of health programs. Fortunately, machinery has been set up in the Office of Indian Affairs to assist the Indian in his economic development. Programs involving reciprocal assistance remain to be developed between industrial and health personnel.

The Indian as yet appears to have acquired comparatively little understanding of the factors involved in health and disease. An increase in the content of his knowledge should be a primary consideration of the health workers, but an incentive must be supplied since it is necessary that the Indian participate in the improvement of his own health. These desirable ends cannot be accomplished by health workers pursuing a program of remedial service only. On the other hand, something more than a purely intellectual approach is required. All units of the Indian agency responsible for the several aspects of Indian life must combine on programs in which health education is correlated with whatever function may be discharged by the different specialized groups.[3]

It may be observed that the quoted summary of the Indian health situation prepared by the Public Health Service stresses, directly or by implication, such factors associated with minority status as inadequate medical facilities, nutrition, housing, sanitation, poverty, physical and social environment, culture conflict, inadequate education, and lack of incentive. Such health influences are all exceptionally important in the circumstances of every American minority people, though in varying degree. They are functions of the degree of acculturation and assimilation, and of class and caste discrimination. It is consequently clear that it is through these social processes that the depression influence on minority health has made itself felt and may best be understood.

To put the minority health problem in another and more compact way, "The three possible major factors in mortality and morbidity are racial immunities and susceptibilities, ignorance of healthful habits and practices, and inadequate health resources. Of the three, the first is of the least importance, and authoritative recourse to it in explaining differential rates is becoming increasingly rare."[4] The second is layman's language for cultural disparity. The third calls attention to the significance of inferior group status in terms of remedial and preventive health facilities.

---

[3] Mountin, Joseph W. and Townsend, J. G. *Observations in Indian Health Problems and Facilities.* U. S. Treasury Department, Public Health Service, Public Health Bulletin No. 223. Washington, D.C.: U. S. Government Printing Office. February 1936. Pp. 35-36

[4] Young, Donald. *American Minority Peoples.* New York: Harper & Brothers. 1932. P. 336

The depression inevitably must have affected the health of minorities unevenly because of their cultural disparity. What was the relation between minority consumption standards and habits, including notoriously inferior housing, clothing, diet, and sanitation, and depression hardship? It is not even known whether or not predepression low levels of living made minority adjustment to depression circumstances relatively less of a hardship than otherwise might have been the case. Had the badly unbalanced diets of the Negro, the Indian, and the recent immigrant weakened the resistance of these peoples so that the depression affected their health more seriously than that of others? To what extent did relief practices allow for disparate minority consumption standards, improve living habits from the point of view of health, and serve as an assimilative influence? Was there any relation between the depression and dependence on folk medicine in contrast with scientific medical practice? Did the depression in any way modify the willingness of minorities to alter their customary living habits which are known to have important bearings on health to bring them more into line with modern medical knowledge? It is not likely that such questions as these will be answered directly by primary research with regard to the last depression, but there is no reason why present knowledge of minority cultures and vital statistics should not be more closely integrated through the interpretative process than has yet been attempted.

It is also inevitable that the depression must have affected the health resources, both private and public, available to minorities.[5] Assuming that minorities suffered income changes exceptional in degree because they were minorities during the

---

[5] For "a brief and somewhat sketchy presentation of the Negro medical, hospital and health situation in the country at large, with special reference to New York" and a report on "the professional, environmental and administrative features of the Harlem Hospital in New York," see Corwin, E. H. L. and Sturges, G. E. *Opportunities for the Medical Education of Negroes.* New York: Charles Scribner's Sons. 1936. Pp. xv+293

depression—and this is a broad assumption concerning which little is now definitely known—it would follow that private health resources were materially curtailed. Unfortunately, exact knowledge concerning the relation between mortality, morbidity and income and income change is scanty for the population in general. Much general groundwork needs to be done before any guesses concerning minority health and depression income changes, together with all that such changes imply with regard to medical facilities and the material necessities of physical well-being, may be hazarded. It seems inevitable that minority private health resources must have been severely limited by the depression, but that is another thing from asserting that minority sickness and death rates must therefore have been increased by the depression.

Public health resources available to minority groups may well have increased during the depression, as may have a willingness on their part to take advantage of them. There was, for example, a marked tendency to shift the burden of economic and social welfare measures for the needy from local governmental units to the national government. This probably meant, particularly in regions of strong anti-minority prejudice such as the South and the Indian country, an appreciably more favorable situation for minorities. Furthermore, the increased acceptance of public aid in the form of food, housing, and cash, along with advice and compulsion concerning consumption habits, may have prepared individuals for the acceptance of public health services and reliance on modern medical advice with decreased reluctance. It is not at all inconceivable, although lacking in proof, that the peoples farthest down in the economic and social scale may have had some aspects of their living physically improved by public aid in the depression. It is not hard to find individuals for whom this was true with regard to health factors; it is another matter to establish any generalization of this nature for a racial or national minority.

The health of American minority peoples was definitely improving in the decades prior to the depression. In the years between 1900 and 1930, "The death rates of whites and of Negroes decreased at about the same rate. The death rate of whites at ages under 45 fell faster and at higher ages slower than the average; that of Negroes at ages below 15 fell faster, and at ages from 15 to 35 slower than the average. At ages above 35 the death rate of Negroes was higher in 1930 than in 1900. The death rate of native whites decreased in the 30 years more than three times as fast as that of foreign-born whites, but if allowance is made for the fact that the foreign-born averaged about 7 years older in 1930 than in 1900 the decrease in the death rate of the native whites was only about one and one-half times that of foreign-born whites."[6] Trends such as these may be found for other minority groupings not here cited, such as the Orientals, and by country of origin, by age, sex, place of residence, etc. They should then be carried into the depression years to determine what changes may have occurred during the period of severe economic crisis.

The Public Health Service has pointed out that "There are three general sources of recent information concerning births, deaths, and illness among the Indians: Special surveys, hospital records, and routine vital statistics reports."[7] The same categories of sources apply to the other minorities. In using these sources, it should be borne in mind that depression relationships gain significance in proportion with the homogeneity of the minority class or caste studied. Thus, rates for the foreign-born are most valuable when broken down by specific nationalities, by sex, by age, length of residence in the United States, place of residence, occupation, and so forth. Similarly, Negro vital statis-

---

[6] Willcox, Walter F. *Introduction to the Vital Statistics of the United States, 1900 to 1930.* U. S. Department of Commerce, Bureau of the Census. Washington, D.C.: U. S. Government Printing Office. 1933. P. 4

[7] Mountin, Joseph E. and Townsend, J. G. *Op. cit.* P. 7

tics for the country as a whole are much less revealing than when broken down in a comparable manner. Such processes of refinement, however, although promising of tremendously increased meaning when carefully performed, introduce a major difficulty, particularly in the intercensal years of the depression, because of the meager data for calculating accurately bases for rate determination. The total foreign-born population, for example, may be calculated with reasonable accuracy for any year, and may with some confidence be broken down by country of origin, but further refinements become progressively inconclusive. There is no insuperable barrier in statistical theory to the accomplishment of the necessary refinements, however, and the prospects of increased interpretative values justifies the risks involved.

As a warning against the too ready assumption that the depression must have had an unqualifiedly harmful effect on the health of minorities there may be cited the record of the industrial policyholders of the Metropolitan Life Insurance Company: "During the depression mortality has been very low, and not high, as might have been expected. While these facts are clear, the reason for them is very much a matter of speculation. Is it possible that retrenchment in certain activities and pursuits, or in diet, has actually had a beneficial effect? Or is it a very fortunate accident that during the greater part of the depression we have had the advantage of unusually favorable weather conditions? Be this as it may, we must not overlook the fact that health departments have continued to function with more enthusiasm and drive than ever before. The momentum of a powerful force like the public health movement will carry on for years. The relief measures that have been taken, also, have been sufficient in most states to take care of the immediate and primary needs of the people."[8]

[8] *Statistical Bulletin.* New York: Metropolitan Life Insurance Company. February 1935. Vol. 16, No. 2, p. 3

Whatever may have been the depression health story for the population as a whole, there is ample reason to suspect that the depression experiences of specific minority groups did not exactly parallel national experience. It would be astounding if unique population dispersions, cultural traits, class and caste status, and the concomitant variant material and social resources, had not led to unique health problems. More specific generalizations than this can not now be ventured, but the possibility of their formulation is remote only in so far as there is but little interest on the part of qualified research workers and a lack of research facilities.

Especial importance is given to the question of the health of minority peoples because of the common accusation that they have been menaces to the health of the nation. It is now generally conceded that, given adequate medical inspection of immigrants at the nation's borders, minorities are about as much of a threat to the health of the country as they are permitted, or even forced to be, by virtue of neglect and discrimination. Elements in minority cultures which are predisposing to high disease rates are susceptible to constructive modification through programs of assimilative education. Unhealthy living standards and practices consequent to inferior economic status are not a consequence of minority choice. Exactly similar conditions, including the entire range of health handicaps from dangerous folk medicine to economic insufficiency, may be found among handicapped and exploited groups of old white American stock. Whether the depression increased the health hazards of the nation deriving from the presence of minority peoples consequently seems to be a question of the extent and effectiveness of public health measures, in the broadest sense of the term, which have been offered such groups. The answer can be derived only from an understanding of the total picture of the way in which specific minority peoples live.

THE FAMILY[9]

It may be accepted without question that the depression caused hardship among a large proportion of the families in the United States that depended upon the continuous wage earning power of their members. This was just as true of well-established majority families who had financial resources as it was of those families of low income that never had been in a position to create a financial reserve. It is more than likely that those majority families who had been financially independent in a sense suffered even more than families in the low-income class. While our immediate problem does not concern itself with the stresses and strains undergone by families of the native-born whites, nevertheless, it is necessary to avoid implying that only certain types of families experienced difficulties. All types of families, from the lowest income family of the Southern Negro to the most favored marital group of early colonial descent were affected to some extent by unemployment or diminishing assets.

While the foregoing statements are true, they need considerable qualification. The difficulties experienced by American families, and by that is meant families in the United States of whatever racial or cultural origin, were not equally distributed in kind or quantity. The families of minority status probably were subjected to greater stresses and strains than families not readily recognized as "different." It is likely that native families found the trying period of economic dislocation more easy to withstand and assimilate than minority families of the same economic class, if only because the native white family would normally be in a position to call upon more social resources than either the foreign-born or Negro family in the same economic class.

In order to understand the manner in which the depression affected minority families it is necessary to approach the effects

---

[9] *Cf.* in this series Stouffer, Samuel A. and Lazarsfeld, Paul F. *Research Memorandum on the Family in the Depression.*

from the functional point of view. We must assume membership in such a family group in order to see the problems emerg-
ing as seen by the members of such families. If, for example,
economic stress impinged upon the Negro family, it is quite
likely that the reactions of the constituent members of the
Negro family would not be psychologically identical with the
reactions of the members of the majority white family in the
same situation.

The problem which suggests itself is whether the difficulties
experienced by minority families were different in kind from
those experienced by majority families of the same economic
level. On the whole, it may be assumed that the problems which
the depression revealed to low-income families in general may
be regarded as roughly the same as those which faced minorities,
but with the important exception that the latter faced special
difficulties associated with their minority status and cultural
divergencies. We are not here interested in what happened to a
minority family because of its position in the economic scale,
valuable as such information might be, except as its economic
status is a function of minority characteristics. The question now
before us concerns the effect of the depression upon the minority
family because it is a minority family.

The first answer to any question with respect to depressions
and existing families is to be found in family budgets. Curtailment of expenses was not an exclusive phenomenon of minorities, although it may have been far more critical in their cases.
On the other hand, the arrival of unemployment to the casual
Negro laborer may in many instances have been most welcome
since relief checks may have been more nearly in the amount
needed than the pittance earned at casual labor. In fact, critics
of relief held just that view, that many Negro families were
far better off during the depression because of the existence of
work- and home-relief than they had ever been. Whether this
was true would need a certain amount of testing. There can be

no doubt that a large number of Negroes receiving public aid would have preferred steady employment for self-support, rather than the make-work policy which made their existence possible during the depression.

Even granting the tenuous hypothesis that relief made for a higher standard of living among casual Negro labor, there still remains the problem of what happened within the Negro family. The Negro family for historical reasons differs appreciably from the majority of native-born families. It also differs from the European immigrant family. We may illustrate by contrasting two radically different types of minority families: the conservative Jewish family, no matter how long on American soil, and the indigenous Negro family. In the first the family appears to be to a great extent an end in itself with values interpreted in terms of the younger members. That is, the Jewish family may be referred to as the "child-centered family." The Negro family, however, is essentially a functional group, a means to an end, with the end or ends somewhat vague and varying. Where in the well-organized and highly-integrated Jewish family we find membership a sine qua non, in the more loosely organized Negro family, there appears to be less of the compulsions found in the cultural configuration which determines the form and content of the Jewish family. In other words, these types of minority families do not mean the same thing in form or function, nor indeed does the family of any one distinctive population group correspond exactly to that of any other.

The functions and purposes of the family, whether minority or majority, are cultural products.[10] Where a definite hierarchy of authority and a scalar organization of descending impor-

---

[10] For a localized cultural study of the changing rôle of Indian women in a period of transition which is both intellectually stimulating and methodologically suggestive with relation to any and all minorities see Mead, Margaret. *The Changing Culture of an Indian Tribe*. New York: Columbia University Press. 1932. Pp. xiv+313

tance and prestige inheres within the family itself, it is safe to conclude that any disturbing factors which tend to upset the traditional equilibrium of the group must affect different members differently. And therein lies the most important problem associated with the depression. When members of a family organization have a definite rôle and part to play, and this rôle or part is disturbed by whatever factors, there must of necessity be resulting implications which make for greater tension than mere fact of reduced income. Conceivably, we might find the process of segmentalization going on within such families.

We may illustrate this point by reference to the highly organized patriarchal family of many immigrants. It is not necessary to labor the obvious fact that in the ordinary European immigrant family each member has a place and that freedom to change one's place in the familial framework is limited. The eldest boy has his place, the marriageable daughters have very definite rôles and responsibilities. The wife and mother has her traditional sphere of activity. The father generally is the head of the family and the main source of authority. This type of family may be looked upon as a traditional psychological unit whose very existence is predicated upon observance of certain forms and ceremonials. It encountered the depression in an area of secondary culture. If such had happened in the old world, its social resources might have been sufficient to weather the storm without too great a stress being placed upon its members and functions. During the depression, however, in an alien land the problem is quite different. The traditional head of the house and the authoritative spokesman may be relegated to the rôle of boarder.

This constitutes a very difficult problem in personality research. Just what happens to the personalities which now have been forced to change positions within a configuration of relationships which has been defined over the centuries? The implications of this process are even more important, since the father's relationships with the rest of the family and even the minority community are also involved. Some of the case material indicates that where it was possible, some heads of families who underwent this type of change of status within their own families attempted the familiar method of escape, through drunkenness. Others became even more domineering to compensate for loss of place in the family. All manner of compensation mechanisms have been tried.

It is not likely that the Negro suffered similar travail to anything like the same extent as the immigrant because of shifts in the rôles of family members enforced by the depression. His orientation toward family maintenance has not assumed such fixed notions of rights and responsibilities. There is a pronounced tendency for the individual as an individual to be of greater relative importance in the Negro family than in that of European origin. Further, the wife and mother is relatively more important in the Negro in comparison with the European family. Beyond saying that these differential tendencies seem to have a natural explanation in historical experiences and present day circumstances, including the exceptionally high rate of employment of Negro women outside the home, we are not concerned with the reasons for their existence, but rather with their existence. They raise the question whether Negro families because of their differential tendencies in functions and organization were better able to cope with depression exigencies with respect to both psychological and material needs than those of other minorities or of the majority.

Problems of personality changes and of modifications in the traditional character of minority families are clearly in need of further investigation both in general and in connection with the depression. The difficulties in the way of developing satisfactory techniques and procedures for such investigation cannot be overstated. Regrettable as it is, the only suggestion which may be made is that such problems be approached opportunistically and with due regard for previous research experience in the field of the family as a whole.

Aside from the tensions and rôle-changes within the minority family, there is an allied problem which appears to grow out of the primary problem, that is, the changing function of the minority family. Where minority families were regarded as self-sufficient, the rude jolt of the depression which threw them on relief must have revealed to their members their dependence upon the community rather than upon themselves. It is commonly believed that certain minorities hesitate long before accepting help from outside agencies. This belief appears to be in keeping with the attitude favoring private mutual aid in times of need. When the time of need exceeds capacity of the group to care for its dependents, just what happens to the family from the standpoint of the future? Will it more easily and readily accept outside aid in any future crisis? There is good reason to believe that the philosophy of the family which dictates the necessity of caring for one's own, perhaps in diluted form, will continue to motivate these minorities in future periods of economic crisis.

Among the most common depression family methods of attempting to meet hopeless financial stringency have been migration, extreme economy, interfamily pooling of resources, relief through public and private agencies, and downright surrender to circumstances. Minority migration to regions of supposedly better opportunities already has been discussed, and needs no further mention here. Economy of crippling intensity already has been pointed out as of significance in the study of minorities in the depression only because there is some reason to believe there are variations in the degree of group adaptability to this measure because of variations in group behavior patterns and standards of living. The other major methods listed, however, require comment in connection with the family.

Interfamily pooling of resources, like all the other devices mentioned, is neither a depression invention nor a unique minority recourse. It is found in greater or lesser degree among all groups of low-income families. Theoretically, because of the fact that the American Negro family is probably the most opportunistically functional of all common types found in the United States, it might be expected that it would be most readily subject to depression enlargement into what could be called the doubled-up household. Enforced residential segregation, through the restriction of housing facilities, definitely contributes to such practice. On the other hand, the functional family is also the one which most easily disintegrates when it loses its practicality as a functioning unit. The question consequently resolves itself into one of determining whether the family as an institution is as well adapted to serving depression needs as is individual freedom from family obligations. With respect to housing, it seems clear that it is better; in other respects the matter is more doubtful. It would be valuable to know the extent to which living quarters were pooled by Negroes and immigrants during the depression, the frequency of financial pooling for food and other purposes, and whether in fact doubling up of all kinds tended to be a family or an individual matter.

Unfortunately there seems to be no satisfactory way to compare recent depression interfamily pooling with earlier pre-depression practices. It is possible, however, to make comparisons of Negro depression practices with majority and immigrant experiences during the same period. How did the more formalized family of European origin adapt itself to this type of depression defense? Did the immigrant more strongly resist any merging of families for the purpose of meeting physical needs in an effort to preserve the identity of the family unit from the encroachments of enlarged household organization? Were the moral and health hazards of doubling up recognized as threats to individual welfare and family solidarity? Was there any difference in behavior in this respect between nationalities corresponding to differences in family solidarity, or between various generations of the same nationality? How quickly did the various groups break away from doubling up arrangements when the opportunity offered? The fact that the evidence on which answers to such questions as these must be made is sparse should not be permitted to serve as an excuse for avoidance.

The problem of relief for minority families has been customarily viewed as though it were one entirely of positive anti-alien and anti-Negro discrimination. That such discrimination was widespread cannot be denied, nor can its influence on minority family living during the depression have been minor. On the other hand, at least as important, if not more so, has been the unconscious discrimination by well-intentioned administrators and case workers who failed to understand the need for recognition of characteristic minority family patterns in the distribution of relief benefits. For illustration, in the granting of relief to a patriarchal type of family it is much more necessary to guard against breaking down paternal authority and self-respect than in taking care of a more individualistic family. Further, relief policies need to recognize that some minority families more than others require special facilities for what might be called luxuries or nonessentials, such as for religious participation or for customary ceremonial occasions. Cultural projection tinged with smugness was all too common in social work in the depression as well as before. Minority-majority differentials in transfer from home to work relief on government projects show clearly that during the depression American relief was for Americans, but this is merely evidence of discrimination; what is needed is more detailed understanding of inadequate family aid through ignorance and complacency.[11]

If there is one way in which to make assimilation difficult it

---

[11] Cf. White, R. Clyde and Mary K. *Research Memorandum on Social Aspects of Relief Policies in the Depression;* Chapin, F. Stuart and Queen, Stuart A. *Research Memorandum on Social Work in the Depression.*

is by the nativistic technique of reminding persons of their minority status constantly, whether intentionally or otherwise. There can be little doubt that one effect of such depression stimulated reminders was to drive minority families farther away from the majority community and force them to rely increasingly upon their own cultural devices for continuance in the face of hostility.

Turning now to a group of problems which are more quantitative in nature, the question may be raised concerning the depression influence on minority marriage, divorce, desertion, and birth rates. It is assumed that the inclusion in this series of the *Research Memorandum on the Family in the Depression* makes unnecessary any discussion of the statistical data on these subjects, beyond recognition of the fact that minority classifications are frequently omitted and that when included they must be used with extreme caution because of inaccuracies.

All classes more or less postponed marriage during the depression because of the financial obligations involved. It is probable that the amount of postponement varied between minorities, other factors being equal, in rough proportion to the traditional group concept of marital responsibility, but with allowance for cultural emphasis on marriage as an ideal. Although no attempt will be made here to verify this suggestion statistically, a technical problem which is entirely feasible, the theoretical implications for selected minorities may be ventured. Thus, the marriage rate for Negroes should have fallen the least of any important population group, for their individualistic, functional view of the family imposes comparatively little fixed responsibility. Any attempt to test this interpretation must take into account the fact that the Negro functional view of the family has favored the recognition of de facto marriages without legal ceremony. In contrast, the European immigrant family in general may be cited as involving responsibilities difficult of fulfillment for a large number of individuals in a depression, with a consequent increase in postponement of marriage. In the case of the Oriental, the importance of the family in the scale of social values should to some extent counteract the desire to escape impossible responsibilities. The high sex ratio of the Chinese in the United States makes this interpretation impossible to test in his case, but it should be capable of verification or refutation in the case of the Japanese. The Filipino sex ratio, it will be recalled, is also very high. Again referring to the fact that the Indian has been exceptionally fortunate in the matter of government aid during the depression, it is hazarded that his marriage rate was not seriously affected by the depression.

Divorce also is subject to depression postponement among all population classes. The amount of postponement among minorities should have varied with relation to the relative emphasis on the family as an end in itself or as a means to an end. If previous assumptions in this connection have been correct, the trend in the Negro divorce rate should have been affected the least and the immigrant rate the most. A complicating factor is the economic status of the groups compared, for legal divorce is expensive and closely related to questions of property rights.

Desertion, another way of severing the family relationship, is a phenomenon of poverty. Minorities are generally poor, and a tendency toward desertion should be observable among them. The poorest minority, the Negro, has long been known for a high desertion rate. This circumstance is largely explainable in terms of the functional family, for under such a system the natural thing to do when a given family unit ceases to serve its purposes is to abandon it. A formalized family, such as that of the Oriental and the European, however, tends to be preserved for itself. No reliable statistical data are available concerning minority desertion, for as a form of extralegal behavior it is not readily observable except as it comes to the attention of public officials who themselves are little concerned with the marital difficulties of colored people and immigrants. Such conclusions about minority desertion as may be ventured must continue to rest on inference from their economic status and degree of family integration.

However the marriage, divorce, and desertion rates may have been modified by the depression, the rate of reproduction among certain minorities has apparently failed to vary with any certain correspondence. Depression years revealed notably low marriage rates in this country and also notably high illegitimacy rates. Of course, not all minorities contributed equally to the rise in the illegitimacy rate, and it may be that the native whites contributed their due share, but the available figures indicate that the great-est increases from 1929 to 1934 were in states heavily Negro. Further, New Mexico, which suggests the Mexican, rose from 76.9 in 1929 to 130.3 in 1934. No other states showed comparable rises. Just what these figures mean in detail is another matter, but it would not be too violent a distortion of reality to believe that the increase in illegitimacy was in part a natural concomitant of the depression.[12]

There is reason to believe that while the birth rate generally fell off during the depression years, the birth rates of minorities did not decrease to the same degree. This opinion cannot be checked against the figures readily, but in view of the total situation and the strong traditional influences among the foreign-born favoring children, it may be accepted as at least worth debating. In the case of the Negro and of the Indian there is no obvious reason why their birth rates should have decreased materially if previous assumptions concerning the nature of the Negro family and the general belief that there was some improvement in the level of living of many Indians during the period of relief are sound. Another factor tending to maintain minority birth rates may be differential familiarity with contraceptives but this is

---

[12] For foreign-born and Negro illegitimacy data in 1932 and the immediately preceding years see Holmes, S. J. and Dempster, E. R. "The Trend of Illegitimate Birth-Rate in the United States," *Population*. Vol. II, No. 2. November 1936

again speculation.[13] While beyond doubt there are minority differences in status, both economic and social, and in cultural standards and practices affecting minority birth rates, their nature and extent is known but vaguely and incompletely, so that inferences may be drawn only with extreme caution. On the other hand, statistical sources are no less unreliable and incomplete, particularly with reference to white minorities. Crude rates for the larger minority groups may be estimated year by year through the statistical correction of available data, but the refinements necessary for the determination of depression influences might just barely be justified by the validity of results in causal terms.[14]

The initiation and termination of a family relationship, family size, and intra-familial attitudes and behavior are all products of a complex network of factors involving every aspect of life. Except change in family size through birth or death, there is disagreement among technicians concerning the definitions of units to be measured. There are even many conflicting definitions of the family itself. Is a family created only by compliance with legal requirements? If so, a large number of Negro extralegal matings having the social status of families in their own groups are eliminated from consideration as such. What validity has the concept of divorce as a statistical unit in minority studies when it is prohibited by the religion of some peoples and commonly disregarded as too expensive and functionally unnecessary by others? Shall we regard as illegitimate, and if so, to what purpose, the child of an unassimilated Indian girl won by custom marriage of no legal standing, of a central European im-

---

[13] Raymond Pearl, for example, found in a study of some 30,000 women that "43 per cent of the white women and 16 per cent of the Negro women in the sample had practiced birth control of some sort." *The Next Steps in Public Health.* New York: Milbank Memorial Fund. 1936. P. 58

[14] For detailed information concerning minority birth rates see Lorimer, Frank and Osborn, Frederick. *Dynamics of Population.* New York: The Macmillan Company. 1934. Pp. xiii+461. The bibliography included in this volume is both well selected and comprehensive.

migrant girl deserted after granting her favors in accordance with alien betrothal custom not recognized in this country, or of a Negro couple who may live devotedly together throughout their lives without seeing any need for legal marriage? What patterns capable of quantitative statement may be used to express husband-wife-child obligations, rights, and relationships? The immediate prospect is discouraging, but reliance must nevertheless be on just such questionable concepts for the study of all families as well as of those of American minorities in depression.

The probable futility of attempting any generalization concerning the depression influence on overt family trends applicable to all American minorities should be evident from the obviously tremendous variations in the composition and histories of the separate groups and even individuals.[15] If any tendency is to be found, it should not be expected to be visible in uniformity of minority symbolic and functional behavior, but rather in similarity of the mechanisms through which depression forces operated. By definition minorities have social visibility and inferior social status; by observation they have distinctive cultural traits and are viewed by others with active prejudice as dangerous competitors. Further, in spite of handicaps, all minorities have begun and continued the process of acculturation from the moment of arrival in this country, with a consequent universal if uneven trend toward family organization patterned on that of their new home community. The probability is that the depression has modified the rate of familial acculturation, as it

---

[15] Compare, for example, Mead, Margaret. *Op. cit.* With Thomas, W. I. and Znaniecki, Florian. *The Polish Peasant in Europe and America.* New York: Alfred A. Knopf. 2nd edition. 1927. I: xv+1116; II: 1117-2250; Frazier, E. Franklin. *The Negro Family in Chicago.* Chicago: University of Chicago Press. 1932. Pp. 294; Fishberg, Maurice. *The Jews.* London: The Walter Scott Publishing Company. 1911. Pp. xix+578; Ruppin, Arthur. *The Jews in the Modern World.* London: The Macmillan Co. 1934. Pp. xxxi+423

This list could be extended indefinitely, for every competent social analysis of a minority necessarily illustrates its unique characteristics.

probably has acculturation in general. Most likely, depression privations and pressures have as a whole retarded this assimilative process. Such modification, however, whatever its direction, does not necessarily express itself similarly in the overt behavior of two groups, or even of two individuals; for example, through retardation of the assimilation of several immigrant groups with distinctive family patterns, it may have been the common factor in reinforcing distinctive types of family behavior. The heart of the matter is perhaps not the seemingly capricious sex and familial behavior of minorities during the depression but rather the crisis-induced changes in the rate of progress toward greater family uniformity.

A final question concerns intergroup marriages. Did the depression stimulate minority inbreeding or outbreeding? It is a truism that two or more peoples living in the same geographical area, participating in the same economic system, no matter how divergent originally in racial or national origin, cannot be kept biologically separate; ultimately they become one stock. Both legally and extra-legally this process has been going on in this country since its founding. It may be viewed as a special problem of research in family behavior, for interracial and internationality families have aspects not shared by intra-group families. The problems of such marriages may also be looked upon as problems of class and caste distinctions, and the implications in this respect are no less equally fundamental. Since questions of this nature already have been raised in the latter connection in a previous chapter, they will receive no further consideration here.

RECREATION AND LEISURE[16]

Leisure time is essentially a residual concept loosely embracing the waking hours not devoted to the more pressing activi-

---

[16] For more general discussion see, in this series, Steiner, Jesse F. *Research Memorandum on Recreation in the Depression.*

ties necessary to existence. Of doubtful validity as a scientific unit of discrimination, the concept nevertheless possesses utility as a practical designation for the periods of more or less random activity.

The somewhat random leisure time activities, however, fall roughly into three categories from a functional point of view: namely, (1) those which may be said to have some intellectual value (2) those tending to improve physical development and health and (3) those which are primarily pleasant aids to the passage of time. It goes without saying that these categories are not mutually exclusive, but rather matters of emphasis. From another point of view, leisure time activities may be classified on the basis of relative emphasis on personal, commercial or public resources. Other divisions may be made, depending on the purpose in mind, but these two classifications are perhaps the most useful for present needs.

The predominating type of leisure time activity for any population group is naturally a function of cultural standards and available facilities. This being the case, it is obvious that the various American minority peoples may be expected to show various patterns of leisure time activities. For example, as a normal consequence of the Negro's inferior caste status, with its attendant limitation on both public and commercial recreational facilities through segregation policies, of his limited financial resources, and of his variant cultural history, he has been forced into dependence to an exceptional degree on leisure time activities requiring little money, little reliance on agencies controlled by the white man, and little formal educational background. In other words, the Negro's leisure time is spent more largely on purely individual pursuits and on "partying" than is the case of his white neighbor.[17] Similar group biases in the expenditure

---

[17] Cf. Washington, Forrester B. *Recreational Facilities for the Negro* in "The American Negro," by Young, Donald. *The Annals of the American Academy of Political and Social Science.* 140:272-282. No. 229. November 1928

of leisure time are evident in the cases of other minorities, the rôle of cultural differences being larger for the more recent immigrant groups than for the Negro, that of segregation being lesser, particularly for the non-colored, and that of inadequate income being also of less significance.[18]

With so little known about minority leisure time activities in general except on a priori grounds, and with the field as a whole relatively undeveloped, it is almost impossible even to ask questions concerning the influence of the depression which may reasonably be considered feasible for research attack.[19] Any number of specialized studies of depression trends may, of course, be framed with reference to such data as are available concerning minority theatres, actors, segregation policies, playground utilization, reading habits, sports, travel, and the like. The records, however, are generally thin, spotty, and unreliable, and it is improbable that the results in terms of the understanding of minority depression changes in leisure time activities would be worth more than a small fraction of the trouble and cost. The alternative is to approach the problem with frank dependence on inference from the total picture of minority life and with no more reliance on direct leisure time data than is warranted by their minor research value.

A plausible hypothesis is that the depression, through a general curtailment of income, increased dependence on inexpensive and personal leisure time resources. For such a tendency minorities were perhaps better prepared by predepression standards and experience than large elements of the majority population. It is suggested that psychologically the result was a smaller gap between minority recreational desires and depression satisfac-

---

[18] *Cf.* Young, Donald. *American Minority Peoples.* New York: Harper & Brothers. 1932. Chapter VIII

[19] For information concerning the data available for the study of leisure time activities see Steiner, Jesse F. *Americans at Play.* New York and London: McGraw-Hill Co. Vol. xiv. Pp. 201. 1933

tions. If this is correct, it may be assumed that minorities consequently encountered less serious problems of individual and social adjustment than the majority as a whole. On the other hand, there is the possibility that the depression reduction in income available for leisure activities may have had just as serious an influence on the physical health of minorities as on that of the majority—or even more serious—and intellectual development may have been retarded. These possible dangers, however, must have been offset to some extent by depression governmental activities which brought standard health practices and educational programs for all age groups to minorities to an extent which, however inadequate, transcended previous experience. Another problem which needs consideration is the extent to which minorities utilized their leisure time during the depression for activities expressive of group solidarity in contrast with predepression activities of a similar nature.

The most promising research expectation is that the direction of the main currents of minority trends with respect to leisure time activities may be determined with reasonable accuracy by inferences drawn from observations ranging over all aspects of life. More intensive, sharply defined research projects in this area of depression experience offer but slight prospect of profit.

RELIGION AND THE CHURCH[20]

Freedom of worship is one liberty which has been enjoyed by American minorities, largely as a matter of majority indifference and as a result of historic tradition of toleration and separatism of church and state. In consequence of this freedom, minority churches have as a whole been subject to minority control and have been responsive to minority functional needs.

Limitations on minority religious institutions and practices have, however, always been in force to some extent, but on the

---

[20] See, in this series, Kincheloe, Samuel C. *Research Memorandum on Religion in the Depression.*

whole they have been casual, unplanned, and loose.[21] Thus the Negro became a Christian both through compulsion and through the natural processes of acculturation, but the form and content of his Christianity has to a great extent been his own concern. The European and Mexican immigrants have brought their own creeds and forms of worship with them, and while they have undergone great changes in ideological structure and practice, the changes have been in response to new life circumstances rather than to direct majority pressures. The Japanese in the United States have been able to maintain both Christian churches and Buddhist temples of their own. The Chinese, migrating to this country as individuals separated from their families, have been unable to retain the integrity of their own family-linked form of worship, nor have they gained control of the Christian institutions introduced by missionaries. The Indian, too, has largely failed to maintain his own religious faiths and forms and those of the white man are administered to him rather than by him. Recognizing that the broad generalizations which have just been made are subject to numerous qualifications and re-finements, it is nevertheless true that only the latter two groups mentioned, the Chinese and the Indian, do not today have well-developed religious institutions relatively free of purposeful

---

[21] The following references on minority religious organization may be found helpful: Bowen, Trevor. *Divine White Right.* New York: Harper & Brothers. 1934. Pp. xv+310; Mays, B. E. and Nicholson, J. W. *The Negro's Church.* New York: Institute of Social and Religious Research. 1933. Pp. xiii+321; Gillard, John T., S.S.J. *The Catholic Church and the Negro.* Baltimore: St. Joseph's Society Press. 1929. Pp. xv+324; Daniel, W. A. *The Education of Negro Minis-ters.* New York: George H. Doran Company. 1925. Pp. 187; Strong, E. K. "Religious Affiliation." Chapter IX. *Japanese in California.* Stanford University, California: Stanford University Press. 1933; Meriam, Lewis. "Missionary Ac-tivities among the Indians." Chapter XIV. *The Problem of Indian Administra-tion.* Baltimore: The Johns Hopkins Press. 1928; Brunner, Edmund deS. "The Church in the Immigrant Community," Chapter VI. *Immigrant Farmers and Their Children.* Garden City, New York: Doubleday, Doran & Company. 1929; Fry, C. Luther. *The U. S. Looks at Its Churches.* New York: Institute for Social and Re-ligious Research. 1930. Pp. xiv+183

majority domination. It is also true that freedom from majority domination tends to favor functional adaptation to specific group circumstances and needs.

One function which a minority religion may serve is that of reconciliation with inferior status and its discriminatory consequences. Evidences of religious service of this function may be found among all American minority peoples. On the other hand, religious institutions may also develop in such a way as to be an incitement and support of revolt against inferior status. Thus, the Christianized Indian, with due allowance for exceptions, has tended to be more submissive than the pagan. Special cults such as those associated with the use of peyote, the Indian Shaker Church, and the Ghost Dance, all three containing both Christian and native elements, were foredoomed attempts to develop modes of religious expression adapted to individual and group circumstances. The latter, with its emphasis on an assured millenium of freedom from the white man, encouraged forceful revolt. The Christianity of the Negro, in spite of appreciable encouragement of verbal criticism of the existing order, has emphasized acceptance of present troubles in the knowledge of better times to come in the life hereafter. The numerous varieties of Christianity and the Judaism brought by immigrants from Europe and Mexico, in spite of common nationalistic elements, also stressed later rewards rather than immediate direct action.[22]

Hence, it may be reasonably enquired whether the minority churches in general were not exceptionally well qualified to offer their congregations comforting assurances of the relative unimportance of present ills intensified by the depression. For the acceptance of such assurances minority congregations should have been well prepared by previous religious experiences. Evidence of any militant reaction to the depression among minor-

---

[22] *Cf.* Young, Donald. *American Minority Peoples.* New York: Harper & Brothers. 1932. Chapter XV

ity churches is not apparent. If it existed to any significant extent it should not be difficult to uncover through the simple examination of religious publications and minority newspapers.

In view of the past history of minority religious expression, it might be expected that new minority cults and schisms would have arisen during the depression, and that altered trends in the strength of existing cults and denominations would reflect minority reactions to the depression. This expectation is based on the hypothesis that there is a tendency in time of crisis for handicapped and oppressed groups to build religious institutions of their own either through the independent formation of new cults or through splitting fragments from established organizations out of their control. The rise of Father Divine in recent years is startling, but it is difficult to associate this religious movement with the depression in a causal sense on the basis of facts now known.[23] Indeed, there seems to have been no marked minority attempt to adjust religious organization to unique group needs during the depression through either new or separatist religious movements. This, however, is a guess based on somewhat casual observation and without research foundation.

If this guess is accurate, it suggests either that minority religious institutions were surprisingly adequate for minority religious needs as influenced by the depression or that other agencies than the church were found satisfactory for purposes previously served by the churches. A third logical possibility that minorities encountered no exceptional stresses during the depression may perhaps be discarded in the light of contradictory evidence.

Which of the two likely possibilities has the greater factual support should be determined minority by minority with-

[23] Cf. Hoshor, John. God in a Rolls-Royce, the Rise of Father Divine, Madman, Menace or Messiah. New York: Hillman-Curl Inc. 1936. Pp. xii+272; Parker, R. A. The Incredible Messiah. Boston: Little, Brown and Company. 1937. Pp. xiii+323

out any attempt in the initial stages of investigation to make one generalization cover all minorities. Differences in culture and in economic and social status are too great between minorities and too important in religious development to justify any over-all approach. Within each minority, the problem is one of determining the relations of individuals with organized religion. This means investigation of such matters as church membership, actual attendance, financial contributions, changes in affiliation, and aid received. The only sources of such data are the individual himself and church records. Both sources should be used, and on a sample basis. It has been customary to disparage church records as a source of data for social research, but with proper entree, records of minority churches adequate to establish trends may be utilized. A neglected but feasible type of study which is inexpensive and flexible, yet highly promising, is the case history of individual religious institutions. No prophecy is here ventured concerning the trends which might be uncovered by the use of such materials.

In view of the doctrine of the brotherhood of man held in common by the dominant religious denominations in the United States there is logical justification for inquiry into the question of the degree to which human troubles of depression origin led to a turning by minorities to the stronger majority churches for spiritual and material aid, to more generous granting of such aid, and to increased interest of minority churches in secular affairs.

EDUCATION AND THE SCHOOLS[24]

Minority education, both formal and informal, although fundamentally of a piece with education in general, nevertheless is distinguished by special problems of background, objectives, and procedure. There is, of course, no trustworthy evi-

---

[24] For more general treatment see, in this series, Educational Policies Commission: *Research Memorandum on Education in the Depression.*

dence that individuals of minority status are by racial heredity incapable of exactly the same education as anyone else. Social differentiation, however, plainly requires special educational provision in accordance with group characteristics, just as within the majority there are subgroups requiring modification of the general educational pattern. In these days it may be assumed that educational uniformity should be kept at the necessary minimum demanded by available facilities and administrative limitations. Minorities present merely one more type of basis for individualization.

The factors distinguishing minority educational problems include cultural differences, limitations of occupational and other activities for which education is preparation, and majority pressure for segregated schooling with restricted educational objectives. Cultural differences necessitate special planning to overcome language handicaps, to meet the problem of reeducation of adults matured in a variant milieu and of children growing up on the margins of conflicting cultures, and perhaps to clarify confused national and group loyalties. The restriction of minority activities raises the question of the relative merits of aiming an educational program directly at a goal known to be attainable in later life or of accepting an idealized democratic objective in education regardless of barriers to free expression of individual capacities. Majority pressure tends to force the joining of the issue on all these problems by favoring separate education of minorities with objectives customarily based on a concept of minority differences as inferiorities to be destroyed or utilized to keep such groups "in their places." Beyond suggesting that the depression probably tended to increase majority pressures and thus sharpen the focus of minority educational issues, it is best not to attempt a single generalization concerning such a complex of problems.

If economic hardship includes among its consequences increased minority-majority tensions, one consequence should be an extension and increased rigidity in compulsory separation of the children of conflict groups in both public and private schools of all levels. As a corollary, under such circumstances there should also be a demonstrable increased discrimination against minorities in such matters as new school buildings and equipment, teachers' salaries, expenditures per pupil, and other measures of educational facilities. These are matters of relatively simple determination from the records of federal, state, and local governmental units, practically all of which are well known, accessible, fairly detailed, and reasonably reliable. There may, however, be offsetting factors to such differential treatment of minority education in depression, such as the higher cost of a dual school system, the power of minority votes and other pressures in special situations, and federal support of local governments and special educational ventures, such as adult forums and the National Youth Administration, in time of crisis.

The Negro, of course, has been most commonly subjected to educational segregation.[25] Because of precedent and ameliorative interest in the most handicapped American minority, the temptation in dealing with Negro educational segregation is to measure quantitatively evidences of discrimination and then fail to make correlations with possible local and national causative factors. There is perhaps no other major minority item on which

[25] For general information and suggestions of special fields of investigation and sources of data see Bond, Horace Mann. *The Education of the Negro in the American Social Order.* New York: Prentice-Hall, Inc. 1934. Pp. xx+501 (bibliography) ; Redcay, Edward E. *County Training Schools and Public Secondary Education for Negroes in the South.* Washington, D.C.: The John F. Slater Fund. 1935. Pp. xvii+168 (bibliography) ; Caliver, Ambrose. "Education of Negro Teachers." *National Survey of the Education of Teachers.* Vol. IV, Bulletin 1933, No. 10. Office of Education, U. S. Department of the Interior. Washington, D.C.: U. S. Government Printing Office. 1933. Pp. ix+123; McCustion, Fred. *Higher Education of Negroes.* Southern Association, Colleges and Secondary Schools. 1933. Pp. 39. Jones, Thomas Jesse. *Negro Education.* Bulletins, 1916, Nos. 38 and 39. Bureau of Education, U. S. Department of the Interior. Washington, D.C.: U. S. Government Printing Office. 1917. Pp. xiv+423; v+724

so many and so good basic data are available as on Negro segregated education. Admitting room for improvement, the need is not in this case for more statistics, but for the reworking of those already available so that they will give information not only about the amount of discrimination but also about the causal sequences and concomitant variations involved.

Did the depression, for example, increase pressure by Negroes themselves for separate schools so that unemployed colored teachers might find jobs, or for some other reason? Did similar white pressures vary in any definite relationship to regional or local economic stringency? In northern cities was there any connection between the importance of the Negro vote and the segregation of colored school children, the employment of colored teachers, and the per capita Negro and white educational expenditures? How did experience in Philadelphia, where education is not under the direct control of the political machine, differ during the depression from that in New York, where the relation between politics and the schools is closer? How did experience vary as between different educational levels, including the primary, secondary, collegiate, professional, agricultural, industrial and academic and public and private schools? Did the interest of philanthropists lag or shift as between the policies of segregated and joint education? What happened to the length of the school term, the equipment, the qualifications of teachers, attendance and achievement, and why? The "what" in such questions is readily determinable; the "why" is more difficult but not impossible; most obscure of all are inquiries concerning the consequences.

Public and private educational segregation is not restricted to Negroes, and to take only Negro experience into account in studying this field is a certain way of distorting conclusions. The Jew, for example, while not legally segregated in the public schools, encounters serious discrimination ranging from covert distaste to forthright exclusion in private schools, colleges, and professional institutions. Did the need of privately supported institutions for money during the depression succeed in lowering barriers against the Jews, or was group feeling strong enough to maintain or even raise them under some circumstances in the face of financial adversity? When admitted to private institutions and in public schools, did they encounter greater or weaker evidences of group feeling on the part of administrators, teachers, and fellow students? Has there been any increase in the enrollment of Jews, and, for that matter, of students of other minority membership, in institutions of learning located in regions outside the main focus of prejudice against them? For example, did Jewish enrollment increase in southern and western universities because of the depression? Because Jewish educational limitation and exclusion is usually concealed in a way that Negro restraints are not, some difficulty will be encountered in efforts to study the various "quota systems" and other bars used. Since educational institutions and their students, however, have been long accustomed to utilization as social science guinea pigs, and since research personnel has exceptional entrée to such sources, the problems in the way of securing data should not be insuperable.

Another group subjected to some segregation is the Oriental student—not the temporary foreign visiting student, but the more permanent American resident. Although subject to some discrimination, collegiate and professional Oriental students are so few in number and have such a wide range of institutional facilities available to them that there would probably be little profit in examining their experience as compared with that of Negro and Jewish advanced students. With only a handful of Oriental school children in the United States (the number of Chinese and Filipino parentage being particularly restricted by extraordinarily high sex ratios), there would probably be no segregated Oriental schools were it not for the concentration of these groups on the West Coast. It is significant for our purposes in studying the effects of the depression to note that the order by the San Francisco School Board, requiring all Japanese in the public school system to attend the Oriental school established in 1885, was passed not because of any educational need but as a political measure, "by a school board under the domination of the labor party, and the corrupt city government of Schmitz and Ruef."[26] Payson J. Treat, in *Japan and the United States* (1921), p. 254, says: "Although various explanations of this resolution were given at the time, the real reason was to start the process of discrimination which would eventually lead to the enactment of an exclusion law."[27] This suggests an economic basis for school segregation which might be expected to be intensified in a depression. The small number of Oriental students now segregated on the West Coast is in one sense a research advantage which should facilitate the study of depression influences, particularly since there are nearby non-segregated Oriental school children for comparative purposes. Historical investigation is also facilitated by the relative recency of the beginning of Oriental immigration, the localization of the school segregation of their children, and the availability of both primary and secondary materials. The study of the rôle of labor and labor unions should be especially fruitful in this case.

Children of Mexican laborers also are subject to irregular segregation in the lower public school grades. To some extent this is approved and encouraged by some Mexicans themselves because of difficulty encountered by their children in making progress in the general schools where Spanish is not always spoken by the teacher and little or no recognition is usually given problems of cultural adjustment. Friction between minority and majority students is also offered as an explanation of the need for separate schools, as it is in the case of every other educa-

---

[26] Strong, E. K. *The Second-Generation Japanese Problem.* Stanford University, California: Stanford University Press. 1934. P. 41

[27] Quoted by Strong, E. K. *Ibid.* P. 40

tionally segregated minority. The Mexican immigrant is primarily a cheap laborer, and not infrequently in conflict with native labor. Under the circumstances the depression should be reflected in segregation policies and practices. In comparing Mexican school segregation with that of other minorities, one should bear in mind that the Mexican is a recent and frequently temporary immigrant, hence the language and cultural factors involved probably play a much larger rôle even than in the case of the Oriental. The strength of the language and cultural variables in the case of the Mexican should make possible significant comparison with other minorities where they are weaker or absent.

The native Indian has been offered education in all possible types of schools, including the segregated and the mixed. Formal Indian instruction in European culture began with the missionaries in colonial days. The slogan until recently was the substitution of European civilization for tribal ways in both private and public education efforts. Although there never has been complete segregation of Indian students, the history of separate Indian schooling goes back to the seventeenth century. The first federal appropriation for Indian education was in 1877, the year when Lieutenant Pratt took a group of Indian prisoners of war to Hampton Institute. The first government Indian school was founded at Carlisle in 1878, and we may confine our consideration of Indian segregation to the period following this date.[28]

The main objective of Indian education, whether in mission school, reservation boarding school, non-reservation boarding school, separate reservation day school, or general public or

---

[28] For the background of Indian education and discussion of modern problems see: Lindquist, G. E. E. *The Red Man in the United States.* New York: George H. Doran Company. 1923. Pp. xxviii+461; Meriam, Lewis and Associates. *The Problem of Indian Administration.* Baltimore: The Johns Hopkins Press. 1928. Pp. xxii+872; Schmeckebier, Laurence F. *The Office of Indian Affairs.* Baltimore: The Johns Hopkins Press. 1927. Pp. xiv+591

private school, has been cultural assimilation. The almost universal acceptance of assimilation as the major objective of Indian education by the public as well as by school officials suggests a motive for segregation considerably at variance with that leading to the segregation of other colored minorities. The policy of the present Indian administration under the leadership of Commissioner John Collier in using the schools and other instrumentalities to preserve Indian tribal culture in so far as feasible also leads to the same conclusion. That benevolently intended assimilation and cultural preservation of a numerically unimportant minority of national sentimental interest were not the only motives in segregation is, however, indicated by instances of public opinion in regions of heavy Indian population against mixed schools. In some Southern areas the presence of Negro blood has also been a factor in Indian segregation. Here, as in the cases of the other minorities, all with incomplete compulsory school segregation, there is opportunity for comparative and historical studies of the effects of economic stringency, complicated in the instance of the Indian by federal dominance over local desire.

Compulsory school segregation cannot be understood by itself; it must be studied in comparison with separate education which is of minority voluntary origin. Much voluntary school segregation is a consequence of minority residential segregation, although this type is usually not complete. Some is predominantly religious in origin, although the subjects taught may include the secular, as in the Roman Catholic or Lutheran parochial schools. There are also minority schools intended to supplement or perhaps counteract the influence of the public schools by instruction in a group's native language, history, and tradition, as in the cases of the Japanese continuation schools and Jewish institutions designed to keep the younger generation from growing up in ignorance and disrespect of the ways of their fathers. Schools giving instruction only in religious subjects, narrowly defined, may be here omitted from consideration.

Since all such institutions are in essence attempts at the preservation of group cultures, or fragments of them, the basic question of concern here is the relative influence of the depression on minority loyalties and group consciousness as evidenced by the support, attendance, and curricula of voluntary segregated schools. This, of course, is but one aspect of a problem previously raised in connection with the general question of the effect of the depression on the disintegration or consolidation of minority loyalties. It is not expected that a simple answer may be found, but rather that diametrically opposite results of the depression may be noted with respect to different groups and different individuals within any one group. This, however, does not mean that the field must remain chaotic, but rather that through knowledge of varying group and individual reactions to opportunities for special education in the ways of one's ancestors there may come a synthesis of understanding concerning cultural, individual, and situational influences on minority loyalties in depression.

Fluctuations in the intensity of group antagonisms are difficult to distinguish by any means. Attitude tests as developed by the social psychologists, valuable as they are, remain suspect as producing verbalizations indefinitely correlated with behavior in life situations. Studies of newspapers, magazines, fiction, and other printed materials may yield rich returns in the hands of a genius at interpretation, but the data they contain are difficult of quantitative expression. Records of most classifications of adult behavior are difficult to obtain. Schools, however, are tangible affairs, with remarkably complete records of their activities. Both compulsory and voluntary school segregation is subject to objective observation from year to year on a local, regional, or national scale. The phenomenon is not limited to any one minority. Instances for comparative study may be found in Germany, where Jewish children are excluded from some public schools;

in South Africa, where Negro students are segregated, or where they are not. It is an overt expression of intergroup attitudes which the controlling generation believes important enough to instill in the minds of oncoming generations. It is a form of actual behavior on which a wide range of data is regularly collected and preserved, and more may be obtained. It is a matter of scientific regret that thus far data on the subject have been used almost exclusively as evidence supporting claims of discrimination and unfair treatment.

The formal education of minorities has been characterized not only by segregation policies but also by planned emphasis on special educational objectives. Reference already has been made to efforts by minorities themselves to utilize voluntary school segregation to preserve group culture traits and loyalties. Compulsory school segregation under majority control has been defended not only as a means for shielding children of superior group status from undesired contacts, but also as a device for facilitating the achievement of differential minority goals. Reduced to the simplest terms and stripped of detailed refinements and rationalizations, these goals have been the development of efficient manual laborers and the destruction of minority cultural traits in favor of so-called American ways of life. The preservation of selected minority traits judged to be of social value has also been advocated, but in the main ineffectively.[29]

Manual education for both agriculture and industry has been characteristically associated with the school programs offered the Negro and the Indian, but not exclusively so. It does not seem to be an accident that training for work with the hands has received the greatest stress in connection with colored minorities. Regardless of the common argument that group prog-

[29] It is suggested that persons interested in the literature of minority education refer to Monroe, Walter S. and Shores, Louis. *Bibliographies and Summaries in Education*. New York: H. W. Wilson Company. 1936. Pp. xiv+470

ress must be founded on a firm basis of physical labor on jobs toward the bottom of the economic ladder, majority support has been given such schools as the Hampton Normal and Agricultural Institute, the Tuskegee Normal and Industrial Institute, and Haskell Institute, because of the harmony of their publicized curricula with the concept of a productive colored peasantry, urban and rural, which knows its place in the hierarchy of castes and classes.

Did the depression increase support of such institutions? No more can now be said than that the factors involved are conflicting. From the majority point of view it might be assumed that increased competition for employment should increase the pressure to keep minorities at the bottom of the economic ladder, but the same sharpened struggle for work may also be expected to increase the interest of majority workers in holding even the most inferior jobs for themselves. Furthermore, vocational education is more expensive than college preparatory work, with the consequence that there has been in the depression an increased reluctance on the part of white school officials to offer facilities for such work to colored pupils. Incidentally, the cost of vocational training may explain in part the lack of emphasis on this type of schooling for immigrant minorities, although it is likely that a more important factor in this situation has been the recognition of the inevitable rapid assimilation of the descendants of white immigrants in the future as in the past—a process which obviously blocks the establishment of an immigrant worker-peasant class. In the case of colored immigrants from Mexico and the Orient, expense has undoubtedly played a leading rôle in preventing the initiation of an educational program for work with the hands, particularly during the depression.

At least one minority, the Negro, seems to have become increasingly skeptical of vocational training as a means for group advancement during recent years. This skepticism, however, is of ancient origin and was growing rapidly before the depression began. Nevertheless, it is possible, and even probable, that the depression strengthened Negro opposition to a racial educational program in harmony with present caste discriminations in occupation and a vague theoretical promise that today's concessions will be rewarded by more solid gains in the future. The study of curricular changes in Negro institutions, with special reference to shifts in emphasis between vocational and other subjects, together with analysis of trends in student enrollment and financial support, should throw light on any trends in the attitude of the Negro toward an educational program founded on caste distinctions. The examination of both the public and private financial support given Negro institutions of all types should aid the understanding of trends in the white man's attitude on the same subject.

In passing, it may be remarked that Indian vocational education has been a prominent feature of the work under the Indian Office not so much because of any implications with reference to the maintenance of caste distinctions as to a philosophy of practical education, to the necessity for using student help because of small appropriations, and to the inertia of an ancient policy. The educational program of the Indian Office under the administration inaugurated in 1933 is one which has long been advocated by unquestioned friends of the Indian free from any suspicion of desire to keep him in "his place." The major rôle of the depression, as in other matters of Indian administration, has been to facilitate the introduction and extension under government auspices of educational policies by no means novel.

Changes in the Indian educational program stimulated by depression circumstances in planned form, if not yet entirely so in practice, are distinctly progressive in nature. As such, important attention is paid to aboriginal cultural elements both for narrowly pedagogical purposes and for the enrichment of later life. Its linkage with the depression is almost entirely fortuitous, and there is consequently no reason for further discussion here, however interesting it may be as an experiment in minority education.

In contrast with the Indian Office insistence on the salvaging and preservation of minority culture traits is the persistent popular attitude that the education of immigrants and their children may be considered successful in direct proportion to the extent to which their cultures are destroyed. The dominating objective has been the rooting out of all traits of recent alien origin, including language, dress, traditions, customs, and social values of all varieties. True, there have been protests that homogeneity means full uniformity, that the civilizations of the world have much to contribute to the United States, that language and dress have little or nothing to do with loyalties, and, in general, that potential immigrant contributions to American life should be utilized to their fullest to avoid stagnation and aid national development.[30] There has also been some confusion concerning the exact nature of the "American standards" to be taught the immigrant. Such protests, however, have not prevailed, and their total effect on the education of the alien and his children has been relatively slight.

Much more far-reaching has been the development of special educational programs for the cultural and political absorption of immigrants known as Americanization. These efforts, under both public and private auspices, have been characterized by the predominating purpose of modifications of the individual im-

---

[30] Protests of this nature have been most prominent in connection with Indian arts, including weaving, pottery, and jewelry manufacture, immigrant folk dancing, needlework and other peasant arts, and Negro music and other cultural (in the esthetic sense) achievements. For illustration see Burton, Henrietta K. *The Re-establishment of the Indians in Their Pueblo Life Through the Revival of Their Traditional Crafts.* New York: Teachers College, Columbia University, Bureau of Publications. 1936. Pp. vi+96; Eaton, Allen H. *Immigrant Gifts to American Life.* New York: Russell Sage Foundation. 1932. Pp. 2+185; Locke, Alain. *The New Negro.* New York: Albert & Charles Boni. 1925. Pp. xviii+446

migrant's ways of life in the direction of pre-conceived notions of American ways of life, and, in spite of sporadic protestations, both their theoretical basis and their consequence have been a disparagement of alien traits. Following an apparent decline in popularity in the late twenties, the depression seems to have given new impetus to the movement while at the same time altering somewhat its nature. The name "Americanization" has fallen into disrepute and almost disappeared as an official designation for educational work with immigrants, but the work itself has been stimulated under the title of "adult education" as a consequence of the program of government depression measures. This again is most likely an illustration of the manner in which a proposed social program may be vitalized somewhat fortuitously by depression circumstances, for in view of the multitude of factors involved it is inconceivable that in any real sense the movement actually stems from the depression as such.

Nevertheless, it should be urged that trends in adult immigrant education be examined over a period not shorter than three decades. What have been the characteristics of the immigrants reached with regard to national origin, time of arrival in the United States, age, sex, occupation, and the like? What subjects have been taught them by teachers how qualified, and with what relative emphasis on mere language ability, American patterns of behavior, economic efficiency, and national loyalty? What funds have been available and where did they come from? What have been the characteristics of administration? Who have been the powerful supporters of the movement in the various phases of its history, and what opposition has it encountered? How may regional differences in policy be explained?

The problem of depression influences on adult immigration education is so large from the physical point of view alone, and has so many facets, that it may be attempted as a whole only if unusual research facilities are available. The most feasible recommendation is perhaps that selected facets, or clusters of facets, be studied state by state or community by community. An obviously important consideration in the framing of such projects is that the geographical area selected for study correspond with a unit of educational administration. Initial preference might well be given industrial states, or at least the larger cities in them, such as New York, Massachusetts, or Illinois.[31]

Classroom adult immigrant education, of course, can be but a fraction of the total process of Americanization under any definition of the word. Since the popular concept of Americanization, however, has come to have a definitely nationalistic connotation, it may be advisable to avoid it altogether in favor of the nationally neutral and more inclusive term "acculturation."[32] Whichever word is used, it must still be self-evident that formal instruction in language, history, tradition, custom, behavior patterns, economic techniques, social attitudes and values, and loy-

---

[31] For a review of the nature and problems of immigrant education work from the educator's point of view down to the date of publication see Sharlip, William and Owens, A. A. *Adult Immigrant Education.* New York: The Macmillan Company. 1925. Pp. xviii+317

[32] For an outline of the range of social phenomena covered by the term see Redfield, Robert, Linton, Ralph, and Herskovits, Melville J. "Memorandum for the Study of Acculturation." *American Anthropologist.* 38:149-152. No. 1. January-March 1936

It is essential that the student of race relations possess a comprehensive understanding of culture in all of its aspects and interrelations, and for this purpose we cannot recommend any more satisfactory work than Linton, Ralph. *The Study of Man.* New York: D. Appleton-Century Company. 1936. Pp. viii+497. As an illustration of the application of a combined anthropological and sociological study of actual processes of cultural adaptation on an extensive scale there may be recommended Thurnwald, Richard C. *Black and White in East Africa.* London: G. Routledge & Sons. 1935. Pp. xxii+419. For a simple, stimulating statement of the biological, psychological, and cultural approaches to the study of racial problems there may be suggested Klineberg, Otto. *Race Differences.* New York: Harper & Brothers. 1935. Pp. ix+367. Although the book makes but passing reference to minority peoples, the problems so well discussed in it are of such importance in our subject that serious attention must be given to Plant, James S. *Personality and the Cultural Pattern.* New York: The Commonwealth Fund. 1937. Pp. x+432

alties is inevitably dwarfed under the existing social order by the experiences of everyday life.

There is justification for saying that to the extent that the multitude of minority-majority relationship depression problems may be stated in general terms as one central problem, that problem is the determination of the relationship between depression phenomena and the social processes involved in the long run reconciliation of the cultures of the peoples of the United States. Each minority group in the country has culture traits which distinguish it from all other groups. These culture traits may have been imported almost if not quite as they now stand, or they may be merely vestigial remnants of the alien culture. In addition, there are also cultural divergencies of American origin through necessary adaptation because of restricted circumstances of life in this country as an unavoidable concomitant of class or caste status, involving as they do locational, occupational and social segregation in varying degree. It may be inferred with confidence that the most significant influence of the depression on all American minority peoples, as minority peoples, has been through its net effect on the processes of acculturation.

Whether this net influence may ultimately be found to be one of retardation or of acceleration cannot now be said. The evidence has not yet been put in a form which permits the casting of even a trial balance. It is reasonably certain, however, that the forces of acculturation were not free from serious depression interference, for they are part and parcel of economic and social forces in general.

If it is thought that the integrating hypothesis just offered does violence to the physical factors involved, including both the environmental and the biological, and perhaps neglects the rôle of the individual, it can only be said that minority status does not derive from the natural physical environment, nor is it ever a consequence of biological heredity or of individual action except under the tutelage of culture.

Appendixes

Definitions of racial and national minority membership for purposes of enumeration and administration

APPENDIX A

Minority classifications in the population census[1]

The strictly personal characteristics which appear in the census classifications are three, namely, color, sex, and age. Color is significant primarily because of the social and economic differentiation between the white and the Negro population, especially in the Southern states, though statistics by color or race are of importance in many other connections. This classification is made less accurately than some of the others because of difficulty in getting reliable information with respect to persons of mixed blood. A person with any fraction of Negro blood is theoretically classified as a Negro. Actually, however, many individuals of mixed blood whose Negro characteristics are not physically prominent are without doubt classified as white. The same difficulty affects the classification of persons as Indians, though because of the relatively small number of Indians, this difficulty is of much less importance—except to those who are making a special study of the Indians. The quasi-color class designated "Mexicans," established and used for the first time in 1930, offers the same difficulties and suffers further disadvantage of not having, even theoretically, a definition quite as specific as the other two non-white classes just mentioned.

Nativity, mother tongue, country of birth, and country of birth of parents, belong primarily to the group of personal characteristics, though in their analysis one finds many features which are social rather than individual in their nature. The classification by nativity, that is, the one which separates persons born in the

[1] Truesdell, Leon E. *Value of the Population Census for Research* in Dublin, Louis I. "The American People." *The Annals of the American Academy of Political and Social Science.* 188:331-333, November 1936

United States or its possessions from those born in foreign countries, is based on the census question asking for the place of birth of each person. There is little uncertainty in the returns on which this general classification is based, and the very few doubtful cases are assumed to be native. In the classification by specific country of birth, however, considerable difficulty was experienced in the censuses of 1920 and 1930 because of changes in the political geography of central Europe. The enumerator was instructed to find out in what country the birthplace of each foreign-born person was located according to the boundaries in force at the time of the census; but appreciable percentages of the returns were ambiguous and assignment to one or another of the new countries had to be made on the basis of mother tongue or of other supplemental information.

In the census reports beginning with 1890 there is given not only a classification of the foreign-born population by country of birth, but also a classification of the children of the foreign-born by country of birth of parents. In some presentations these are combined under the designation "foreign white stock."

From the returns for place of birth were tabulated also for the native population the census data on state of birth. This provides almost the only material in the census reports affording any tangible clue to the geographic course of the internal migration of the population. It does not give directly the number of persons who migrated from one state to another during a decade, but by comparing figures for several censuses approximate migration data between one state and another can be worked up.

APPENDIX B

U. S. Census instructions to enumerators with respect to races[2]

151. Negroes.—A person of mixed white and Negro blood should be returned as a Negro, no matter how small the percentage of Negro blood. Both black and mulatto persons are to

---

[2] *Fifteenth Census of the United States: Population.* II:1398-1399. 1930

be returned as Negroes, without distinction. A person of mixed Indian and Negro blood should be returned a Negro, unless the Indian blood predominates and the status as an Indian is generally accepted in the community.

152. Indians.—A person of mixed white and Indian blood should be returned as an Indian, except where the percentage of Indian blood is very small, or where he is regarded as a white person by those in the community where he lives. (See par. 151 for mixed Indian and Negro.)

153. For a person reported as Indian in column 12, report is to be made in column 19 as to whether "full blood" or "mixed blood," and in column 20 the name of the tribe is to be reported. For Indians, columns 19 and 20 are thus to be used to indicate the degree of Indian blood and the tribe, instead of the birthplace of father and mother.

154. Mexicans.—Practically all Mexican laborers are of a racial mixture difficult to classify, though usually well recognized in the localities where they are found. In order to obtain separate figures for this racial group, it has been decided that all persons born in Mexico, or having parents born in Mexico, who are not definitely white, Negro, Indian, Chinese or Japanese, should be returned as Mexican ("Mex").[3]

155. Other mixed races.—Any mixture of white and non-white should be reported according to the non-white parent. Mixtures of colored races should be reported according to the race of the father, except Negro-Indian (see par. 151)

APPENDIX C

Census classification of the population of the United States by color or race, nativity, and parentage[4]

The classification of the population of the United States by color or race distinguishes in many cases only three main groups,

---

[3] It would be more in accordance with actual practice if the phrase "having parents born in Mexico" were replaced by "of Mexican ancestry."

[4] *Fifteenth Census of the United States: Population.* II:25-27. 1930

namely, white, Negro, and "other races." The "other race" group includes Mexican, Indian, Chinese, Japanese, Filipino, Hindu, Korean, Hawaiian, Malay, Siamese, and Samoan—and the last three are represented by less than 100 persons each.

In classifying the population by nativity, all persons born in continental United States or in any of the outlying territories or possessions are regarded as native and all other persons as foreign-born. In the classification by parentage there are three primary groups, as follows: (1) native parentage, that is, having both parents born in the United States or in the outlying possessions (2) foreign parentage, that is, having both parents foreign-born (3) Mixed parentage, that is, having one parent native and the other foreign-born. In many of the tables persons of foreign parentage and those of mixed parentage are combined into one group designated "foreign or mixed parentage." Conversely, in a few tables the mixed parentage group is separated into two parts, designated (a) father foreign, and (b) mother foreign.

The distinction as to parentage is generally confined to the native white population, so that in most of the tables there are five principal classes: (1) native white of native parentage (2) native white of foreign or mixed parentage (3) foreign-born white (4) Negro (5) other races. The number of classes is expanded to six in many cases by the separate presentation of native white of foreign parentage and native white of mixed parentage. The group designated "other races," being relatively unimportant in most areas, is frequently omitted from the tables altogether. Figures are presented however, for this group and for its constituent races—Mexicans, Indians, Chinese, Japanese, etc.—in separate tables containing such details in each case as the number of persons in the group seems to justify.

Statistics of color or race, nativity, and parentage are presented in this chapter for continental United States, by states, and for cities of 25,000 or more. Less detailed statistics are presented for counties and townships, and for incorporated places of 1,000 or more, in Volume III of the Fifteenth Census Reports on Population; and statistics for the outlying territories and possessions enumerated at the Fifteenth Census are presented in a volume entitled *Outlying Territories and Possessions.*

The 1930 figures for the various color or race groups are shown by nativity in Table 1.

TABLE 1

POPULATION OF THE UNITED STATES BY COLOR OR RACE AND NATIVITY: 1930

(Per cent not shown where less than 0.1 or where base is less than 100)

COLOR OR RACE	TOTAL POPULA- TION	NATIVE		FOREIGN-BORN		PER CENT DISTRIBUTION		
		NUMBER	PER CENT OF TOTAL	NUMBER	PER CENT OF TOTAL	TOTAL	NA- TIVE	FOR- EIGN- BORN
Total	122,775,046	108,570,897	88.4	14,204,149	11.6	100	100	100
White	108,864,207	95,497,800	87.7	13,366,407	12.3	88.7	88.0	94.1
Negro	11,891,143	11,792,523	99.2	98,620	0.8	9.7	10.9	0.7
Mexican. . .	1,422,533	805,535	56.6	616,998	43.4	1.2	0.7	4.3
Indian. . . .	332,397	328,845	98.9	3,552	1.1	0.3	0.3	—
Chinese . . .	74,954	30,868	41.2	44,086	58.8	0.1	—	0.3
Japanese. . .	138,834	68,357	49.2	70,477	50.8	0.1	0.1	0.5
Filipino . . .	45,208	45,026	99.6	182	0.4	—	—	—
Hindu. . . .	3,130	412	13.2	2,718	86.8	—	—	—
Korean . . .	1,860	816	43.9	1,044	56.1	—	—	—
Hawaiian . .	660	654	99.1	6	0.9	—	—	—
Malay. . . .	96	48	—	48	—	—	—	—
Siamese	18	7	—	11	—	—	—	—
Samoan . . .	6	6	—	—	—	—	—	—

Correction for 1870. The corrected figures for 1870 in Table 4 and for the decades 1860 to 1870 and 1870 to 1880 in Table 5 are based on estimates of the true population in 1870, the census taken in that year having been generally deficient in the Southern States. The number of omissions in these states in 1870 is estimated to have been 1,260,000, comprising 748,000 whites and 512,000 Negroes. (See reports of the Eleventh Census, *Population*, Pt. I, pp. xi, xii, and xvi.)

White population. The proportion of whites in the total population, which was a little over 80 per cent in 1790, has increased at each succeeding census, except for a slight decline in 1810 as compared with 1800 and a decrease from 89.0 per cent (for the white population excluding Mexicans) in 1920 to 88.7 per cent in 1930. . . . This last decline is the result of a very considerable influx of Mexicans between 1920 and 1930. If Mexicans had been classed as white in 1930, the proportion in 1920 would have been slightly higher than in 1930.

Accepting the estimate for 1870 as approximately correct, each decade since 1790, except the decade 1910 to 1920, has shown for the white population a numerical increase greater than for the decade immediately preceding; and the percentage of increase for the white population has exceeded that for the Negro population in every decade since 1810. . . .

In considering the growth of the white population it must be kept in mind that in the case of only one of the four nativity and parentage classes is the increase due in any measure to the excess of births over deaths within the class itself. The number of natives of native parentage is increased in part by the children born to natives of native parentage and in part by the children of the natives of foreign or mixed parentage; the number of natives of mixed parentage is increased by the children of intermarriages between the native and the foreign-born; the number of natives of foreign parentage, by the children born to immigrants after their arrival in this country; and the number of foreign born, by immigration.

Of the four classes of whites, therefore, the natives of native parentage constitute the only one whose increase is affected in any degree by its own reproductivity, since the children born in this country to each of the other classes belong to a class different from that to which their parents belong (except that in some cases one parent of a native of mixed parentage is also a native of mixed parentage). While the increase in the number of native whites of native parentage must, so long as there is any element of foreign birth or parentage in the population, necessarily exceed the natural increase by excess of births over deaths within this class, the numerical increase of any of the other classes may or may not exceed the natural increase which would result if the children were included in the same class with the parents. The numerical increases within the several nativity and parentage classes, therefore, bear no specific relationship to the natural increase.

TABLE 2

WHITE POPULATION OF THE UNITED STATES BY NATIVITY AND PARENTAGE: 1930

Nativity and Parentage	Number	Per Cent of Total Population	Per Cent of White Population	Per Cent of Native White Population
Total White.	108,864,207	88.7	100	—
Native	95,497,800	88.8	87.7	100
Native parentage	70,136,614	57.1	64.4	73.4
Foreign or mixed parentage . .	25,361,186	20.7	23.3	26.6
Foreign parentage	16,999,221	13.8	15.6	17.8
Mixed parentage.	8,361,965	6.8	7.7	8.8
Father foreign.	5,459,530	4.4	5.0	5.7
Mother foreign	2,902,435	2.4	2.7	3.0
Foreign-born	13,366,407	10.9	12.3	—

The 1930 figures for the white population classified by nativity and parentage are summarized in Table 2. For comparative figures for earlier censuses, see Table 6. (Not here reproduced.)

Negro Population. The distinction between white and colored is the only racial classification which has been carried through all the 15 censuses. There is some doubt as to whether the small number of taxed Indians were counted with the white or with the colored population prior to 1860.

With adjustment for the undercount of Negroes in 1870, the

proportion of Negroes in the total population has decreased at each census since 1810. The rate of increase in the Negro population has also shown a downward trend since 1810, but the rates, even with adjustment for 1870, show fluctuations which are difficult to explain. For example, the rate of increase dropped from 22.0 per cent (adjusted) in the decade 1870 to 1880 to 13.5 per cent between 1880 and 1890, and then rose to 18.0 per cent in the following decade.

In the face of this fluctuation in the decennial rate of increase, the Census Bureau has admitted the possibility of an undercount of Negroes in 1890. A similar fluctuation in the rate of increase was that from 11.2 between 1900 and 1910 to 6.5 in the decade 1910 to 1920, followed by a rate of 13.6 between 1920 and 1930. This fluctuation is even greater than that of 30 years earlier, and suggests the probability of an undercount of Negroes in 1920, as well as in 1890. It would be a mistake, however, to assume that the entire fluctuation in the latter period was due to an undercount. The decade 1910 to 1920 included the years of the World War, with its consequent disorganization of the Negro population through military service and labor migrations, and also the influenza epidemic of 1918 and 1919. The disorganization of the War and migration period would tend to decrease births, and the epidemic probably increased the number of deaths of Negroes within the decade by at least 100,000. The number of deaths in the decade 1910 to 1919 of Negroes living at the census of 1910, on the assumption that the death rate of Negroes in the registration area was typical of that for Negroes in the United States as a whole, was 1,754,956, as compared with 1,522,665 Negro deaths similarly calculated for the decade 1920 to 1929 in the population living at the census of 1920. A comparison by five-year periods of the Negro population in 1910, 1920, and 1930, arranging these periods by groups of birth years and allowing for calculated deaths in each birth-year group, would indicate a shortage of about

150,000 in the Negro enumeration of 1920, as compared with the enumerations of 1910 and 1930. This shortage in the enumeration is in addition to the usual shortage of perhaps 100,000 in the enumeration of Negro children under 5 years old. This latter shortage can be shown for every census by comparing the number of children under 5 with the number 10 to 14 in the following census, taking into account deaths within the ten-year period.

The following statement shows the rates of increase in the Negro population for the last six decades, first as reported, and second, with the adjustments suggested above:

DECADE	AS REPORTED	ADJUSTED
1920-1930	13.6	12.0
1910-1920	6.5	8.0
1900-1910	11.2	11.2
1890-1900	18.0	13.8
1880-1890	13.5	17.6
1870-1880	34.9	22.0

The rapid downward trend in the decennial rate of increase in the Negro population from 1870 to 1920 can only be accounted for by the assumption of declining birth rate, parallel with the decline which has been recorded for the white race. The Negro death rate apparently remained stationary or declined less rapidly than did the birth rate. In the decade 1920 to 1930, both birth and death registration figures for Negroes are for the first time sufficiently complete to be used as a check on the indicated decennial increase. These figures show that during the decade the Negro death rate declined more rapidly than the Negro birth rate. This offers an explanation of the apparent reversal in the trend of the rate of increase. Whether this reversal is temporary or permanent remains to be seen.

Mexican population. The Mexican element in the population has increased very rapidly in certain parts of the United States during the past ten years. By reason of its growing importance, it was given a separate classification in the census returns for

1930, having been included for the most part with the white population at prior censuses. The instructions given to enumerators for making this classification were to the effect that "all persons born in Mexico, or having parents born in Mexico, who are not definitely white, Negro, Indian, Chinese, or Japanese, should be regarded as Mexican." Under these instructions, 1,422,533 persons were returned as Mexican in 1930, and 65,968 persons of Mexican birth or parentage were returned as white. Using as a basis the 1920 returns for persons born in Mexico and persons having one or both parents born in Mexico, it has been estimated that there were in that year 700,541 persons who would have been classified as Mexican under the 1930 instructions.[5] Similarly it was estimated that there were included in the white classification in 1910, 367,510 persons who would have been counted as Mexican in 1930.

Indian population. The census of 1860 was the first at which Indians were distinguished from the other classes, but no enumeration was made of the Indians in Indian Territory or on Indian reservations until 1890. Prior to that time the enumeration of Indians was confined to those found living among the general population of the various states. The returns for Indians are subject to some degree of uncertainty because of the practice of treating as Indians all persons having any trace of Indian blood. Such persons in many cases cannot be distinguished by their appearance from pure-blooded white persons, and as a result some of them have doubtless been reported as white at one census and as Indian at another, since the enumerators are not always able to interview directly the persons whom they

---

[5] This estimate is based on the assumption that the ratio between white persons of Mexican birth or parentage and persons who should be classified as "Mexicans" was the same in 1920 as in 1930, when the total number of persons of Mexican origin (1,488,501) comprised 1,422,533 Mexicans and 65,968 white persons of Mexican birth or parentage. The total number of white persons of Mexican birth or parentage in 1920 was 731,559.

enumerate but are obliged to secure information regarding them from other sources.

At the census of 1910 a special effort was made to secure a complete enumeration of all persons having any perceptible amount of Indian blood, for the purpose of preparing a special report showing tribal relation, degree of Indian blood, etc.; and it is probable that this resulted in the enumeration as Indian of a considerable number of persons who would ordinarily have been reported as white. In 1920 no special instructions were given to the numerators on this point, and the returns showed a much smaller number of Indians than in 1910.

In 1930, however, a special effort was again made to secure a complete count of persons of Indian blood, and the enumerators were instructed specifically to return as Indian all persons of mixed white and Indian blood, except where the percentage of Indian blood was very small, or where the person was regarded as white in the community where he lived. The results of this enumeration show 87,960, or 36.0 per cent more Indians than were returned in 1920, but for reasons already indicated, it seems likely that this figure overstates the actual increase in the number of Indians.

APPENDIX D

Indians variously defined[6]

The 1910 census[7] classed as Indians "all persons of mixed blood who have any appreciable amount of Indian blood"—obviously a flexible and uncertain criterion. Enumerators of the 1930 census were instructed to include persons of mixed blood

---

[6] Supplementary Report of the Land Planning Committee to the National Resources Board. Part X. *Indian Land Tenure, Economic Status, and Population Trends.* Washington: United States Government Printing Office. 1935. P. 62 (Section IV, by Ray Ovid Hall and Harry I. Nettleton of the Office of Indian Affairs, Department of the Interior.)

[7] *Indian Population in the United States and Alaska.* P. 10

"except where the percentage of Indian blood is very small" or where the individual "is regarded as a white person in the community where he lives." A person of mixed Indian and Negro blood was to be returned as a Negro, "unless the Indian blood predominates and the status as an Indian is generally accepted in the community." Enumerators were directed to include Mexican laborers in the Southwest trying to pass as American Indians.

The Indian Office, on the other hand, aims specially to count what might be termed official Indians. It has usually defined Indians as persons on the official roll of any tribe, and hence has sometimes included in its count many of negligible Indian blood, besides intermarried whites; but the definition is disregarded in its extensive estimating, described later herein. Furthermore, tribal rolls have sometimes had only a mythical existence or have been years out of date, except at reservations where per capita payments are made regularly to tribe members. Needless to say, many Indians on a given tribal roll do not live on the reservation which counts them—a further cause of discrepancies between the Indian Office and the Census Bureau.

APPENDIX E

Legal definitions of immigrants, non-quota immigrants, and quota immigrants[8]

Sec. 3. When used in this act the term "immigrant" means any alien departing from any place outside the United States destined for the United States, except (1) a government official, his family, attendants, servants, and employees (2) an alien visiting the United States temporarily as a tourist or temporarily for business or pleasure (3) an alien in continuous transit through the United States (4) an alien lawfully ad-

---

[8] United States Department of Labor, Immigration and Naturalization Service. *Immigration Laws and Rules of January 1, 1930.* Washington, D.C.: United States Government Printing Office. 1935. Pp. 2-4

mitted to the United States who later goes in transit from one part of the United States to another through foreign contiguous territory (5) a bona fide alien seaman serving as such on a vessel arriving at a port of the United States and seeking to enter temporarily the United States solely in the pursuit of his calling as a seaman, and (6) an alien entitled to enter the United States solely to carry on trade under and in pursuance of the provisions of a present existing treaty of commerce and navigation. (Sec. 203.)

Non-Quota Immigrants

Sec. 4 (as amended by sections 1 and 2 of joint resolution approved May 29, 1928, 45 Stat. 1009). When used in this act the term "non-quota immigrant" means—

(a) An immigrant who is the unmarried child under twenty-one years of age, or the wife of a citizen of the United States, or the husband of a citizen of the United States by a marriage occurring prior to June 1, 1928;

(b) An immigrant previously lawfully admitted to the United States who is returning from a temporary visit abroad;

(c) An immigrant who was born in the Dominion of Canada, Newfoundland, the Republic of Mexico, the Republic of Cuba, the Republic of Haiti, the Dominican Republic, the Canal Zone, or an independent country of Central or South America, and his wife, and his unmarried children under eighteen years of age, if accompanying or following to join him;

(d) An immigrant who continuously for at least two years immediately preceding the time of his application for admission to the United States has been, and who seeks to enter the United States solely for the purpose of, carrying on the vocation of minister of any religious denomination or professor of a college, academy, seminary, or university; and his wife, and his unmarried children under eighteen years of age, if accompanying or following to join him;

(See act of July 3, 1936, pp. 94-95.)

(e) An immigrant who is a bona fide student at least fifteen years of age and who seeks to enter the United States solely for the purpose of study at an accredited school, college, academy, seminary, or university, particularly designed by him and approved by the Secretary of Labor, which shall have agreed to report to the Secretary of Labor the termination of attendance of each immigrant student, and if any such institution of learning fails to make such reports promptly the approval shall be withdrawn; or

(f) A woman who was a citizen of the United States and who prior to September 22, 1922, lost her citizenship by reason of her marriage to an alien, but at the time of her application for an immigration visa is unmarried.

(Sec. 204.)

Quota Immigrants

Sec. 5. When used in this act the term "quota immigrant" means any immigrant who is not a non-quota immigrant. An alien who is not particularly specified in this act as a non-quota immigrant or a non-immigrant shall not be admitted as a non-quota immigrant or a non-immigrant by reason of relationship to any individual who is so specified or by reason of being excepted from the operation of any other law regulating or forbidding immigration.

(Sec. 205.)

Index

Studies in the Social Aspects
of the Depression

AN ARNO PRESS/NEW YORK TIMES COLLECTION

Chapin, F. Stuart and Stuart A. Queen.
Research Memorandum on Social Work in the Depression. 1937.

Collins, Selwyn D. and Clark Tibbitts.
Research Memorandum on Social Aspects of Health in the Depression.
1937.

The Educational Policies Commission.
Research Memorandum on Education in the Depression. 1937.

Kincheloe, Samuel C.
Research Memorandum on Religion in the Depression. 1937.

Sanderson, Dwight.
Research Memorandum on Rural Life in the Depression. 1937.

Sellin, Thorsten.
Research Memorandum on Crime in the Depression. 1937.

Steiner, Jesse F.
Research Memorandum on Recreation in the Depression. 1937.

Stouffer, Samuel A. and Paul F. Lazarsfeld.
Research Memorandum on the Family in the Depression. 1937.

Thompson, Warren S.
Research Memorandum on Internal Migration in the Depression. 1937.

Vaile, Roland S.
**Research Memorandum on Social Aspects of Consumption in the
Depression.** 1937.

Waples, Douglas.
Research Memorandum on Social Aspects of Reading in the Depression.
1937.

White, R. Clyde and Mary K. White.
**Research Memorandum on Social Aspects of Relief Policies in the
Depression.** 1937.

Young, Donald.
Research Memorandum on Minority Peoples in the Depression. 1937.